# Reading Virginia Woolf

For Jon, Simon and Jeremy

# Reading Virginia Woolf

Julia Briggs

Edinburgh University Press

Edinburgh University Press Ltd
22 George Square, Edinburgh

Typeset in 10.5/13 Adobe Sabon
by Servis Filmsetting Ltd, Manchester, and
printed and bound in Great Britain by
MPG Books Ltd, Bodmin, Cornwall

A CIP record for this book is available from the British Library

ISBN-10 0 7486 2434 1 (hardback)
ISBN-13 978 0 7486 2434 8
ISBN-10 0 7486 2435 X (paperback)
ISBN-13 978 0 7486 2435 5

# *Contents*

# *Acknowledgements*

More scholars and friends have contributed to these essays than I can acknowledge, but I particularly want to thank those who made my year in Paris such a pleasure, notably Richard Wilson, François Laroque, Ann and Jean-Jacques Lecercle, Catherine Bernard and Daniel Ferrer; my many friends across the Atlantic, and in particular Mark Hussey, Jane Marcus, Vara Neverow, Merry Pawlowski and Ted Bishop; my former students Kathy Laing and Alice Staveley, my current students Marion Dell and Deborah Gerrard, and my colleagues at De Montfort University. David Stocker has talked, listened and encouraged, Hans Gabler has been characteristically generous with his thoughts and ideas, and Stuart Clarke has helped me greatly at every stage, with patience, kindness and his extraordinary knowledge of Woolf's work. I have enjoyed working with my copy-editor Sarah Hall, and my editor, Jackie Jones.

* * *

The occasions of these essays are listed below. I am grateful to all those who invited me to speak or write for them, and for their permissions to reprint.

Essay 1 was read at the International Shakespeare Conference at Stratford-upon-Avon, Summer 2004, and published in *Shakespeare Survey 58: Writing About Shakespeare*, ed. Peter Holland (Cambridge: Cambridge University Press, 2005).

Essay 2 was read at a conference on literary biography organised by the English Institute, and later published in *The Art of Literary Biography*, ed. John Batchelor (Oxford: Clarendon Press, 1995).

Essay 3 was written as the introduction to my edition of *Night and Day* (London: Penguin, 1992).

An early version of essay 4 was read as the Byron Lecture at Nottingham, 1994.

An early version of essay 5 was read at the 13th International Woolf Conference at Northampton, MA, 2003, and published in *Woolf in the Real World: Selected Papers from the Thirteenth International Conference on Virginia Woolf*, ed. Karen V. Kukil (Clemson, SC: Clemson University Digital Press, 2005).

An early version of essay 6 was read at the 14th International Woolf Conference held in London, 2004.

An earlier version of essay 7 was read at the 'Text and Border' Colloquium at Innsbruck to celebrate the work of Hans Walter Gabler, January 2003, and has been published in *Variants 4* (Amsterdam: Rodopi, 2005).

Essay 8 was read to the Virginia Woolf Society of Great Britain as their second Annual Birthday Lecture, January 2001, and published by the Society in a limited edition.

An early version of essay 9 was read at the 'Vortex' colloquium on 'L'empreinte des choses', organised by André Topia at Paris III, October 2003.

Essay 10 was read at the 'Virginia Woolf Across Cultures' symposium held in Moscow, June 2003, and published in *Woolf Across Cultures*, ed. Natalya Reinhold (New York: Pace University Press, 2004).

Essay 11 was read at the Colloquium of the Société d'Etudes Woolfiennes on 'Conversation in Woolf's Work' organised by Catherine Bernard and Christine Reynier at Montpellier, June 2003, and published in *Etudes britanniques contemporaines* (Automne 2004), and in *Etudes Anglaises: Littérature et théories critiques II* (janvier–mars 2005) 58/1.

Essay 12 was written for *Trespassing Boundaries: Virginia Woolf's Short Fiction*, ed. Kathryn N. Benzel and Ruth Hoberman (Basingstoke and New York: Palgrave Macmillan, 2004).

Essay 13 was read at the Graduate School, CUNY, and subsequently at the Smithsonian Institute, Washington in September 2000, and will be published in *Inroads and Outposts: British Women in the Thirties*, ed.

Robin Hackett, Jane Marcus and Gay Wachman (Gainesville, FL: University of Florida Press, 2006).

Essay 14 was published in *TEXT* 12, ed. W. Speed Hill and Edward M. Burns (Ann Arbor, MI: University of Michigan Press, 1999).

The author and publishers would like to thank the Society of Authors as the literacy representative of the Estate of Virginia Woolf for permission to quote from Woolf's manuscript drafts and their transcriptions; and to the executors of the Estate of Virginia Woolf and the Random House Group Limited for permission to quote from Woolf's diaries, letters, journals and unpublished shorter fiction; to the Henry W. and Albert A. Berg Collection in the New York Public Library for permission to quote from *The Years* notebooks; to Hope Mirrlees's executors and the University of Sussex Library for permission to quote from Mirrlees's letters to Woolf and from her poem *Paris*; and finally to Cambridge University Press, Oxford University Press, Pace University Press, Penguin Books and Palgrave for permissions to reprint essays first published by them.

# *List of Abbreviations*

| | |
|---|---|
| BA | *Between the Acts* (1941), edited by Stella McNichol, with an introduction by Gillian Beer (London: Penguin, 1992) |
| CE | *Collected Essays*, vols i–iv, edited by Leonard Woolf (London: Chatto and Windus, 1966–7) |
| CSF | *The Complete Shorter Fiction*, edited by Susan Dick (London: Hogarth Press, revised edition 1989) |
| *Diary* | *The Diary of Virginia Woolf*, vols i–v, edited by Anne Olivier Bell with Andrew McNeillie (London: Hogarth Press, 1977–84) |
| *Essays* | *The Essays of Virginia Woolf*, vols i–iv, edited by Andrew McNeillie (London: Hogarth Press, 1986–94) |
| J's R | *Jacob's Room* (1922), edited with an introduction by Sue Roe (London: Penguin, 1992) |
| *Letters* | *The Letters of Viriginia Woolf*, vols i–vi, edited by Nigel Nicolson with Joanne Trautmann (London: Chatto and Windus, 1975–80) |
| MB | *Moments of Being: Autobiographical Writings*, edited by Jeanne Schulkind, with an introduction by Hermione Lee (London: Pimlico, 2002) |
| MD | *Mrs Dalloway* (1925), edited by Stella McNichol, with an introduction by Elaine Showalter (London: Penguin, 1992) |
| ND | *Night and Day* (1919), edited with an introduction by Julia Briggs (London: Penguin, 1992) |
| O | *Orlando* (1928), edited by Brenda Lyons, with an introduction by Sandra Gilbert London: Penguin, 1993) |

P *The Pargiters: The Novel–Essay Portion of 'The Years'*, edited with an introduction by Mitchell A. Leaska (London: Hogarth Press, 1978)

RF *Roger Fry* (1940), edited by Diane F. Gillespie (Oxford: Blackwell, Shakespeare Head Press, 1995)

ROO *A Room of One's Own* and *Three Guineas* (1929, 1938), edited with an introduction by Michèle Barrett (London: Penguin, 1993)

TG *A Room of One's Own* and *Three Guineas* (1929, 1938), edited with an introduction by Michèle Barrett (London: Penguin, 1993)

TTL *To the Lighthouse* (1927), edited by Stella McNichol, with an introduction by Hermione Lee (London: Penguin, 1992)

VO *The Voyage Out* (1915), edited with an introduction by Jane Wheare (London: Penguin, 1992)

W *The Waves* (1931), edited with an introduction by Kate Flint (London: Penguin, 1992)

Y *The Years* (1937), edited with an introduction by Jeri Johnson (London: Penguin, 1998)

# Introduction

Such attics cleared of me! Such absences![1]

If a single theme runs through these essays, it is that of absence, the theme of so much modernist writing. As Woolf herself recognised, but never formulated to her own satisfaction, gaps and absences are what bring the very different processes of reading and writing together, for the writer works by filling the gaps with her imagination, and so, if rather differently, does the reader. Jane Austen, Woolf observed, 'stimulates us to supply what is not there' (*Essays* iv, 149). Readers co-ordinate the signs supplied by the text in order to 'make a whole' (in Woolf's phrase), in the process of assimilating the reading to their own inner world.

For Woolf, the concept of absence brought together a series of linked ideas. In emotional terms, it resulted from the experience of loss, and in particular the series of losses she had endured as an adolescent and a young woman – her half-sister Stella in 1897, her father in 1904, her favourite brother Thoby in 1906, and, most devastating of all, that of her mother when she was only thirteen, in 1895. Julia Duckworth Stephen was eventually memorialised as Mrs Ramsay in *To the Lighthouse*, where she unconsciously foresees her own absence as she reads Shakespeare's sonnet 98, 'From you have I been absent in the spring' (TTL, 131). Woolf published *To the Lighthouse* on 5 May 1927, the anniversary of the day her mother died, thirty-two years before. The gap that severs the present from the past, yet also bridges the gap between the young Virginia's early losses, and those of so many others during the Great War, is represented in the novel as the ten years of 'Time Passes', one of her most far-reaching experiments,

Loss and absence lie at the heart of Woolf's art. Her late, unfinished memoir, 'A Sketch of the Past', records how she turned to writing as a way of dealing with their pain:

> the shock-receiving capacity is what makes me a writer . . . it is or will become a revelation of some order; it is a token of some real thing behind appearances; and I make it real by putting it into words. It is only by putting it into words that I make it whole; this wholeness means that it has lost its power to hurt me. (MB, 85)

Recalling the conception of *To the Lighthouse*, she acknowledged that the process of writing about her mother had affinities with the practice of psychoanalysis: 'I expressed some very long felt and deeply felt emotion. And in expressing it I explained it and then laid it to rest.' And yet as soon as she had written this, she felt dissatisfied with the type of 'explanation' provided by psychoanalysis. 'But what is the meaning of "explained" it? Why, because I described her and my feeling for her in that book, should my vision of her and my feeling for her become so much dimmer and weaker?' (MB, 93).

In terms of Woolf's art, absence takes on a range of forms, expressing itself spatially and historically as gaps or chasms, and textually as silences, including the active silence of thought, articulated in *The Waves* as speech, where it reverses the normal convention of the novel that dramatises dialogue, rather than interior monologue. This text alternates between individual soliloquies and shared feelings, expressed as unspoken choruses, as its six characters meet for their two ceremonial last suppers. Gaps and absences can be experienced as disruptive, as a series of 'jerks and jumps' in *Jacob's Room*, but Woolf's next novel, *Mrs Dalloway*, offsets these with a series of unifying devices, of shared sights in the sky, or sounds in the public streets.

Woolf's experience of loss as disruption characterised her vision of history, both political and literary. The significance of '[o]n or about December 1910 human character changed' (*Essays* iii, 421) lies less in the political events of that year (interesting though they were – see pp. 130–1 for further details), than in the fact that it constituted a break, even a 'chasm' between the past – the world of the Victorians, the world of Woolf's parents – and the present, in the same way that the Great War would later make a break in people's lives, although in the case of the War,'the fracture differs, according to what is broken' (RF, 160). Woolf located that break between the thirteenth and fourteenth chapters of *Jacob's Room*, half-way through the 1914 section of *The Years* (though she would later sacrifice the second half, the 'September' sequence, as one of the 'two enormous chunks' cut out to reduce the novel's overall length), but above all in 'Time Passes' – the horizontal stroke of the letter 'H', the short beam of the lighthouse, the moment when the loss of her mother/Mrs Ramsay, the social and structural changes of 1910, and the Great War all combine to create a kind of quintessence '[o]f absence, darkness, death; things which are not'.[2] Time Passes' is the narrative of a house emptied of its inhabitants, a narrative of 'something mystic, spiritual; the thing that exists when we aren't there' (*Diary* iii, 114). Now it is not merely the attics but the whole house that is cleared, producing a long-drawn-out cry of yearning, a vision of emptiness that is at once painful, yet oddly consolatory.

The past is always a felt absence, even when memory summons threads and strands of it back again, supplementing them from imagination, probability or surviving records – a process explored in Woolf's unfinished memoir known as 'A Sketch of the Past'. Admitting that whatever is remembered is determined by the moment of remembrance, what Woolf termed 'the little platform of present time' (MB, 96), she there recalled her earliest memories of childhood, and of the long-lost dead – her mother, Stella, her father and Thoby – in a series of reminiscences written in the months leading up to the declaration of war on Germany on 3 September 1939, and then again during the Battle of Britain in the following summer. Now the violence and disruption of the present colour the pleasures and pain of the past. Surprisingly, given the relationship between her memories and the moment of their remembering, Woolf asserts that the present needs to run peacefully in order to allow past time to be recollected in tranquillity: 'The past only comes back when the present runs so smoothly that it is like the sliding surface of a deep river' (MB, 108). In reality, nothing could have been less tranquil than the moments at which she wrote those memoirs. Instead of the present affording a quiet setting for the recovery of a distressing past, her memories of Talland House – the garden and the beach, her mother shopping or Thoby steering a boat across the bay – provide a safe anchorage for her thoughts during those two stormy summers.

Now the past became a place of retreat from imminent or actual war. Yet it may also be that these were exactly the conditions she needed to record memories of childhood that, until then, she had rehearsed only as fiction. Though she here recalled her mother's death, she still found herself shying away from the 'dark years' that followed, when her father's grief overshadowed the naturally high spirits of the growing family. As Lily Briscoe had put it, 'this was tragedy – not palls, dust and the shroud; but children coerced, their spirits subdued' (TTL, 162–3). 'A Sketch of the Past' survives in two versions, in manuscript and typescript: in the process of typing out her manuscript, Woolf deleted some passages and expanded others, changing them in response to the constantly shifting 'platform of present time'. Like her great contemporary, Marcel Proust, Woolf's central concern had always been with lives in time, and how best to represent time, since its steady falling away endlessly recreated the experience of absence and loss, in a range of shapes and at a variety of levels.

These fourteen essays explore themes that have engaged my attention since I began studying Woolf, as the general editor of a series of reprints of Woolf for Penguin at the beginning of the 1990s when her work came out of copyright (temporarily, as it turned out). Among the earliest here reprinted is my own introduction to *Night and Day*. But the majority of them are more recent, and several were written in Paris in 2003, as I was completing my study of her writing process, *Virginia Woolf, An Inner Life* (2005). In the course of assembling them for this book, I have revised all the essays to a greater or lesser extent, and in doing so, could not help noticing how certain phrases, passages, ideas or networks of associations determine my thinking about Woolf, but though these recur, they do so as variations on a theme: Woolf's concern to construct a 'significant form' for her work is the subject of the two central essays (6 and 7), but it also introduces essay 10, on the quite different topic of the role of Constantinople in Woolf's work.

The essays are arranged along loosely chronological lines, because I am still fascinated by the unfolding shape of Woolf's career, but many of them range backwards and forwards across her work in pursuit of their individual topics, and these I have set at the beginning and end, or else in the middle. I start with the most recently-written essay, concerned with a curious absence from Woolf's canon – the essay she never wrote on Shakespeare – a topic that reveals Woolf at her most ambitious as a writer, yet one that she handles with characteristic subtlety and self-mockery. This essay introduces several themes central to the volume as a whole, notably Virginia's relationship with her brother Thoby and with her eminent father Leslie Stephen, and through them with the male-dominated literary culture of her times. From her reading of Shakespeare sprang the hope that a woman poet, through some almost supernatural 'second coming', might one day rival Shakespeare's unique achievements as a writer.

The next essay opens the chronological sequence by exploring Woolf's earliest short stories, and their use of different forms of life-writing. It corresponds to the twelfth essay, which offers readings of her late short stories, written in the 1930s, stories that return, by way of social caricature, to the processes of writing, remembering and recording. Woolf used the short story as a space for active experiment, for trying out within its narrow confines ideas that would later call for lengthier treatment. From the beginning, she experimented with fictionalising biography and (auto)biographical fiction, experiments that culminated in 'The Mark on the Wall', where Woolf launched herself into inner space as she described 'the shower of ideas [that] fell perpetually from some very high Heaven' (CSF, 85) (she was writing of Shakespeare, but thinking of herself). My third essay introduces *Night and Day*, Woolf's second and most consistently neglected novel, a novel characterised by significant absences – most notably that of any reference to the Great War, during which it was written, or to the long breakdown she suffered during the early stages of its composition. The result is a social comedy, yet one that suggests that day-dreams and inner thoughts may, after all, turn out to be the determining factors in life. This piece is followed by an account of Woolf's unfinished introduction to an unwritten book on 'Reading', 'Byron and Mr Briggs', where she explores the way reading – whether the reading of texts or the semiotic reading of other people from their appearance – involves bridging or otherwise negotiating gaps in information, reconstructing from hints, 'not exactly what is said, nor yet entirely what is done' (J's R, 24) to create something of greater consistency, of great constancy, in the process of 'making a whole'.

Woolf's relationship with Hope Mirrlees, and her typesetting of Mirrlees's poem *Paris* in the early months of 1920 are the subject of the fifth essay, which grew out of my work on an edition of the poem.[3] It argues that if we knew more about their friendship, it might figure as largely in Woolf's biography as does her friendship with Katherine Mansfield (which it parallels in certain respects). Certainly, *Jacob's Room*, with its innovative form, its use of measured gaps (white lines) between the blocks of text and its scenes of young painters in Paris, registers the impact of Mirrlees's 'very obscure, indecent, and brilliant poem' (*Letters* ii, 385). Both *Paris* and *The Waste Land* (1922) suggested the need to find an appropriate form for modern fiction, and the closely-linked sixth and seventh essays pursue this question: the first focuses on Roger Fry's concept of 'significant form', seen as a distinctive shape or structure within the novel or short story. The second examines Woolf's use of numbers, and in particular her numbering of parts, sections or divisions in her work, and how she linked these to the rhythms of time. These two essays are followed by an account of Woolf's sense of the gap or chasm that cut off the past from the present, the Victorians and Edwardians from the Georgians – the gap that conflated her mother's death, and the misery of the years that followed, with the Great War, bringing the two together in 'Time Passes'.

'Like a Shell on a Sandhill' focuses upon the use of this image in 'Time Passes', exploring absence as emptiness, the empty vessel that once held a former life, and the links between the empty shell, the empty house and the skull, that most traditional of 'memento mori', that appears both in *Jacob's Room* and *To the Lighthouse* as a silent warning. Yet the skull is also the home of the writer, the place of creativity, and in *Jacob's Room* the dome of the British Museum Library is pictured as a 'vast mind', an enormous skull: '[s]tone lies solid over the British Museum, as bone lies cool over the visions and heat of the brain. Only here the brain is Plato's brain and Shakespeare's' (J's R, 94). It is a dome of wisdom, like that of Santa Sophia in Constantinople, a city Virginia had visited with her brothers and sister in the autumn of 1906, shortly before Thoby's death. The domes of that city, glittering in the sunlight, also recur as symbols of creativity, as bright and evanescent as soap bubbles – an image Woolf used to describe the conception of *To the Lighthouse*: '[b]lowing bubbles out of a pipe gives the feeling of the rapid crowd of ideas and scenes which blew out of my mind' (MB, 92–3). The tenth essay examines Woolf's treatment of Constantinople, and its variety of associations.

The eleventh essay considers some words and thoughts that could not be spoken or written in public in the early twentieth century, suggesting that, while Woolf sometimes resented such censorship (particularly where it applied only to women writers), she also took some pleasure in vaulting over the obstacles it put in her path. Restrictions have their own contribution to make to the creative process. The twelfth essay, on Woolf's later short stories, ranges from the fantasia of 'The Lady in the Looking Glass' to the social satire of 'The Shooting Party', concluding with her preoccupation in the last months of her life with 'The Searchlight' and 'The Symbol', stories about the operation of loss and memory, here represented by a telescope or field glasses whose close-up on a distant spot isolates and focuses a particular experience. She wrote at least nine versions of 'The Searchlight', each one different from the rest, though each, in one way or another, turns upon the themes that underpin 'A Sketch of the Past' – the operation of distance and memory, and the effect of 'this moment I stand on' upon what the telescope or searchlight reveals, the scene that memory calls back.

Two final essays look back across Woolf 's work, one from a cultural and the other from a textual standpoint. The thirteenth explores Woolf's embarrassment at being so English. Bloomsbury found patriotism distasteful, and Roger Fry in particular had no patience with little England, its weather, its light, or its values. Such views complicated and contradicted her own love of English literature and the English landscape, a love inherited from her parents and linked with nostalgia for her lost childhood. I end with an attempt to fill a significant gap in Woolf studies by examining the editing problems her work throws up. A further purpose of this particular essay, as of several others, is to nudge Woolf studies towards some remaining gaps and absences – towards unfinished works such as 'Byron and Mr Briggs' and towards what remains to be published of her manuscripts (though Woolf studies have already benefited greatly from the published transcriptions of manuscript material that are available). In addition to the intriguing pile of notes for *Three Guineas* (not identical, I suspect, with the manuscript of the text put up for auction), only the first section of the eight manuscript notebooks of *The Years* has been transcribed. The second notebook includes the first nineteen page of *Flush* – among the most comically exuberant of her writings, while the long section in volume 4, later to become the '1910' sequence, is fascinating for what it tells us about Woolf's feminism, as well as being an important source for *Three Guineas*. And 'A Sketch of the Past' deserves a fuller and more informative edition. There is more to be done on Woolf's practice of revision, as well as on the hidden structures, skeletons and frameworks, that support her novels. And we still know far too little about the history of her texts – as my final essay indicates, our current assumptions must remain provisional until further evidence appears. Such tasks are as endless as they are inviting. For those prepared to listen, Woolf's empty spaces are always on the point of bursting into song, like the silent dining room in *Between the Acts* that becomes a Keatsian urn, 'a shell, singing of what was before time was' (BA, 14).

## Notes

1. Philip Larkin, 'Absences', *Collected Poems*, ed. Anthony Thwaite (London and Boston, MA: Marvell Press and Faber and Faber, 1988), p. 49.
2. John Donne, 'A Nocturnal upon St. Lucy's Day', *The Complete English Poems of John Donne*, ed. C. A. Patrides (London and Melbourne: J. M. Dent, 1985), pp. 90–1 (my modernisation).
3. In *Gender in Modernism*, ed. Bonnie Kime Scott, (Chicago: University of Illinois Press, 2006).

Essay 1

# Virginia Woolf Reads Shakespeare: or, Her Silence on Master William

> If [the] number 18 [bus] still runs, let us take it, when the owling time is at hand, down to London Bridge. There is a curious smell in this part of the world, of hops, it may be; & also a curious confraternity . . . The gulls are swooping; & some small boys paddle in the pebbles. Above the sky is huddled & crowded with purple streamers . . . because it was here that the Globe stood.[1]

Near the end of her life, probably in January 1941, Virginia Woolf tried once again to make her way to the Globe theatre, to net Shakespeare in a web of words; yet even before she began, she experienced a sense of defeat:

> One reason why Shakespeare is still read is simply the inadequacy of Shakespearean criticism . . . it is always autobiographical criticism. It is a commonplace to say that every critic finds his own features in Shakespeare. His variety is such that every one can find scattered here or there the development of some one of his own attributes. The critic then accents what he is responsive to, and so composes his own meaning, in Shakespeares words . . . But there always remains something further . . . that lures the reader. And it is this quality that finally eludes us. gives him his perpetual vitality, he excites perpetual curiosity . . . One reading always supercedes another. Thus the truest account of reading Shakespeare would be not to write a book with beginning middle and end; but to collect notes, without trying to make them consistent.[2]

Which is largely what she did.

In this unrevised paragraph from an unwritten book, to be entitled 'Reading at Random' or perhaps 'Turning the Page', Woolf represents Shakespeare as at once mirror and mystery. She attempts to stalk her elusive subject through a series of drafts, but the essay devoted to Shakespeare continued to elude her. She felt defeated by the weight of what had already been said, as she had admitted fifteen years earlier in her essay 'On Being Ill' which argues that the recklessness of illness is essential to break down the barriers between Shakespeare and the reader:

> his fame intimidates and bores . . . Shakespeare is getting flyblown; a paternal government might well forbid writing about him, as they put his monument at Stratford beyond the reach of scribbling fingers. With all this buzz of criticism about, one may hazard one's conjectures privately, make one's notes in the margin, but, knowing that someone has said it before, or said it better, the zest is gone. (CE iv, 436)[3]

Woolf's difficulties with Shakespeare were deeply rooted, going back to her childhood where Shakespeare had been part of the literary world inhabited by her elder brother and her father. Leslie Stephen was a professional literary biographer and a founding editor of the *Dictionary of National Biography*, though it was his co-editor, Sidney Lee, who contributed the life of Shakespeare (Lee's massive two-volume life grew out of that initial research).[4] As a young woman, Virginia Stephen had felt daunted by all those 'lives of great men': her response anticipates that of the feminist Julia Hedge who, in *Jacob's Room*, sits beneath the dome of the British Museum Reading Room reading the names of authors written around it in gold letters – Shakespeare's, of course, among them: 'the names of great men which remind us – ' "Oh damn," said Julia Hedge, "why didn't they leave room for an Eliot or a Brontë? " ' (J's R, 91).[5]

Woolf began work on 'Reading at Random' in the autumn of 1940 as she was writing the unfinished memoir now known as 'A Sketch of the Past'. There she recalled her initial difficulties with Shakespeare and how she and her older brother Thoby had disagreed about the plays:

> A play was antipathetic. How did they begin? With some dull speech; about a hundred miles from anything that interested me. I opened [Twelfth Night] to prove this; I opened at 'If music be the food of love, play on . . . ' I was downed that time. That was, I had to admit, a good beginning.[6]

Their letters continue the debate. Virginia read *Cymbeline* (then very much admired, in the wake of Swinburne's enthusiasm), finding herself as exasperated by the characters as she was entranced by their language:

> Why aren't they more human? Imogen and Posthumous and Cymbeline – I find them beyond me – Is this my feminine weakness in the upper region? But really they might have been cut out with a pair of scissors – as far as mere humanity goes – Of course they talk divinely. I have spotted the best lines in the play – almost in any play I should think – Imogen says – Think that you are upon a rock, and now throw me again! And Posthumous answers – Hang

> there like fruit, my Soul, till the tree die. Now if that doesn't send a shiver down your spine, even if you are in the middle of cold grouse and coffee – you are no true Shakespearian![7]

Was Shakespeare too difficult for women to understand? Woolf's complex and at times uneasy relationship with Shakespeare is reflected in a series of divagations, rejections and rediscoveries that closely parallels her retrospective relationship with her Victorian parents and what they stood for – a simpler, more ideal and more romantic vision of the world than she normally allowed herself, an outlook that risked becoming 'sentimental'. *To the Lighthouse* is the novel that depicts her parents and herself as a child, a novel she feared might also be regarded as 'Sentimental? Victorian?' (*Diary* iii, 107). In a scene at the end of the first part, 'The Window', Mr and Mrs Ramsay (portraits of Leslie and Julia Stephen, as Woolf readily admitted) sit together at the end of the day, each with a book in hand. Mr Ramsay is reading from Scott's novel *The Antiquary*. Mrs Ramsay is reading sonnet 98, 'From you have I been absent in the spring': she

> raised her head . . . She was climbing up those branches, this way and that, laying hands on one flower and then another.
>
> Nor praise the deep vermilion in the rose,
>
> she read, and so reading she was ascending, she felt, on to the top, on to the summit. How satisfying! How restful! All the odds and ends of the day stuck to this magnet; her mind felt swept, felt clean. And then there it was, suddenly entire shaped in her hands, beautiful and reasonable, clear and complete, the essence sucked out of life and held rounded here – the sonnet. (TTL, 131)

Their different reading experiences are subtly gendered: Mr Ramsay is reading prose and participating vicariously in a masculine world of action – the drowning of Steenie – while Mrs Ramsay reads poetry as if climbing through the branches of the text and enjoys a world of feeling – perhaps of feminine feeling? – exemplified by the Shakespeare sonnet. As Jane Marcus suggests in her subtle analysis of this scene, 'Mr Ramsay reads to find himself, Mrs Ramsay to lose herself'.[8]

This is a moment of brief but perfect poise and harmony, yet Shakespeare could have a very different significance for women, and indeed does so in a passage from the first draft of this novel. It occurs during the early stages of the family dinner party near the end of 'The Window' but was excluded from the final version, whereas the account of Mrs Ramsay reading sonnet 98 was added at a late stage and did not appear in the manuscript version. In this draft sequence, Shakespeare is absorbed into the misogyny of Charles Tansley whose assertion, 'Women can't write, women can't paint', threatens the painter Lily Briscoe, undermining her confidence when she most needs it. Her reaction takes the form of a soliloquy:

> Why, then, did one mind what [Charles Tansley] said, Lily Briscoe wondered. – insignificant as he was! O it's Shakespeare, she corrected herself – as a forgetful person entering Regent's Park, & seeing the Park keeper was coming towards her menacingly; might exclaim Oh of course I remember dogs must be on a lead! So Lily Briscoe remembered that every man has Shakespeare & women have not. What then could she say? inferior as she was; & was it not much easier to be inferior after all? – That is the whole secret of art, she thought to herself. To care for the thing: not for oneself: what does it matter whether I succeed or not?[9]

Here Shakespeare is cast as an official, policing the park of literature. The imagery of Lily's soliloquy anticipates those scenes early in *A Room of One's Own* where the narrator is ordered off the college lawn by a Beadle and out of the Wren Library by a librarian because she is an outsider and a woman. Misogyny such as Charles Tansley's was the irritant that prompted Woolf to write *A Room* where his sentence 'Women can't write, women can't paint' (TTL, 94) is translated into the assertion of an unidentified old gentleman, 'Cats do not go to heaven. Women cannot write the plays of Shakespeare' (ROO, 42). These two episodes from *To the Lighthouse* point in opposite directions: Mrs Ramsay's reading of sonnet 98 suggests that Shakespeare supremely expressed the life of feeling and imagination that Woolf associated with her mother and herself, while Lily Briscoe's thoughts link Shakespeare with a territory exclusive to men, a parade ground for the masculine intellect. Was writing about Shakespeare a form of trespassing for Woolf? Taking up *Romeo and Juliet* as a young woman, she had wondered 'Who shall say anything of [it]? Do I dare?'[10] Is this the reason she never formally wrote about Shakespeare?

By the beginning of the twentieth century, the difficulties of doing so were almost as daunting as they are today: Shakespearean scholarship had become the 'Shakespeare industry', reflected in the mass and solidity, the monumental character of Sidney Lee's two-volume *Life*, while productions of the plays tended to be richly costumed, elaborately set, and often suggested Royal Academy paintings in their attention to physical (and naturalistic) detail. During the nineteenth century, scenes from Shakespeare had become particularly popular as subjects for paintings, so much so, indeed, that Katherine Mansfield in a moment of exasperation exclaimed of Gertrude's curious account of Ophelia's death (so visually detailed, but so difficult to explain plausibly), 'Dear Shakespeare has been to the Royal Academy . . . for his picture.'[11]

The modernist project of demythologising Shakespeare has continued to the present day with occasional pauses or backlashes, moments when a more dignified or a more patriotic version was called for. Oppressed by ancestral voices (among which Shakespeare's was the most pervasive), modernism had to confront the too-familiar words, to rework the 'orts, scraps and fragments'[12] it had inherited. The process of interrogating those echoes was already under way when Virginia Woolf began writing. The ninth chapter of Joyce's *Ulysses*, the 'Scylla and Charybdis' chapter, is set in the National Library of Dublin, the repository of so many English words. Here the so-called Quaker librarian, Lyster, and his assistant, Mr Best, listen as Stephen Dedalus propounds his theories on Shakespeare and argue with him about Wilde's *Portrait of Mr. W. H.* and the relative merits of Shakespeare's recent biographers, George Brandes, Frank Harris and, of course, Sir Sidney Lee. But before Stephen unveils his mystery, he evokes a little local colour:

> It is this hour of a day in mid June . . . The flag is up on the playhouse by the bankside. The bear Sackerson growls in the pit near it, Paris garden. Canvasclimbers who sailed with Drake chew their sausages among the groundlings.[13]

Stephen Dedalus rejects the romantic identification of Shakespeare with Hamlet, arguing that when Shakespeare wrote the play he was too old to identify with the young prince just back from university. Associating the physical and metaphysical modes of begetting makes Shakespeare simultaneously the author of *Hamlet* and the father of Hamnet, his real-life son. According to a long theatrical tradition, Shakespeare played Hamlet's father's ghost,[14] a role that enabled him to warn both his real and fictional sons against their mothers' infidelities. Through the figure of Stephen Dedalus, Joyce thus confronted Shakespeare as rival poet and ghostly (fore)father, while endowing him with his own methods of composition, for Joyce had drawn upon the narrative of his own life for 'Stephen Hero' and, later, for *A Portrait of the Artist as a Young Man* and *Ulysses*. Stephen's disquisition on Shakespeare's biography is thus self-reflexive. It is also retrospective in one sense, since (though he does not know it) Stephen is about to step down in favour of the more universal figure of Leopold Bloom who materialises at the Library at the end of the chapter.

While Joyce thus covertly acknowledged the autobiographical nature of his own fiction, he also insisted upon the artist's necessary distance from his material – he must be god-like and stand back from his work, 'paring his fingernails'.[15] T. S. Eliot declared that 'the more perfect the artist, the more completely separate in him will be the man who suffers and the mind which creates'.[16] The ninth chapter of *Ulysses* was published in the *Little Review* in May 1919. When Eliot reviewed J. M. Robertson's book *The Problem of Hamlet* for the *Athenaeum* in September of the same year, he recalled the debate in the National Library as he argued that

Shakespeare's problem in *Hamlet* was that he had become too personally involved, had failed to establish the necessary artistic distance, to find what Eliot termed 'the objective correlative' for his emotions, with the result that the play was 'most certainly an artistic failure'.[17]

If *Hamlet* posed one sort of problem, *Henry V* created another: before the First World War, Henry V was widely regarded as the epitome of the English gentleman, though one Irish gentleman, W. B. Yeats, protested that he occasioned 'the admiration . . . that schoolboys have for the sailor or soldier hero of a romance in some boys' paper', and contrasted him unfavourably with Richard II, a version of the Yeatsian dreamer ('I cannot believe that Shakespeare looked on his Richard II with any but sympathetic eyes').[18]

The disillusion brought by the War led to a new and very different interpretation of Henry V – as a callous hypocrite – from the poet and critic Gerald Gould.[19] For Virginia Woolf in her earliest novel *The Voyage Out* (begun in 1907 and completed in 1913, though not published until 1915), *Henry V* was still a touchstone for patriotism and Englishness. In this novel, Clarissa Dalloway and her husband Richard, an ex-Tory MP, make their first appearance as absurd and sentimental imperialists, satirised for their chauvinism. At the end of the fourth chapter, as the sinister shape of the *Dreadnought* battleship comes into view, Clarissa squeezes the heroine's hand, demanding ' "Aren't you glad to be English! " ' (VO, 60).

Earlier, Mr Grice, the ship's steward, shows Clarissa his collection of sea creatures, while reciting in

> an emphatic nasal voice:
> Full fathom five thy father lies,
> 'A grand fellow, Shakespeare,' he said . . .
> Clarissa was so glad to hear him say so.
> 'Which is your favourite play? I wonder if it's the same as mine?'
> '*Henry the Fifth*,' said Mr Grice.
> 'Joy!' cried Clarissa, 'It is!'
> *Hamlet* was what you might call too introspective for Mr Grice, the sonnets too passionate; Henry the Fifth was to him the model of an English gentleman. (VO, 46)

As if to counterbalance this note of satire in her first novel, Shakespeare figures quite differently in Woolf's second novel, *Night and Day* (1919), where he is comfortably assimilated into the eccentric and feminine world of Mrs Hilbery, mother of the heroine, who sees her daughter as Rosalind and herself as a Shakespearean fool (ND, 260; also 146):

> Beginning with a perfectly frivolous jest, Mrs Hilbery had evolved a theory that Anne Hathaway had a way, among other things, of writing Shakespeare's sonnets; . . . she had come half to believe in her joke, which was, she said, at

> least as good as other people's facts . . . She had a plan . . . for visiting Shakespeare's tomb. (ND, 258–9)

Mrs Hilbery's jest (like Mrs Hilbery herself) was inspired by Anny Thackeray Ritchie, daughter of the great Victorian novelist and elder sister of Leslie Stephen's first wife. 'Aunt Anny' was her father's biographer and a novelist in her own right. When Samuel Butler was working on *Shakespeare's Sonnets Reconsidered* (1899), she had asked him 'O, Mr Butler, I hope you think they were written by Anne Hathaway to Shakespeare?' Her joke was in part an allusion to Butler's previous book, *The Author of the Odyssey* (1897), which had argued that the great Greek epic had been written by a woman (Butler, apparently, was not amused).[20]

In Woolf's novel, Mrs Hilbery sets off for Shakespeare's tomb, 'the heart of the civilized world','with a passion that would not have been unseemly in a pilgrim to a sacred shrine'. It seems that she is planning to dig up the tomb in search of the buried manuscripts of Anne Hathaway's sonnets – a scheme that threatens 'the safety of the heart of civilisation' (ND, 364) through its challenge to the myth of the supreme male author.[21] At the novel's climax, Mrs Hilbery returns from Stratford weighed down by branches of laurel and garlands of spring flowers – ' "From Shakespeare's tomb!" exclaimed Mrs Hilbery, dropping the entire mass upon the floor, with a gesture that seemed to indicate an act of dedication' (ND, 408). 'Old gentlemen' were not slow to inform Mrs Woolf that leaves and flowers do not grow on Shakespeare's grave, but she refused to alter it – the scene was artistically right, if not precisely 'true to the facts'.

Gender complicated Woolf's response to Shakespeare, as did his appropriation for patriotic propaganda, and, while the beauty of Shakespeare's language and the beauty of Shakespeare's landscapes always held a strong appeal for her, she was well aware that they could be borrowed for unwelcome political ends.[22] *Mrs Dalloway* (1925) alludes pointedly to the exploitation of Shakespeare to attract young men into the army. Septimus Warren Smith 'was one of the first to volunteer. He went to France to save an England which consisted almost entirely of Shakespeare's plays and Miss Isabel Pole in a green dress walking in a square' (Miss Isabel Pole had been his adult education tutor) (MD, 94). When Septimus Warren Smith returned shell-shocked from the War, his disillusion coloured his reading of Shakespeare. He saw '[h]ow Shakespeare loathed humanity – the putting on of clothes, the getting of children, the sordidity of the mouth and the belly! This was now revealed to Septimus; the message hidden in the beauty of words' (MD, 97). *Mrs Dalloway* is also the novel in which Clarissa and Richard Dalloway reappear, but now their 'Kensington' conventions and high Tory politics have been displaced onto more minor characters such as Hugh Whitbread, a stuffy official at 'the Palace', and Lady Bruton who has somehow absorbed Shakespeare instinctively: her 'love for "this isle of men, this dear dear land" was in her blood (without having read Shakespeare)' (MD, 198).[23]

Woolf did not actually visit Stratford and Shakespeare's tomb until May 1934 when she and Leonard were motoring back from their first (and only) visit to Ireland, a visit that, given Ireland's recent troubled history, must have prompted thoughts about nationalism and its effects. She liked the town of Stratford, finding it surprisingly unspoiled, and imagined the spirit of Shakespeare close at hand, in the mulberry tree at New Place, where

> [a]ll the flowers were out in Sh[akespea]re's garden . . . He is serenely absent-present; both at once; radiating round one; yes; in the flowers, in the old hall, in the garden; but never to be pinned down . . . there was no impediment of fame, but his genius flowed out of him, & is still there, in Stratford. (*Diary* iv, 219–20)

If Shakespeare's spirit, hovered, an Ariel unconfined, around his birthplace, the aura of the national poet also imbued his native county: in January 1941, when the war was at its darkest, Woolf told her friend Ethel Smyth that London was her 'only patriotism: save one vision, in Warwickshire one spring when we were driving back from Ireland and I saw a stallion being led, under the may and the beeches, along a grass ride; and I thought that is England' (*Letters* vi, 460).

Woolf deeply distrusted patriotism and nationalism, believing they fomented wars; such feelings were particularly ill-suited to women living in a patriarchy, whose stake in society was significantly different from that of men. And just as gender affected or inflected her sense of patriotism, so it could not be kept entirely separate from her response to Shakespeare even though (as we have seen) she also read him as a writer who spoke directly to women through his insight into the inner life. Such conflicting responses waited to be reconciled.

From an early stage, no doubt encouraged by the *Zeitgeist* and her friendships with Rupert Brooke and T. S. Eliot, Woolf had read widely among Shakespeare's contemporaries, writing essays on Elizabethan drama ('Notes on an Elizabethan Play'), as well as on Gabriel Harvey (in 'The Strange Elizabethans'), Sidney, Spenser, Donne, and more than once on Hakluyt whom she had loved since childhood. Yet there is no single essay devoted to Shakespeare, not, it seems, from any lack of enthusiasm on her part, nor from any shortage of invitations on the part of others – a letter to David Garnett politely thanks him for inviting her to do so, adding, by way of explanation,

> I have a kind of feeling that unless one is possessed of the truth, or is a garrulous old busybody, from America, one ought to hold one's tongue. So I will. I mean I wont. Send it [an unidentified book on Shakespeare] to Logan [Pearsall Smith] is what I mean, and take my blessing. (*Letters* v, 257)

The closest she came to doing so was a review of Tyrone Guthrie's production of *Twelfth Night* at the Old Vic in September 1933, a review written reluctantly and from a sense of duty, since Lydia Lopokova (now Lydia Keynes) was playing Olivia in an attempt to convert her career as a dancer to that of an actress.[24] Woolf carefully avoided direct comment on Lopokova's performance by taking up the old debate on the difference between a play read and a play acted (Dr Johnson had claimed that '[a] play read affects the mind like a play acted'). The shortcomings of Lopokova's performance could thus be represented as resulting from the inevitable difference between a private reading and a public performance. Woolf's account is so carefully worded that, at first glance, one might mistake it for praise.

One reason Woolf never wrote directly about Shakespeare was that for her fiction usually came first and theory afterwards, and in dealing with controversial topics (such as sex or Shakespeare – or even both together) 'one cannot hope to tell the truth. One can only show how one came to hold whatever opinion one does hold . . . Fiction here is likely to contain more truth than fact' (ROO, 4). Yet the fiction which might have been expected from its title and historical moment to portray Shakespeare only does so obliquely: *Orlando: A Biography* (1928) begins as the story of a young man in love with a girl dressed as a boy, the story of a hero run mad for love (behind Shakespeare's choice of 'Orlando' as the name of the third son of Sir Rowland de Bois lay Ariosto's epic, *Orlando Furioso* – Orlando maddened[25]).

*Orlando* can be read as an act of homage to Woolf's androgynous aristocratic friend Vita Sackville-West or even to Shakespeare, the dramatist whose comedies celebrate the possibilities of gender change and fluidity, yet, if so, both 'begetters' are notable for their absence though they are never very far off. But if Shakespeare is absent, or very nearly so, his dark shadow, the Salieri to his Amadeus, is present in the character of Nick Greene, almost (if not quite) the rival playwright and pamphleteer Robert Greene. For Nick Greene in Woolf's novel, the writing of the modern age – of any modern age – is to be deplored. The envious Greene becomes Orlando's treacherous pensioner, his overweaning protégé.[26]

At the heart of Woolf's novel lies the identity of Orlando with Woolf's beloved Vita, and the unspoken (because at that time unspeakable) history of their friendship (Radclyffe Hall's novel of lesbian love, *The Well of Loneliness*, was prosecuted in November 1928, a month after

*Orlando*'s publication). With this open secret at its heart, the text makes great play with disguise and concealment, with masks and masquing. In an episode later abandoned, Greene gives Orlando a letter he just happens to have on him – it is 'Shakespeares own account of his relations with that Mr W H & the dark Lady written by him with great fulness & spirit'. But instead of relating its contents, the narrator consigns it to the fire on the grounds that

> when Truth and modesty conflict (as they so often do) who can doubt which should prevail? . . . No one of British blood will censure us for the course we took; & as for the rest, their opinions on a matter of this sort, scarcely matter.

Thus, an officious – and properly 'British' – propriety deprives the reader of a possible solution to the most notorious of all literary mysteries.[27]

Greene was not the only Elizabethan pamphleteer to figure in *Orlando*: Thomas Dekker's 'The Great Frost or Cold Doings in London, except it be at the Lottery' provided Woolf with an unforgettable vision of London and the River Thames in the grip of the Great Frost of 1608 – which parallels the frozen passion that grips Orlando. For those brief weeks, it possesses him as he and Sasha sweep and swoop over the ice. As it thaws, her love melts, carrying Sasha back to Muscovy and Orlando into the frenzy of grief that links him to Ariosto's hero, a frenzy anticipated by seeing a performance of *Othello* on the ice (O, 40–1).

Orlando – both the character and the novel – is haunted by a mysterious figure glimpsed when Queen Elizabeth visits Orlando's great house, a house never named just as this figure is never named – his identity is confined to the liminal column of the index (O, 230). Glancing into the housekeeper's sitting room as he passes, Orlando catches sight of 'a rather fat, rather shabby man' in a dirty ruff, holding a pen in his hand. He

> seemed in the act of rolling some thought up and down, to and fro in his mind till it gathered shape or momentum to his liking. His eyes, globed and clouded like some green stone of curious texture, were fixed. He did not see Orlando . . . the man turned his pen in his fingers . . . and gazed and mused; and then, very quickly, wrote half-a-dozen lines and looked up.

This vision haunts Orlando for the rest of his/her life (O, 16, and 56, 116–17, 215–16, 226), perhaps as it had haunted Woolf herself, for ten years earlier, in the first short story she wrote for the Hogarth Press, she imagined just such a figure sitting in an arm-chair and gazing into the fire (as the story's narrator is doing), while '[a] shower of ideas fell perpetually from some very high Heaven down through his mind. He leant his forehead on his hand, and people, looking in through the open door –' as Orlando would later do ('The Mark on the Wall', CSF, 85). Woolf's next novel, *The Waves*, is similarly haunted by a vision of an unidentified writer – the lady of Elvedon, who 'sits between the two long windows, writing' (W, 11, and also 18, 93, 147, 164, 185, 191, 196, 206).

To discover the nature of the relationship between the stranger in Mrs Stewkley's parlour and his female equivalent, the absent figure of Vita or Orlando herself, we must turn to Woolf's next book, her polemic, *A Room of One's Own*, a book twinned with *Orlando* in terms of theme and construction. Where *Orlando* had dramatised the difficulties encountered by the woman artist, *A Room of One's Own* theorises them, and it is here that Woolf finally confronts the old gentleman's assertion that 'Cats do not go to heaven. Women cannot write the plays of Shakespeare' (though cats 'have, he added, souls of sorts', ROO, 42). Woolf's work up to this point had in various ways been asking 'To whom does Shakespeare belong? To men or to women?' The conclusion she reached lies in the unexpected connection she now found between the two absent presences of *Orlando*. Orlando, like Vita (or Shakespeare), was a poet and as a poet s/he was marked out by the quality that also characterises Vita and Shakespeare – that is, a refusal to be pinned down, to be confined, and in particular to be confined to a single gender role. Shakespeare, like Vita and like Orlando, is androgynous. Coleridge, greatest of all Shakespearean critics, had observed that 'a great mind is androgynous' (ROO, 88).[28] Here lay the explanation for Shakespeare's plenitude: 'If ever a human being got his work expressed completely, it was Shakespeare. If ever a mind was incandescent, unimpeded . . . it was Shakespeare's mind' (ROO, 52).[29]

> [Coleridge] meant, perhaps, that the androgynous mind is resonant and porous; that it transmits emotion without impediment; that it is naturally creative, incandescent and undivided. In fact, one goes back to Shakespeare's mind as the type of the androgynous, of the man-womanly mind. (ROO, 89)

Shakespeare, in other words, is Orlando's ideal/ised double (rather as Nick Greene is Shakespeare's darker shadow).

But Woolf hadn't quite finished with the old gentleman, the cats that don't go to heaven and the women who cannot write Shakespeare's plays. Unexpectedly, she now agrees that the old gentleman was 'right at least in this; it would have been impossible, completely and entirely, for any woman to have written the plays of Shakespeare in the age of Shakespeare', an age when women had little status and no history, for 'nothing is known about women before the eighteenth century' (ROO, 42).[30] This explains why Orlando cannot become a woman until then, and her first incarnation must inevitably be as a man. Now, in an act of imaginative resistance, Woolf invents yet another double for Orlando (and perhaps for Shakespeare too) in the form of Shakespeare's imaginary sister Judith who aspires to become a playwright. Her history is not so much a blank as a series of disasters – and that echo of Viola in *Twelfth Night* is deliberate, since the invention of Judith Shakespeare as a kind of extension of her more famous brother echoes Shakespeare's own invention in *Twelfth Night* when he transforms the androgynous Viola/Cesario into the heavenly twins, Viola and Sebastian, in order to untie the play's love-knot.

Judith Shakespeare flees from her parental home at Stratford to London and the playhouses, hoping to become an actress and a writer. There, she is inevitably seduced by the odious Nick Greene (familiar from *Orlando*), and finds herself pregnant. She, for

> who shall measure the heat and violence of the poet's heart when caught and tangled in a woman's body? – killed herself one winter's night and lies buried at some cross-roads where the omnibuses now stop outside the Elephant and Castle. (ROO, 44)

The Old Vic, with its tradition of Shakespearean performance, stood close by. Judith Shakespeare's dark fate no doubt precluded her from figuring in the essentially comic narrative of *Orlando*, though her close connections with that novel and its hero are reflected in the structural similarities between the two books. Judith Shakespeare appears and dies at the heart of chapter 3 of *A Room* . . . at a point closely corresponding to Orlando's sex-change at Constantinople in chapter 3 of the earlier novel. Judith Shakespeare is thus Orlando's sixteenth-century female self, frustrated and finally destroyed by the patriarchal culture of her time. But even now, Woolf hasn't quite finished with her – she must undergo a further transformation. Though 'despised and rejected' in her first incarnation, 'the dead poet who was Shakespeare's sister will put on the body which she has so often laid down'; 'she will be born' (ROO, 102–3), she will come again, and women must wait and work for her second coming.

The invention of Shakespeare's sister suggests a fundamental difference between Woolf and Joyce in their responses to the complex balance of threat and inspiration that Shakespeare constituted for each of them. Though both responded through fiction, they did so in diametrically opposed ways and along contrasting axes. The 'Scylla and Charybdis' chapter begins with Lyster talking of Goethe as 'a great brother poet',[31] yet Joyce read his relationship with Shakespeare in terms of father and son, on what is essentially a 'vertical' axis. Shakespeare plays the ghost that haunts his son, and Stephen identifies with young Hamlet. Though Stephen tosses in an argument about Shakespeare's brothers, Gilbert and the more sinister Edmund and Richard,[32] it is the impact of his father that predominates, while old Hamlet is obscurely linked with Simon Dedalus, another primal story-teller, according to the opening lines of *A Portrait of the Artist*. The ghost of old Hamlet suggests the Oedipal anxieties involved in resisting a father's influence, for Freud has also made a contribution to Joyce's reading. And if the tensions between father and son determine Stephen's relationship with Shakespeare, it is further complicated by nationality, so that his language is and is not Shakespeare's.[33]

While Joyce's relationship with Shakespeare is problematised by nationality, Woolf's is complicated by gender – 'Women cannot write the plays of Shakespeare', so is there any point in trying? Unlike that of Joyce, Woolf's relationship to Shakespeare lies along a horizontal rather than a vertical axis: despite her own writing father, she sees herself not as Shakespeare's daughter but his sister. Unlike Eliot, she refuses to be fazed by the problems of Hamlet. 'If you find *Hamlet* difficult, ask him to tea. He is a highbrow. Ask Ophelia to meet him. She is a lowbrow. Talk to them as you talk to me . . . ' ('Middlebrow', CE ii, 201). Shakespeare is Judith's older brother – and this was also true of her personal experience, since Shakespeare had played a key role in her relationship with her older brother Thoby who died young in 1906 and whose death is mourned in *Jacob's Room* and *The Waves*. Thoby had 'consumed Shakespeare . . . had possessed himself of it'. It was 'his other world', and Woolf echoed Hamlet's epitaph, 'Had he been put on, he would have proved most royally' (MB, 141–2). Her arguments with him had had a further function, for they created a bond between them that had excluded Vanessa, Virginia's sister and beloved rival, from their conversation. Thus Shakespeare, for Virginia, was from the beginning bound up with sibling love and rivalry within the family.

So, though in one sense Woolf never wrote about Shakespeare, in another sense she never stopped writing about him, and he continued to hover 'serenely absent-present', as she had sensed at Stratford, until the end of her life. *The Waves*, partly inspired by sonnet 60, 'Like as the waves make towards the pebbled shore', and written as a series of dramatic soliloquies to an epic form and on an epic scale, is arguably Woolf's most Shakespearean work, but Shakespearean imagery and language run through her later novels. In the final section of *The Years*, North opens an unidentified book at random and reads ' "The scene is a rocky island in the middle of the sea " ' – a Victorian stage direction, it seems, for Act I scene 2 of *The Tempest* (Y, 253), and Shakespeare's 'last' play dominates Woolf's final novel, *Between the Acts*. Here Prospero is transformed into the stout middle-aged lesbian, Miss La Trobe (meaning 'finder' or 'inventor'), the artist as magician, yet, like Prospero, troubled and marginalised, presiding uneasily over a pageant that itself includes a scene from an imaginary Elizabethan play. As *The Tempest* does, *Between the Acts* adopts a unified time scheme and setting, and Woolf quietly acknowledges her debt at several points: 'Isa had done with her bills. Sitting in the shell of the room, she watched the pageant fade. The flowers flashed before they faded. She watched them flash' (BA, 128, echoing Prospero's 'like this insubstantial pageant fades', Act IV, sc. 1, 155).

As always, Woolf's echo brings something new to her allusion, transforming and reactivating its words. If Woolf never wrote the essay on Shakespeare that we might have looked for, scattered throughout her writings – her novels and essays, but in particular her diaries – a portrait of Shakespeare emerges: '[s]omewhere, everywhere, now hidden, now apparent in whatever is written down',[34] the result of a serious reading of one great writer by another. And, as one might have suspected, that reading is often formalist in its emphasis, exploring how it is that Shakespeare achieves his effects and wondering what might be learned from his example. In particular, as Woolf was working on the huge and (as she felt), inchoate material that eventually became *The Years*, she wondered at the extraordinary ease with which Shakespeare apparently jumped from one mood and level of experience to another, from scenes of simple action to scenes of great inwardness – especially when she herself was finding it difficult to make such transitions.[35]

At other times, she abandons herself to an 'O altitudo!' as in this passage from her diary, written during the writing of *The Waves*:

> I read Shakespeare *directly* I have finished writing, when my mind is agape & red & hot. Then it is astonishing. I never yet knew how amazing his stretch & speed & word coining power is, until I felt it utterly outpace & outrace my own, seeming to start equal & then I see him draw ahead & do things I could not in my wildest tumult & utmost press of mind imagine. Even the less known & worser plays are written at a speed that is quicker than anybody else's quickest; & the words drop so fast one can't pick them up. Look at this, Upon a gather'd lily almost wither'd (that is a pure accident: I happen to light on it.) Evidently the pliancy of his mind was so complete that he could furbish out any train of thought; &, relaxing lets fall a shower of such unregarded flowers. Why then should anyone else attempt to write. This is not 'writing' at all. Indeed, I could say that Sh[akespea]re surpasses literature altogether, if I knew what I meant. (*Diary* iii, 300–1)[36]

## Notes

1. Transcribed from Woolf's notes by Brenda R. Silver, in ' "Anon" and "The Reader": Virginia Woolf's Last Essays', *Twentieth Century Literature*, 25, 3/4 (Fall/Winter 1979), p. 434 (with my minor expansions). As Silver points

out, Woolf did indeed visit London on 13 January 1941, probably at the same time as she made this note. She 'went to London Bridge' and 'looked at the river; very misty; some tufts of smoke, perhaps from burning houses'. Her diary entry (for 'Wednesday 15 January' 1941) mourns the destruction of London in the Blitz and reflects on the death of James Joyce at Zurich, also on 13 January. On Woolf's readings of Shakespeare, see Alice Fox's chapter in *Virginia Woolf and the Literature of the English Renaissance* (Oxford: Clarendon Press, 1990), pp. 94–158; Christine Froula, 'Virginia Woolf as Shakespeare's Sister: Chapters in a Woman Writer's Autobiography', in Marianne Novy, ed., *Women's Re-Visions of Shakespeare* (Urbana and Chicago: University of Illinois Press, 1990), pp. 123–42.

2. Brenda Silver, ibid., pp. 431–2.
3. In his edition, Leonard Woolf notes that this essay was first published in 1930 (as a Hogarth Press pamphlet), overlooking its earliest publication in T. S. Eliot's *New Criterion* for January 1926 – see Andrew McNeillie's note to the earlier text in *Essays* iv, 327 (though I have cited the later text).
4. For Sidney Lee's biographies of Shakespeare, see Samuel Schoenbaum, *Shakespeare's Lives* (Oxford: Oxford University Press, 1970), pp. 506–26, and for Virginia Stephen's response to Lee's *Life of Shakespeare* see her letter to Thoby Stephen, [May 1903], *Letters* i, 77.
5. See also J's R, 94, where the stones of the British Museum are the bones covering 'Plato's brain and Shakespeare's'. These stones are protected by the Museum's night-watchmen, while 'the woman in the mews . . . cries all night long, "Let me in! Let me in!" '.
6. 'A Sketch of the Past', in *Moments of Being: Unpublished Autobiographical Writings*, ed. Jeanne Schulkind (1976), p. 139. This section of the text is dated 'October 12th 1940' and the first notes for 'Reading at Random' are dated 18th September 1940 – Silver, p. 356 (I here prefer the earlier version to the revised edition at MB, 142).
7. To Thoby Stephen, 5 Nov 1901, *Letters* i, 45–6; *Cymbeline*, Act V, sc. 6, 264–5. In *Jacob's Room* Jacob is partly based on Thoby Stephen, and his friend Cruttendon quotes this line as one of ' "the three greatest things that were ever written in the whole of literature" ', p. 110. The opening words of Fidele's dirge from the same play, 'Fear no more the heat of the sun', become a repeated refrain in *Mrs Dalloway* where they comment on the death of the young.
8. 'Still Practice, A/Wrested Alphabet: Towards a Feminist Aesthetic', *Art & Anger: Reading Like A Woman* (Columbus: Ohio State University Press, 1988), p. 246. The figure of a primeval 'woman in a tree' reappears in *Women & Fiction: The Manuscript Versions of 'A Room of One's Own'*, ed. S. P. Rosenbaum (Oxford: Blackwell, Shakespeare Head, 1992), pp. 143, 144.
9. *To the Lighthouse: The Original Holograph Draft*, ed. Susan Dick (London: Hogarth Press, 1983), p. 136 (slightly simplified from Dick's transcript). Woolf originally wrote 'Hyde Park', and then altered it to 'Regents Park', perhaps, as Michael Dobson has suggested to me, because there were open-air performances of Shakespeare in Regent's Park from as early as 1900.

10. Cited by Alice Fox from Woolf's Holograph Reading Notes, Jan. 1909–March 1911, at the back of the holograph draft of *Night and Day*, in the Berg Collection of the New York Public Library, op. cit., p. 98.
11. *The Critical Writings of Katherine Mansfield*, ed. Clare Hanson (Basingstoke: Macmillan, 1987), p. 120 (and see pp. 118–19 for Mansfield's hilarious account of her response to *All's Well that Ends Well*). Mansfield probably had John Millais's famous painting of Ophelia in mind.
12. This phrase occurs at BA, p. 111, and it is echoed on pp. 112 twice, 114 and 127, recalling 'The fractions of her faith, orts of her love,/ The fragments, scraps, the bits and greasy relics,/ Of her o'ereaten faith', *Troilus and Cressida*, Act V, sc. 2, 161–3.
13. *Ulysses*, ed. Hans Walter Gabler (London: Bodley Head, 1986), p. 154, lines 154–7.
14. It derives from Nicholas Rowe's 'Account' of Shakespeare introducing his edition of the *Works* (1709), vol. I, p. vi.
15. 'The artist, like the God of the creation, remains within or behind or beyond or above his handiwork, invisible, refined out of existence, indifferent, paring his fingernails', *A Portrait of the Artist as a Young Man* (1916), ed. Hans Walter Gabler (New York and London: Garland, 1993), p. 242, lines 1467–9.
16. 'Tradition and the Individual Talent', *The Sacred Wood: Essays on Poetry and Criticism* (1920; London: Methuen, 1976), p. 54.
17. 'Hamlet and His Problems', *The Sacred Wood*, pp. 100–1, 98.
18. 'At Stratford-on-Avon' (1901), W. B. Yeats, *Selected Criticism and Prose*, ed. A. N. Jeffares (London: Macmillan, 1980), pp. 99, 100.
19. Gerald Gould, 'A New Reading of *Henry V*', *The English Review*, 29 (1919), pp. 42–55; reprinted in *'Henry V', a Casebook*, ed. Michael Quinn (London: Macmillan, 1969), pp. 81–94.
20. Desmond MacCarthy relates this anecdote in his Foreword to *Thackeray's Daughter: Some Recollections*, ed. Hester Thackeray Fuller and V. Hammersley (Dublin: Euphorion Books, 1951), p. 7. Butler's *Shakespeare's Sonnets Reconsidered* had been inspired by Wilde's *Portrait of Mr. W. H.* (1889), which argued that the sonnets were written for a boy actor, Willie Hughes (or Hewes). Butler searched through contemporary records, and discovered a sea-cook of that name; in his account, Shakespeare loves the sailor but is troubled by his coarseness.
21. In *Women & Fiction*, Woolf would imagine an Amazonian tribe whose 'chief poetess, the poet Maya Hina [may be] the superior of Shakespeare', p. 55. Mrs Hilbery is the first of Woolf's attempts to rewrite Shakespeare as a woman and is thus a precursor of Judith Shakespeare.
22. This point is considered at greater length in the thirteenth essay, ' "Almost Ashamed of England Being so English"', pp. 191–2, 196–8. For Woolf's equation of beauty with Shakespeare, see *Diary* ii, 273: 'it was so lovely in the Waterloo Road that it struck me that we were writing Shakespeare . . . somehow it affected me as I am affected by reading Shakespeare.'
23. The allusion is to John of Gaunt's speech, 'This royal throne of kings . . .', (*Richard II*, Act II, sc. 1, 40 ff, esp. 45, 57), a *locus classicus* for patriotic sentiment (we are told on p. 115 that Lady Bruton 'never read a word of poetry herself'). For Richard Dalloway's youthful response to the Sonnets, see below, n. 27.

24. '*Twelfth Night* at the Old Vic', *New Statesman & Nation*, 30 September 1933, pp. 385–6, reprinted in CE i, 28–31. Woolf referred to it as 'Lydia's extortion' in *Diary* iv, 179, and see her letter to Quentin Bell, *Letters* iv, 227.
25. As Woolf indirectly acknowledged in a passage cut from the published text that records the contents of Orlando's library as 'Petrarch; Bocaccio; Ariosto;' – see *Orlando: The Holograph Draft*, ed. S. N. Clarke (London: S. N. Clarke, 1993), p. 145.
26. He is also the contemporary critic Edmund Gosse, as Vita told her husband Harold Nicolson in a letter of 11 October 1928 – see Victoria Glendinning, *Vita: The Life of V. Sackville-West* (New York: Alfred A. Knopf, 1983), p. 202. Michael H. Whitworth, in *Virginia Woolf: Authors in Context* (Oxford: Oxford University Press, 2005), pp. 84–5, argues that Greene's opinions echo those of Logan Pearsall Smith.
27. *Orlando: The Holograph Draft*, p. 72. The theme of homosexual desire gives the sonnets a special relevance to *Orlando*; see also *Mrs Dalloway*, where the young Richard Dalloway at Bourton 'got on his hind legs and said that no decent man ought to read Shakespeare's sonnets because it was like listening at keyholes (besides, the relationship was not one that he approved)', p. 82.
28. See Coleridge's *Table Talk*, 1 September 1832.
29. These sentences may be Woolf's response to Eliot's critique of *Hamlet*.
30. We now know that Woolf's assumption was wrong, but in making it she urged her young women listeners to go out and find out more about women's history, and our knowledge is partly the result of their having followed her instruction.
31. *Ulysses*, p. 151, line 3 (Lyster refers to 'those priceless pages of *Wilhelm Meister*').
32. *Ibid*., pp. 171–4.
33. In chapter 5 of *A Portrait* . . . Stephen discusses the English language with the (English) dean, recalling 'that the man to whom he was speaking was a countryman of Ben Jonson', p. 216, lines 551–2.
34. Said of Sir Thomas Browne in 'Reading', CE ii, 29.
35. See, for example, *Diary* iv, 207: 'An idea about Sh[akespea]re . . . This is working out my theory of the different levels in writing, & how to combine them'. As the remainder of this note indicates, Woolf thought that the realism of drama required Shakespeare to come 'to the surface', and envied his ability to combine this with great depth of feeling.
36. As a note points out, the quotation is from *Titus Andronicus*, Act III, sc. 1, 114. The phrase 'my widest tumult and utmost press of mind' deliberately echoes a favourite Shakespearean word order.

Essay 2

# 'The Proper Writing of Lives': Biography versus Fiction in Woolf's Early Work

'I should like to write a very subtle work on the proper writing of lives. What it is that you can write – and what writing is. It comes over me that I know nothing of the art', Virginia Stephen confided in her brother-in-law, Clive Bell, in 1908 (*Letters* i, 325). Many years later she would fulfil her ambition, writing subtle essays on 'The New Biography' (1927) and 'The Art of Biography' (1940), but her earliest writings are preoccupied with the problems posed by 'the proper writing of lives', exploring them through her writing practice and her comments on its possibilities and constraints. Biography could be seen as an exemplary form in combining history and imagination, fact and fantasy, constraint and freedom, but at the same time she did not subscribe to its rationale, indeed its exemplary nature in that other sense of holding up moral examples. From an early stage, she was committed to extending its range and increasing its flexibility, to writing against it as well as within it, as she would later do with fiction. In her second novel, *Night and Day*, fiction and biography are used to mirror one another, but, although she completed her novel, the biography that is being written within the book remains unfinished.

It is scarcely surprising that the young Virginia Stephen associated the possibilities of (and constraints upon) writing with the writing of biography, given her status as 'Daughter of the *DNB*'. Her father, Sir Leslie Stephen, had gained his knighthood primarily for editing the *Dictionary of National Biography*. Not only in the household in which she grew up but in the wider family group, biography was accorded high status as a literary form, and widely practised: 'when one of them dies the chances are that another of them writes his biography' (ND, 27). Leslie Stephen's commitment to his massive task was at once respected and resented. According to family legend, the Dictionary had been produced at the expense of his younger children's well-being: 'Poor old Adrian!' wrote Woolf of her younger brother,

> the *DNB* crushed his life out before he was born. It gave me a twist of the head too. I shouldn't have been so clever, but I should have been more stable, without that contribution to the history of England. (*Diary* ii, 277)

She sometimes attributed her poor health to 'those 68 black books' (*Letters* iv, 145). At the end of her life, when she was writing her autobiography, she read Freud and borrowed from him the term 'ambivalence' to describe the blend of love and hatred that she felt for her father (MB, 116). Something of those conflicting feelings extended to the literary form with which Leslie Stephen was most closely associated. Her earliest work paid homage to it and accepted it as a literary yardstick even while seeking to modify its influence.

Leslie Stephen had accepted the editorship of the *DNB* in 1882, the year Virginia was born. Its purpose was to keep a national record of the lives of great men, the heroes who 'had sailed with Sir John Franklin to the North Pole, and ridden with Havelock to the Relief of Lucknow' (ND, 26), the greatest British writers, statesmen and thinkers; yet fired though it was by a sense of the inspiration that heroic lives might provide, that ethos was already beginning to be suspect. It was during the 1880s and 1890s, the very years when Stephen was working on his dictionary, that modern biography was born. Woolf would later point out that 'Froude's [biography of] Carlyle is by no means a wax mask . . . And following Froude there was Sir Edmund Gosse, who dared to say that his own father was a fallible human being' (CE iv, 222). A cultural shift in the nature of biography had begun. Both Woolf's later essays on biography – 'The New Biography' (*Essays* iv, 473–8) and 'The Art of Biography' (CE iv, 221–8) analyse this development in which Lytton Strachey played a key role. Over time, she observed, it would bring the intimate, domestic view, with its 'accent on sex' (CE iv, 226) to the centre of biography – the place it occupies today.

Virginia Stephen's first experience of writing biography might have been designed to illustrate the gap between the authorised version and the backstairs view. In the autumn following her father's death in February 1904, the historian Frederic Maitland invited her to contribute to his biography of her father. The resulting sketch, included in *The Life and Letters of Leslie Stephen* (1906), pictures him sailing a toy boat with his children on the Round Pond and reading to them in the evening – intimate scenes from the great man's domestic life, yet, as such, carefully selected (*Essays* i, 127–9). Familiar only to the women in his life were the violent uninhibited tantrums and rages that seemed to his daughters so 'brutal'. His mother, his sister Caroline, his two wives, his step-daughter and his daughters had all put up with them, accepting them as the price of his 'genius'; but according to Woolf's later view, each 'bowing to it, increased the load for the other' (MB, 148). Fred Maitland, she recalled, 'resolutely refused to believe, though tactfully instructed by Carry [Woolf's aunt, Caroline Emelia Stephen], that Leslie's tempers were more than what he called (in his biography) 'coloured showers of sparks' (MB, 148).

Men and women, then, might see the same individual from very different angles. The intimate and sometimes sordid secrets of a man's life, that he 'threw boots at the maid's head, had a mistress in Islington, or was found drunk in a ditch after a night's debauch' (CE iv, 226), were often only too obvious to his wife, his maid, even his daughters, but, as Woolf recognised, truths of that kind were not yet tolerated in middle-class society. Trawling through her father's letters for his biographer, she was urged by Jack Hills, an old family friend, 'Whatever you do, *dont* publish anything too intimate' (*Letters* i, 151). 'The sensibilities of conventional people' demanded that the male subject be portrayed in such a way that he continued to command respect within his family: 'One of the objects of biography is to make men appear as they ought to be, for they are husbands and brothers' ('Sterne', *Essays* i, 281)

Not only were the perspectives of public and private life very different but women were also confined to roles whose most characteristic activities and experiences were often considered too trivial for fiction, let alone for biography defined in terms of 'the lives of great men'. Living mainly at home, feeding rabbits, visiting old ladies, shopping or reading, young middle-class women were virtually invisible as they went about their 'curious silent unrepresented life' (VO, 200). One of the chief problems that Woolf confronted as a biographer was how to write the lives that the *Dictionary* had ignored, those lives of the obscure that remained unrecorded, that were lived out, unconsidered and unvalued, in the shadows. As a reader, reviewer and writer, she committed herself to an exploration of women's lives. Her many biographical sketches of women made a counter-claim to her father's writings, as if setting up a posthumous interrogation of his principles of inclusion, or else directing attention to the major omissions in his coverage.

She was particularly interested in the lives marginalised by the *Dictionary*, lives of women, of outsiders, of the obscure. In 1915 she proposed writing 'a book of "Eccentrics". Mrs. Grote shall be one. Lady Hester Stanhope. Margaret Fuller. Duchess of Newcastle. Aunt Julia [Margaret Cameron]?' (*Diary* i, 23). In 1919, an essay on 'The Eccentrics' (*Essays* iii, 38–41) attempted to revive the idea, and she did indeed write lives of three of these five women at different times.[1] All, in one way or another, had refused to accept traditional pressures and had put their own dreams and visions first, as the writer must also do. The category of lives of the obscure was altogether more problematic: eccentrics usually attracted the attention of their contemporaries, of diarists or memoirists, but obscure lives and ordinary people, the people that historians have so long overlooked and are even now combing the records for, seldom left any account of themselves. When they did, it was largely by chance, as with the letters preserved in the Paston family. From Woolf's short story of 1906, 'The Journal of Mistress Joan Martyn' (CSF, 33–62), to *Between the Acts* and her late, unfinished essay 'Anon',[2] she searched for the voices of those that history and the literary historian had failed to represent. Their silence created a supreme difficulty, while providing an artistic opportunity for the writer who could picture their lives or find words for them to speak.

For her earliest experiments in biography, however, Virginia Stephen turned to friends and members of her family who provided her not only with material to write about but also with a limited but familiar audience. In doing so she was following a family tradition, for not only had her relatives written each other's official lives, but they had also left private papers addressed to one another, and letters, diaries and other family productions were brought out and reread on occasion.[3] After his wife's sudden death, Leslie Stephen wrote an account of her addressed to her children, which they referred to as his 'Mausoleum Book'. In so doing, he may have had in mind his grandfather's memoir of himself intended 'for the Use of His Children'.[4] Late in 1904, Woolf began writing comic lives of her paternal aunt Caroline Stephen and her maternal aunt Mary Fisher (Frederic Maitland's mother-in-law) (*Letters* i, 163). Though these have not survived, the operatically interfering aunts in her novel *Night and Day*, Cousin Caroline and Mrs Milvain, are surely their descendants. Two accounts of her eccentric great-aunt, the photographer Julia Margaret Cameron – an introduction to a selection of her photographs, and Woolf's comedy *Freshwater*, written for private performance – belong to the same tradition.[5]

Her first serious attempt at life writing was that of her sister Vanessa, probably begun in the later summer of 1907, and the subject of the letter to Clive Bell quoted in the opening paragraph.[6] Hers was precisely the kind of life that challenged DNB principles – that of a young woman who had been brought up at home, studied at art school, and had recently married. Even so, the voice Woolf adopted was still her father's, but her father's at its closest approach to domestic intimacy (though still not close enough to discuss any really intimate crisis) – the sentimental style of the 'Mausoleum Book'. Addressing his children there, his dead wife became 'Your Mother'. Woolf adopted this device, addressing herself to the child that Vanessa was now expecting (later, Julian). With it, she adopted her father's mournful tones (she had been more hurt than she could admit by her sister's departure through marriage). Her memoir recalls their earliest games together – 'the great extent and mystery of the dark land under the nursery table, where a continuous romance seemed to go forward' (MB, 1) – and brings out Vanessa's truthfulness and sense of responsibility for her younger siblings. It is chiefly concerned, however, with their mother and their half-sister Stella, and their untimely deaths twelve and ten years earlier.

While this memoir offered Virginia an opportunity to correct the account of Leslie Stephen she had given to his official biographer, it is Maitland's portrait of their mother that is judged inadequate:

> You will not find in what I say, or again in those sincere but conventional phrases in the life of your grandfather, or in the noble lamentations with which he fills the pages of his autobiography, any semblance of a woman whom you can love.

The difficulty lay in the nature of 'written words' that 'drape themselves in smooth folds annulling all evidence of life' (MB, 8). Unfortunately, her sharp-eyed analysis of the problem did not help her to avoid it: the style she was using continually translated Julia Stephen into an abstract, heroic mode, entirely lacking in intimacy. Of her mother's second marriage, she wrote that 'She rose to the heights, wide-eyed and nobly free from all illusion or sentiment, her second love shining pure as starlight, the rosy mists of the first rapture dispelled for ever' (MB, 6); while later, 'she sank, like an exhausted swimmer, deeper and deeper in the water, and could only at moments descry some restful shore on the horizon' (MB, 11). It seemed impossible to portray Julia Stephen or Stella Duckworth as familiar, lovable people. Their lives had been swallowed up in their care for others. Their tragic fates had overshadowed them, precluding humanising laughter or particularity, and exposing a deeper fear that, in inheriting their roles as bride and mother, Vanessa might be similarly lost. In her mourning for them, Virginia concealed her grief at Vanessa's marriage, her private echo of their father's resentful demands. The warmth of Mrs Ramsay lay twenty years and four novels ahead.

Virginia's letter to Clive Bell about 'the proper writing of lives', quoted at the outset, reveals her desire to recover Vanessa vicariously, through writing her life, but what strikes Virginia most forcefully is the inadequacy of her efforts:

> I have been writing Nessa's life; and I am going to send you 2 chapters in a day or two. It might have been so good! As it is, I am too near, and too far; and it seems to be blurred, and I ask myself why write at all? seeing I never shall recapture what you have, by your side this minute. (*Letters* i, 325)

She had not achieved the speaking likeness she had aimed for, and at the first point where scandal threatened – when Vanessa fell in love with Stella's distraught widower, Jack Hills – her narrative ended abruptly. Even in a document intended only for family reading, there was much that could not be said.

In marked contrast to the life of Vanessa, though written a month or two earlier and out of a comparable emotional need, is the life of Virginia's friend Violet Dickinson, entitled 'Friendship's Gallery'.[7] Violet Dickinson was an older woman who had given Virginia motherly love and support, and to whom Virginia, in turn, was passionately devoted. Though in no obvious way exceptional, Violet fitted few of the Victorian stereotypes of womanhood: well bred, clever, affectionate and cheerful, she was also single, middle-aged, and enjoyed making herself useful. She took holidays with the Stephen family, had encouraged Virginia to write her first reviews (contributed to the *Guardian*, a weekly paper for Anglican clergymen), and had nursed her devotedly through her first major breakdown. 'Friendship's Gallery' was a love gift for her, typed out in violet ink and bound in violet leather. But here Violet's humorous approach to life set the tone, releasing Virginia into a vein of fantasy and parody that easily accommodated the prosaic details of her friend's life by making fun of them.

Though the three chapters of 'Friendship's Gallery' differ from one another, the predominant mode is mock-heroic, inflating its subject to the proportions required to justify the celebration of Violet's life, while covertly alluding to her exceptional height. Though hardly a 'great man', Violet qualified as 'great' in the most literal sense – according to Leslie Stephen, her 'only fault is that she is 6 feet high' (Bell i, 82).[8] Woolf makes the most of this new-found imaginative freedom, beginning in the manner of another mock-biography, that of *Tristram Shandy*, with a baptismal search for the right name. The rest of her childhood is passed over in favour of a detailed account of Violet's first 'season':

> I suspect that my artistic skill would have been more consummate had I thrown these first pages into the waste paper basket or enclosed them within the arms of a parenthesis. For when you are writing the life of a woman you should surely begin
>
> Her First Season
>
> and leave such details as birth parentage education and the first seventeen years of her life to be taken for granted . . . But then this biography is no novel but a sober chronicle; and if Life will begin seventeen years before it is needed it is our task to say so valiantly and make the best of it. ('Friendship's Gallery', 279)

The different aspects of Violet's early life are not even separated from one another by commas, and only her arrival in 'society', the announcement of her marriageable status, is judged worthy of record. 'Making the best of it' will become a keynote, characterising both the author's approach to her form and her subject's approach to her circumstances.

The second chapter takes place in a wonderful garden where Violet and her friends Nelly (Lady Elinor) Cecil and Kitty Maxse are distanced and enlarged into

> gigantic women lying like Greek marbles in easy chairs; draped so that the wind bared little gleaming spaces on their shoulders; who laughed as they helped themselves to strawberries and cream as they looked upon a vision of a jocund world. ('Friendship's Gallery', 282)

Their size reflects the special status attributed to them, as it might in the fantasies of Pope or Swift, lending an affectionate absurdity to Violet's prosaic preoccupations with drains and operations. In the third section, a fairy-tale version of Violet and Nelly's world tour of 1905, the two ladies are promoted to goddesses who rescue the city of Tokyo from an invasion of sea monsters with the tips of their umbrellas. Violet Dickinson's size and power within the fantasy register her relative importance and maternal role, and compensate for the failure of conventional biography to value her special talents as they deserve.

As *Orlando* would do twenty years later, 'Friendship's Gallery' solved the problem of how to write the life of an intimate friend by substituting fantasy for realism, by writing it in a manner that proclaimed its fictiveness. Reviewing a life of Sterne in 1909, Woolf took the opportunity to weigh up the attractions and obstacles that biography afforded. Her experience already suggested to her that a degree of intimacy with a subject might need to be disguised as fiction, given contemporary sensibilities: 'A certain stigma is attached to the biography which deals mainly with a man's personal history, and the writer who sees him most clearly in that light is driven to represent him under the cover of fiction' (*Essays* i, 281). At the same time, she recognised that fiction was at a disadvantage compared with biography in that it was taken less seriously by the reader – it lacked 'the aesthetic effect of truth';

> the bare statement of facts has an indisputable power, if we have reason to think them true . . . a real life is wonderfully prolific; it passes through such strange places and draws along with it a train of adventures [so] that no novelist can better them, if only he can deal with them as with his own inventions. (*Essays* i, 281)

To rewrite personal history as fiction, to use the materials of real life as if they were her own inventions – these were the lessons that Woolf learned from her early experiments with biography.

Although real lives were potentially 'wonderfully prolific', her next exploration of the subject moved decisively away from the lives of friends and family, while employing the knowledge she had gained from her earlier experiments – that the determining factors in the writing of biography were the style which dictated what it was possible to discuss and the relationship between biographer and subject, conventionally kept out of sight, but often setting its own hidden agenda. She also drew on her professional experience as a reviewer with a particular interest in women's memoirs. The result was her most complex and ambitious fiction so far, a short story which sets out two competing biographical narratives and in so doing exemplifies the advantages of the new biography over the old, nine years before Lytton Strachey was to do so in *Eminent Victorians* (1918).

'Memoirs of a Novelist' (1909) presents itself as a review of an (imaginary) volume of life-and-letters – 'the book which one may still buy with luck in the Charing Cross road' (CSF, 70). Its subject is an (equally imaginary) Victorian sentimental novelist, Miss Willatt, whose works are now only to be found on the dusty shelves of seaside libraries. It seems that Miss Willatt was a person of determined and powerful character who in life had easily dominated her friend and future biographer, Miss Linsett. Timid and conventional, Miss Linsett was nevertheless pleased to discover how the power dynamic of their relationship had altered with Miss Willatt's death, transferring control over her friend's 'life' to her. She finds 'how pleasant mere writing is, how important and unreal people become in print so that it is a credit to have known them; how one's own figure can have justice done to it' (CSF, 69). Yet far from revealing the facts of Miss Willatt's life, Miss Linsett carefully avoids them, reducing the impact of her subject's life by filtering it through the medium of her own lesser personality. Above all, she has nothing to say when she reaches Miss Willatt's sole experience of passion: 'The most interesting event in Miss Willatt's life, owing to the nervous prudery and the dreary literary conventions of her friend, is thus a blank' (CSF, 73). Only towards the end does the framework loosen, when the reviewer briefly assumes the role of narrator in order to expose the pretentiousness of Miss Linsett's response to her friend's death: 'But afterwards, when she went home and had her breakfast, she felt lonely, for they had been in the habit of going to Kew Gardens together on Sundays' (CSF, 79).

This moment of spontaneous feeling emphasises Miss Linsett's literary self-indulgence by contrast. It also marks the end of the alternative biography of Miss Willatt that the reviewer has been imagining, reconstructing it from her letters and photograph: 'The sight of that large selfish face, with the capable forehead and the surly but intelligent eyes, discredits all the platitudes on the opposite page; she looks quite capable of having deceived Miss Linsett' (CSF, 74). The reviewer's version exposes the inadequacy of the original biography, substituting instead an analysis of the nature of the relationship between the biographer and her subject. In this new reading, Miss Willatt's silly novels and Miss Linsett's pious biography deserve attention for what can be learned from or read into them. Out of their thinness, the reviewer builds a new and altogether more compelling narrative, demonstrating how the new biography could be made by dismantling the old. Woolf's short story brings together criticism, biography and fiction with a sophistication that the simple antitheses of her essay on Sterne had not allowed for. Though it illustrates a process by which dead books can be rendered down into the facts required for a new narrative, the books themselves had been imaginary in the first place, so the story's focus on the process of narrative construction tends to qualify our response to its final moment of 'truth'.

'Memoirs of a Novelist' was submitted to Reginald Smith, editor of the *Cornhill* (a position once held by Leslie Stephen), for whom Virginia Stephen had been reviewing memoirs. It was intended as the first of a series. Understandably, if unforgivably, he found it 'cleverness itself, but . . .' (Bell i, 153–4). It was put away for good, but its lessons were not forgotten: the imaginary biography of an imaginary writer surfaces again in Woolf's second novel *Night and Day*, and its exploration of the boundaries between fiction and biography opened the way for further experiments with existing forms. Rescuing or reconstructing Miss Willatt from her inept biographer became a sort of detective game that Woolf linked with the process of reading and imagining character:

> Our reading is always urged on by that instinct, [to] complete what we read . . . to supply background, relationship, motive . . . this is nothing but a random game, like that we play in railway carriages with people who leave us at Putney . . . a game too perpetually interrupted by life. (*Essays* iii, 482, 483, 485)[9]

An unknown, silent woman seated in the corner of a railway carriage (as she so often is), flitting about London as in 'The Mysterious Case of Miss V.' (CSF, 30–2) or glimpsed through the window of a house opposite (MD, 203–4), fascinates Woolf.[10] The invention or realisation of such fugitive figures was one way of using a 'fact', a person or even a book, as a starting point for the flight of the imagination.

One such figure whom Woolf rescued from oblivion, or at least from the indifference of the *DNB*, was 'Miss Ormerod' (1919; *The Common Reader*, *Essays* iv, 131–40), a Victorian entomologist who had pioneered the use of the chemical 'Paris Green' as an insecticide in

Britain. Her father, a historian of Cheshire, had an entry of his own, but despite her greater contribution to agriculture there was no account of Eleanor. Woolf's biographical sketch takes the form of a series of scenes from her life. She is first shown in her high chair, absorbed in the contents of a tumbler full of pond life, and correcting her father's assumptions about it from her own already sharp observation. Later, she receives the gift of a rare locust and finally (and most significantly) we see her sitting up in bed to discuss with her doctor how she will be remembered. Though Woolf had read a collection of Ormerod's letters and papers, she recreated the forgotten entomologist by reinventing her, supplying the scenes she described from imagination.

The result was yet another hybrid – neither fiction nor biography – and as such Woolf once again had difficulty in placing it. Originally conceived as the first of a series of lives of eccentrics planned for the *Athenaeum*,[11] it did not appear there, nor in her collection of short stories *Monday or Tuesday* (1921), being too fictional for the former, too factual for the latter. It eventually appeared in the American edition of *The Common Reader* (1925) where it joined two other 'Lives of the Obscure', thus maintaining its anomalous status by remaining outside the British canon of Woolf's writings. It was not the only biographical sketch to combine history and fiction: at such moments Woolf's reading became re-imagining, and the boundaries between biography, thought and fiction (and also between the processes of reading and writing) threatened to disappear altogether. But the generic indeterminacy of 'Miss Ormerod' was particularly appropriate for a woman who had firmly identified herself as an outsider.

In the case of Eleanor Ormerod, her existence within her own letters or in her father's *DNB* entry had provided the fact that engendered the fantasy, but its freewheeling element remained suspect. In two further short stories, Woolf explored biographical fantasies occasioned by apparent 'facts' and subsequently dismissed them ('a game . . . perpetually interrupted by life'). In 'Sympathy' (1919; CSF, 108–11),[12] the starting point is that most literal of facts, a newspaper announcement. Reading of the death of a friend, the narrator drifts into a reverie in which she pictures the young man's deathbed, followed by a country walk with his widow. The brevity of his life is mourned in elegiac terms that anticipate those other lost lives, of Jacob Flanders, Septimus Warren Smith, and Percival in *The Waves*: 'his silence is profound. He has laid his life down like a cloak for us to tread over' (CSF, 110). But the final paragraph suddenly reveals that the whole reverie was based on a simple misapprehension. It is the friend's identically named father who has died – thus further facts dissolve fictions (as in Woolf's 'Mark on the

Wall' where the suggestive mark turns out to be a snail). Although the power of the imagination and its enactments are celebrated, they are also exposed as untrustworthy. When the story is finished, it is necessary to reconsider what the imagination has conjured up, and resubmit it to the claims of truth or of fact.

While 'Sympathy' imagines a death and some of its consequences for the living, 'An Unwritten Novel' (1920; CSF, 112–21) creates an imaginary life for Woolf's first archetypal anonymous middle-aged woman in a railway carriage, a woman invisible to historians and novelists alike (and thus the precursor of Mrs Brown in Woolf's essay 'Mr Bennett and Mrs Brown'). This woman's apparently nervous movements and expression stimulate the narrator to imagine for her a Freudian childhood trauma, and a present life of lower-middle-class poverty and loneliness as an object of pity and contempt in her brother's household. But, as in 'Sympathy', this imagined life is abruptly interrupted and effectively ruled out by the appearance of her son, come to meet her at the station. The narrator's initial confusion at the collapse of her story is rapidly succeeded by the invention of a further narrative as mother and son walk away together, and the intervention of fact is recognised as the occasion of a pleasurable shock and the renewal of creativity: 'Wherever I go, mysterious figures, I see you, turning the corner, mothers and sons; you, you, you. I hasten, I follow . . . adorable world!' (CSF, 121).

'An Unwritten Novel' recalls 'Memoirs of a Novelist' in its use of a fact, a moment of reality as a touchstone to dissipate fantasy or self-deception. And, as in the earlier piece, the story's conscious deployment of the processes of fiction-making makes it more difficult to accept that moment – or any moment – as reality. The unwriting of the title is never entirely effected, since the most memorable part of the story is the imagined narrative of a life; its status as speculation had, in any case, been established at the outset. The life writing that can be disposed of by an inconvenient fact is closer to biography than to the novel, where the writer enjoys comparative freedom from facts. And, as in biography, facts may invalidate one line of thought, but are just as likely to engender another (as they do at the end of 'An Unwritten Novel').

Woolf's earliest writings can be read as a series of attempts to reconceive biography by focusing on the kinds of material and technique that it had traditionally avoided – mundane reality or imaginative flight – while at the same time hankering after its characteristic virtue, its claim to truth. Yet that focus had brought her steadily closer to fiction whose greater freedom involved, she believed, a consequent loss of conviction. Woolf's second novel, *Night and Day* (1919), transforms the material of biography – the lives of 'her sisters and her cousins and her aunts', of her father, and aspects of Clive Bell and Leonard Woolf, into fiction. At the same time, it examines the problems of writing fiction in terms of the difficulty of writing a particular (imaginary) biography. Inevitably, this is the novel most directly concerned with the weight of the past, with literary ancestor-worship and its impositions. In it, Woolf set out to exorcise her own literary inheritance, and it may, paradoxically, be a measure of her success that it can be dismissed as 'an exercise in classicism'.[13]

In *Night and Day*, Woolf's determination to master the traditional novel form and at the same time to break away from it is directly reflected in her heroine Katharine's commitment to help her mother to finish her grandfather's biography:

> The glorious past, in which men and women grew to unexampled size, intruded too much upon the present, and dwarfed it too consistently, to be altogether encouraging to one forced to make her experiment in living when the great age was dead . . . sometimes she felt that it was necessary for her very existence that she should free herself from the past. (ND, 29, 32)

Both Katharine's parents are biographers. Mr Hilbery, working away in his study on the lives of the Romantic poets, recalls Leslie Stephen, while Anny Thackeray Ritchie (her mother's friend and her father's sister-in-law) was the main model for Mrs Hilbery. Life at Cheyne Walk is full of echoes of life at 22 Hyde Park Gate and shares the same physical focus: 'The tea table . . . was the centre of Victorian family life – in our family at least . . . the heart of the family . . . the centre . . . the hearth' (MB, 125). The Sunday tea party, its literary credentials guaranteed by the presence of Henry James (Mr Fortescue), constitutes the opening scene of the novel.

Mrs Hilbery is writing a life of her father, the great (imaginary) Victorian poet Richard Alardyce. She has all the 'facts' (the necessary documents) and a fertile imagination, but she is unable 'to face the radical question of what to leave in and what to leave out' (ND, 30):

> [N]o one with the ghost of a literary temperament could doubt but that they had materials for one of the greatest biographies that has ever been written. Shelves and boxes bulged with the precious stuff. The most private lives of the most interesting people lay furled in yellow bundles of close-written manuscript. In addition to this Mrs Hilbery had in her own head as bright a vision of that time as now remained to the living . . . She had no difficulty in writing . . . but nevertheless . . . the book still remained unwritten . . . Here were twenty pages upon her grandfather's taste in hats, an essay upon contemporary china, a long account of a summer day's expedition into the country, when they had missed their train, together with fragmentary visions of all sorts of famous men and women, which seemed to be partly imaginary and partly authentic. (ND, 29, 32)

The steady proliferation of material for this life and Mrs Hilbery's sense of its limitless possibilities carry implications not only for traditional biography, but also for the over-formal structure of the novel Woolf was writing. By contrast, this primal scene of creation with its uncounted tales, memories and discourses is at once fertile and hard to control. In its freedom, it has affinities with the short stories Woolf was writing concurrently, stories such as 'The Mark on the Wall' (1917; CSF, 83–9) that develop extravagantly from a single object, and resist the tyranny of logical or chronological structure, as the unfinished biography of Alardyce also seems to do. His study is cluttered with promising materials, replete with suggestion, yet Mrs Hilbery cannot contemplate the diminution and exclusion that a single narrative would impose.

Mrs Hilbery is at once the model Victorian daughter, piously assembling and standing guard over her father's relics as so many literary daughters had done (Anny Thackeray Ritchie among them[14]), and the woman writer, questioning her culture's order of value and its inherited narratives. She is absent-minded but inspired. Everything is potentially exciting to her and she acts as a powerfully generative figure at the heart of the novel, associated with the freedom of the imagination, while her daughter Katharine, in her self-imposed role as the practical one (for, paradoxically, she too is a secret dreamer), tries vainly to discipline her mother, organising her to work by the clock and trying to sort her endless new beginnings into an ordered sequence. Later, a more subversive side of Mrs Hilbery emerges when she abandons the biography and sets out for Stratford to prove that Anne Hathaway wrote Shakespeare's sonnets, thus challenging 'the safety of the heart of civilisation itself' (ND, 364) in search of a new and more compelling version of the 'truth' about Shakespeare. It is as if, having failed to write the new (that is, the totally frank) biography of her father, she turns to the fantasy version, the biography of what might or should have been, the biography that has freed itself altogether from conventional constraints (as *Orlando* would).

Mrs Hilbery's impatience with traditional methodologies (such as had determined Miss Linsett's approach), and her eagerness to supplant Shakespeare with a convincing woman rival anticipate the author of *A Room of One's Own*, yet in one vital respect she is utterly different, for she is essentially a writer of traditional romance, a historian of love and marriage. She would prefer to represent her father's life as an ongoing romance, yet doing so would inevitably lead the reader back to the most inconvenient of 'facts', that of his failed marriage. Not only is she unable 'to face the radical question of what to leave in and what to leave out. She could not decide how far the public was to be told the truth about the poet's separation from his wife' (ND, 30).

The question of 'what it is that you can write', what can and cannot be said in biography, was the crucial one: it had interrupted Virginia's life of Vanessa and silenced Miss Linsett at a moment of imminent revelation in 'Memoirs of a Novelist'. It would continue to be a problem for Woolf as a woman writer, creating insurmountable difficulties when she wrote her biography of Roger Fry, for Fry's own sexual honesty was likely to offend the sensibilities of the average reader. *Night and Day* initially introduces the problem of sexual scandal in terms of the Alardyce biography: the poet's marriage had turned sour after three months of passion. He and his wife had lived apart, and she had taken other lovers. But this mishap has repercussions for the rest of the novel, since it calls in question the assumption that romantic love finds its natural outcome in happy marriage, an assumption fundamental to the type of novel that Woolf was writing. Katharine Hilbery's cousin Cyril is introduced to amplify this point. Quoting Ibsen and Samuel Butler (ND, 89), he deplores marriage as an institution and refuses on principle to marry the woman who lives with him and bears his children. When those guardians of public morals, the aunts, discover this, they descend on the Hilberys, insisting that the family honour is at stake and that, as head of the family, the reluctant Mr Hilbery must intervene (their behaviour recalling the family reaction to Vanessa's friendship with her half-sister's widower, Jack Hills).

Katharine herself is eager to marry, if only to escape from the problems posed by her grandfather's biography, and to find the freedom and independence she longs for; but when another of her aunts warns her against marrying if she wants to have her own way, its attractions begin to fade (ND, 177–9). The apparently passionless marriages of the older generation seem to justify Katharine's own distrust of passion as well as her recognition that, when love comes, marriage is not the only conceivable arrangement: 'Why, after all, isn't it perfectly possible to live together without being married?' (ND, 411). When Mrs Hilbery fails to rewrite the plot of her father's (or even of Shakespeare's) biography without concealing or altering the known facts, she turns instead to rewriting the plot of 'life' – that is, of course, the rest of the novel. She urges her daughter towards marriage as 'the happiest life for a woman', later correcting this to 'the most interesting' (ND, 179). But Katharine, like the novel's more thoughtful characters, does not share Mrs Hilbery's blind confidence that marriage offers women the greatest happiness, the most fulfilling of lives (her conviction will be shared by Mrs Ramsay in *To the Lighthouse*, but by that stage Woolf's creative women, artists or writers such as Lily Briscoe or Miss La Trobe, had decisively rejected it).

Woolf thus uses the device of Alardyce's unfinished biography to cast doubt on the assumptions of social comedy that otherwise determine the shape of her novel. The problems it raises – of the limitations of the genre and the constraints on what it can say – suggest a critique of the novel she was in the process of writing, and an impulse like Katharine's to escape from an obligation to satisfy the social expectation of her day. *Night and Day* is the only one of Woolf's novels to make use of marriage as a conventional close, but the biography of Alardyce enables Woolf to set up a dialogue between the fiction she is writing and the wider truths ('facts?') about marriage that Mrs Hilbery and the novel's structure do not fully allow for. Mrs Hilbery's hesitation as to 'how far the public was to be told the truth about the poet's separation from his wife' exposes the nature of the reader's expectations in old-fashioned biography and this in turn leads to an interrogation of marriage as a 'happy ending', the literary convention of the type of novel that Woolf was writing, and beyond that of the social myth of marriage in the actual world. In this way, Mrs Hilbery's biographical quandary is crucial, since it opens up a line of questioning that introduces an element of much-needed scepticism into a novel centrally concerned with the nature and power of fantasy and romance.

*Night and Day* makes no attempt to finish its projected biography – instead, it functions to articulate structural and social problems that haunt the novel as a whole. It remains, like the grit in the oyster, the starting point for a critique of 'Modern Novels' that followed,[15] silently acknowledging that the traditional structure of the novel, its social and literary rules, can no longer accommodate the experiences and desires of Katharine's generation. In terms of Woolf's development as a writer, she had reached the point where she was ready to abandon conventional form altogether. Though biography gradually ceased to provide her main model for thinking about the nature of imaginative writing, the issues it raised remained potent for her: *Jacob's Room* contrasts the *DNB* view of the lives of great men with a more prosaic reality, as heroic ideals are simultaneously fulfilled and destroyed by the First World War; *Mrs Dalloway* and *To the Lighthouse* are both forms of imaginative life-writing that draw heavily on Woolf's personal experiences; *The Waves* and *The Years* epitomise the lives of individuals outside and inside history; *Orlando* and *Flush* revise the traditional concept of biography; and late in the 1930s, Woolf wrote a life of Roger Fry (her only 'straight' biography) and began writing her autobiography. Her essays on the subject continued to draw a contrast between the granite of truth and the rainbow of personality, associating truth with scientific fact – in 1927, she compared it to radium ('The New Biography', *Essays* iv, 473). Even in 1940 she was still contrasting the facts of biography with the freedom of fiction, while making the crucial admission that the status and even the nature of 'facts' could change ('The Art of Biography', CE iv, 221, 225–6); but the fertility of the marriage she had effected between the two had long since precluded so stark an opposition.

## Notes

1. See 'Lady Hester Stanhope' and 'The Duke and Duchess of Newcastle-Upon-Tyne' (*Essays* i, 325–9, 345–9); 'The Duchess of Newcastle' (*The Common Reader*, *Essays* iv, 81–8); for Julia Margaret Cameron, see below, note 5.
2. '"Anon" and "The Reader": Virginia Woolf's Last Essays', ed. Brenda R. Silver, *Twentieth Century Literature*, 25 (1979), 356–441.
3. A letter to Violet Dickinson of October 1904 reports her aunt Caroline Stephen ('Nun') showing her family letters and diaries (*Letters* i, 146).
4. *Sir Leslie Stephen's Mausoleum Book*, intro. Alan Bell (Oxford: Oxford University Press, 1977); for his grandfather's ('Jem' Stephen's) memoirs, see Noel Annan, *Leslie Stephen: The Godless Victorian* (London and Chicago: Chicago University Press), p. 7.
5. Her essay introduces *Victorian Photographs of Famous Men and Fair Women* by Julia Margaret Cameron (London: Hogarth Press, 1926) (and *Essays* iv, 375–83); *Freshwater*, ed. Lucio P. Ruotolo (London: Hogarth Press, 1976); Queenie Colquhoun (ND, 95) is also a portrait of her.
6. According to Quentin Bell's biography (vol. i, 122), the life of Vanessa was begun when Virginia was staying at Playden, near Rye (August–September 1907). It is reprinted as 'Reminiscences' (MB, 1–30), though referred to in Woolf's letters as her 'life of Vanessa'. Her life of Violet Dickinson was completed shortly before Virginia went to Playden, and so actually preceded that of Vanessa, but they were closely contemporary. I discuss them in the reverse order of composition in order to follow Woolf's interests as they developed beyond her family.
7. 'Friendship's Gallery', ed. Ellen Hawkes, *Twentieth Century Literature*, 25 (1979), 270–302. An undated note to Violet Dickinson accompanying the life was written early in August 1907 (*Letters* i, 303).
8. Quentin Bell, *Virginia Woolf: A Biography* (London: Hogarth Press, 1972), p. 82.
9. This unfinished and heavily corrected essay was intended to introduce a book on 'Reading' (see essay 4).
10. Other such figures are Mrs Brown in 'Mr Bennett and Mrs Brown' (as 'Character in Fiction', *Essays* iii, 420–36) and Mrs Norman (J's R, 23–4).
11. 'I open this book today merely to note that Miss *Eleanor Ormerod*, destroyer of insects, promises well for Murry: should he take kindly to my first (Eccentrics: I myself rather liked it)' (*Diary* i, 260) – John Middleton Murry was currently editor of the *Athenaeum*. 'Miss Ormerod' first appeared in the American periodical *The Dial*, in December 1924. Its subsequent appearance only in the US edition of *The Common Reader* may be an assertion of (or otherwise connected with) American copyright laws.

12. Woolf jotted down an outline for 'Sympathy' in the second manuscript notebook of *Jacob's Room* under the title 'A Death in the Newspaper' (CSF, appendix A, 315).
13. E. M. Forster, 'The Early Novels of Virginia Woolf', *Abinger Harvest* (1936; London: Penguin, 1974), 122.
14. Anny Ritchie wrote biographical accounts of her father in the form of introductory memoirs to individual novels. She would have had comparable difficulties in writing about her father's marriage, since her mother was a victim of a different kind of scandal – she had become insane – see Henrietta Garnett, *Anny: A Life of Anne Isabella Thackeray Ritchie* (London: Chatto and Windus, 2004), pp. 15–18.
15. 'Modern Novels' (*Essays* iii, 30–6) was revised as 'Modern Fiction' for *The Common Reader* (*Essays* iv, 157–64), a point further discussed in the following essay.

Essay 3

# *Night and Day*: The Marriage of Dreams and Realities

> We walked on the river bank in a cold wind, under a grey sky. Both agreed that life seen without illusion is a ghastly affair. Illusions wouldn't come back. However they returned about 8.30, in front of the fire, & were going merrily till bedtime . . . (*Diary* i, 73)

Virginia Woolf's diary entry for 10 November 1917, with its riverside walk, its glimpse of despair and rapid recovery, is strongly redolent of her second novel, *Night and Day*, on which she was currently at work. This is a novel that fluctuates between the outer and inner life, between social comedy and alienation, between the solid houses and streets of London and the ceaseless flux of the river – for her husband, Leonard Woolf, an emblem 'of the mystery and unreality of human things'.[1]

By 1917, many illusions had been lost: the Great War was in its fourth year and scarcely nearer resolution. As a pacifist, Woolf was sickened by it and by the patriotic sentiment and the 'violent and filthy passions' it aroused (*Letters* ii, 71). She felt herself becoming 'Steadily more feminist', faced with 'this preposterous masculine fiction' (*Letters* ii, 76). To what extent the war had contributed to her breakdown of 1915 cannot be determined, but both her private experience of psychic illness and the public trauma of the war promoted a sense of inner and outer worlds being pulled violently apart. This tension and opposition, explored in all her fiction in one way or another, gradually became the dominant theme of *Night and Day*, completed on 21 November 1918, ten days after the armistice (*Diary* i, 221).

'The war never has been: that is what the [novel's] message is', wrote Katherine Mansfield to her husband, John Middleton Murry. But in her published review of *Night and Day*, she modified this to a complaint about its 'aloofness, [its] air of quiet perfection . . . the absence of scars'; it was 'unaware of what has been happening'.[2] At a superficial level, she was obviously right: the novel is set before the war, at an untroubled

Edwardian tea party and does not include so much as a glance forward to the coming storm.[3] Woolf never wrote of the war directly since it was outside her experience, and even her third novel, *Jacob's Room* (1922), whose subject is Jacob's life thrown away in the war, only reveals his empty room and the undertones of his surname, Flanders. War remains a distant if unignorable presence, like the low thunder of the guns from the Western front, 'strange volumes of sound' that could be heard rolling over the Sussex Downs during the summer of 1916. Woolf described their sinister rumbling in an article for *The Times* and the way in which the war was contributing to local superstition, while understandably shying away from the thing itself ('Heard on the Downs: The Genesis of Myth', *Essays* ii, 40–2).

Though *Night and Day* makes no mention of the war, it is none the less shaped by it and by the sense of crisis it induced. Katharine, its heroine, displays a deep distrust of words and feelings, which corresponds to Woolf's own revulsion against patriotic rhetoric and sentiment, while the novel as a whole calls in question the values on which the rationale for fighting (as well as much traditional fiction) had been based: 'civilisation' and the existing structures of society, especially love, marriage and the family. The interrogation of what was being fought for would become a central feature of wartime writing. In Woolf's novel, these conflicts are played out light-heartedly in what is (in the context of the war) almost a pastoral setting – that of peacetime London, a candle-lit Chelsea drawing room, or the Embankment beneath the stars. 'Let us not take it for granted that life exists more in what is commonly thought big than in what is commonly thought small', Woolf wrote in 1919, simultaneously enunciating modernist principles and a feminist perspective on war ('Modern Novels', *Essays* iii, 34).

Katherine Mansfield was not alone in her criticism. *Night and Day* has been the most neglected of Woolf's novels, partly as a result of her own dismissive account of it. In a long letter to Ethel Smyth written in 1930, she established the place it would thereafter hold in her canon by contrasting it unfavourably with the short stories she was writing at the same time:

> I was so tremblingly afraid of my own insanity that I wrote Night and Day mainly to prove to my own satisfaction that I could keep entirely off that dangerous ground. I wrote it, lying in bed, allowed to write only for one half hour a day. And I made myself copy from plaster casts, partly to tranquillise, partly to learn anatomy. Bad as the book is, it composed my mind and I think taught me certain elements of composition which I should not have had the patience to learn had I been in the full flush of health always. These little pieces [the short stories] . . . were the treats I allowed myself when I had done my

> exercise in the conventional style. I shall never forget the day I wrote The Mark on the Wall – all in a flash, as if flying, after being kept stone breaking for months. The Unwritten Novel was the great discovery, however . . . How I trembled with excitement; and then Leonard came in, and I drank my milk and concealed my excitement, and wrote I suppose another page of that interminable Night and Day . . . (*Letters* iv, 231)[4]

In her anxiety to anticipate adverse criticism, Woolf presents her short stories and *Jacob's Room* as the true forerunners of her major experiments, identifying their radical form as the source of their radical meaning. Yet this letter misremembers (or misrepresents) the actual experience of writing, adjusting it to suit the story she wanted to tell, for although the novel was indeed written very slowly, it was written with an unusual fluency, a certainty of purpose and considerable pleasure. 'I don't suppose I've ever enjoyed any writing so much as I did the last half of N. & D.', she wrote in March 1919, and thought it 'much more mature & finished & satisfactory' than her first novel, *The Voyage Out* (which she had rewritten many times). It was certainly less taxing to write: 'if one's own ease & interest promise anything good, I should have hopes that some people at least will find it a pleasure' (*Diary* i, 259). Her comments are borne out by the sole surviving manuscript which, though composed at a fairly early stage (it is dated 6 October 1916), is already surprisingly close to the published text.

Woolf either began or returned to serious composition late in 1914 or early in 1915, after two years of more or less continuous illness, but her progress was further interrupted by a another breakdown early in 1915 and was only slowly resumed in the following year. Among diary entries for January and February 1915 she records writing '4 pages of poor Effie's story' ('Effie' would soon become Katharine, the novel's heroine). A fortnight later, her diary lists a programme of background reading – 'the Kembles – Tennyson & so on' – 'for the sake of The Third Generation' (*Diary* i, 4, 19).[5] Surviving glimpses of Katharine's grandfather, the great Victorian poet Richard Alardyce, and of his marriage in chapters VII and IX suggest that some of this material had been worked out earlier. At this stage the novel looked as if it would focus on the three generations from Alardyce through his daughter (Mrs Hilbery) to Katharine, charting the changing patterns of marriage and family life from the 1860s to 1910, rather as D. H. Lawrence had done in *The Rainbow* (1915) and *Women in Love* (1920), or as Woolf herself would later do in *The Years* (1937).

By the end of February she was seriously ill again, and there is no further mention of the novel until July 1916 when she wrote to Lytton Strachey, 'I begin to despair of finishing a book on this method – I write one sentence – the clock strikes – Leonard appears with a glass of milk'

(*Letters* ii, 107). Yet by the autumn she had made substantial progress, for the surviving manuscript (entitled 'Dreams and Realities') begins in the middle of the present chapter XI with an entry dated 'October 6th 1916', and runs from there to an entry half-way through chapter XVII, the last date recorded being 5 January 1917.[6] She resumed her diary in October of that year, though work on the novel is not referred to until November. By the following March she was 'well past 100, 000 words' (*Diary* i, 127) and thought that if she stopped accepting books for review she might possibly finish it within a month or two. In fact, it was not completed until late in 1918, and was published by her half-brother, Gerald Duckworth, the following autumn.

The novel's heroine, Katherine Hilbery, has much in common with her author, including her upper-middle-class and very literary family background, her rejection of a 'clever' suitor (William Rodney includes elements of the classical scholar Walter Headlam, Lytton Strachey and, perhaps, of her brother-in-law Clive Bell, all of whom had conducted flirtations with her), and her acceptance of a man who had no money and came from a distinctly lower class, but was full of passionate sincerity. Even so, Woolf advised her friend Janet Case that, in reading *Night and Day*, she should 'try thinking of Katharine as Vanessa, not me' (*Letters* ii, 400). The merging of elements of herself and her adored sister Vanessa in the portrait of Katharine is complex and intriguing: from an early stage Katharine seems to have been consciously based on Vanessa, bitterly missed by Virginia when she married Clive Bell in 1907 and whose affection she continued to need. After visiting Vanessa in the summer of 1916, Virginia told her that she was already thinking of 'writing another novel' about her life (*Letters* ii, 109). The family pressure to be 'practical' upon a heroine who was deeply romantic, her quiet power over others and her general air of 'otherness' all suggest Vanessa whose talent for painting is here translated into the equally non-verbal and unfeminine study of mathematics. In a deleted passage in the manuscript, Katharine observes 'If I had to be an artist . . . I should certainly be a painter; because then at least you have solid things to deal with.' It was Vanessa's blend of the solid with the ethereal that Woolf set out to evoke – 'to crack through the paving stone and be enveloped in the mist' (*Letters* ii, 232).[7]

Contrasted with Katharine is her mother Mrs Hilbery, whom Woolf admitted was inspired by her aunt Anny Thackeray Ritchie, though she added that 'in writing one gets more and more away from the reality, and Mrs Hilbery became quite different to me from anyone in the flesh' (*Letters* ii, 406). Aunt Anny, the elder daughter of the great Victorian novelist, W. M. Thackeray, and sister of Leslie Stephen's first wife Minnie, was herself a writer, a lively, idiosyncratic, highly creative and somewhat absent-minded woman who, like Mrs Hilbery, had been her father's close companion and had helped him with his work. Though she 'lost trains, mixed names, confused numbers', she was also 'a mistress of comedy' and so presides over the novel's happy ending.[8] Her husband Trevor Hilbery has some traits of Leslie Stephen (who had been very fond of Anny[9]) and some of Anny's husband Richmond Ritchie, but he is also a thoroughly literary creation, his love of a quiet life recalling Mr Bennet in *Pride and Prejudice*. The chorus of aunts and cousins correspond to Woolf's numerous highly-placed relatives, while Ralph shares with Leonard Woolf a widowed mother, a sister with whom he is particularly close, and a large family of siblings living in the suburbs. Katharine's initially uneasy encounter with Ralph's family reflects something of Woolf's own embarrassment with her in-laws. But as with *Jacob's Room*, inspired by her brother Thoby, and *To the Lighthouse*, inspired by her parents and her own memories of childhood, such figures provided no more than starting points; they rapidly developed in new directions, taking in the issues and ideas that, for Woolf, had accumulated around them. She dramatised her perception of their roles in society and the meaning of their lives, both for themselves and for others.

While Woolf was writing Vanessa and Aunt Anny into her fiction, she also had before her a curious portrait of herself as mediated through fiction, for on the last day of January 1915, Leonard had finally shown her a copy of his own novel *The Wise Virgins*. Published the previous autumn, it included highly recognisable, and not altogether complimentary portraits of Virginia and Vanessa as the Lawrence sisters, Camilla and Katharine, as well as of himself and his family. Virginia thought it 'a remarkable book; very bad in parts; first rate in others' (*Diary* i, 32). In particular, she found its desolate representation of their courtship so imaginatively gripping that she reworked the main outlines of the story in her own novel, and in doing so took over its thematic counterpointing of dreams, desires and realities. She was also impressed and influenced by its deliberate subversion of the usual fictional closure in a 'happy ever after' wedding.[10]

*The Wise Virgins* is a bleak tale of a Jewish family who move into a comfortable suburb, where their marriageable son Harry tries to educate Gwen, the girl next door, at the same time as he is falling in love with the socially and personally distant Camilla whom he meets, with her gentler sister Katharine, at art school. Camilla becomes the unattainable object of his dreams, and in a perverse mood of self-pity and self-contempt he proposes to Gwen who then pursues him into bed, so that he finds himself obliged to marry her. But these unhappy triangulations were then subjected to Woolf's optimistic feminist revisions. She conflated the two sisters into 'Katharine', thus absolving them of Camilla's coldness, and she allowed her hero to win his dream woman. She also rewrote the dangerously pathetic girl next door as the competent Mary Datchet, whose honesty and independence make her reject Ralph's half-hearted proposal and encourage him instead to win Katharine for himself. Yet what is in many ways the most important element in *The Wise Virgins* is never actually confronted, though it has left traces of itself – and that is the problem of Harry's Jewishness.

This is the source of Harry's difference, and of the blend of suspicion and excitement he arouses in others. The character of Ralph Denham resembles Leonard's self-portrait as Harry Davis rather more than it resembles Leonard himself. Ralph shares with Harry the resentment, the mystery and perhaps the sexual attractiveness of the outcast, yet in *Night and Day* these qualities are never fully explained in terms of his economic or class status. Ralph's initial insistence on the difference between himself and Katharine in terms of money, privilege and family pride seems so extreme, so unjustifiable as to be displaced. He simultaneously insists on his family's lack of distinction, while boasting of their achievements. Woolf adopted the tensions that Harry arouses in others without reference to their actual cause, perhaps because she could not have written about Jewishness neutrally. She had grown up with the unquestioning anti-Semitism of her class and times, and had had to overcome it in marrying Leonard. But she never abandoned it altogether, which may explain why this aspect of *The Wise Virgins*, treated with such fierce honesty by Leonard, left no more than a shadow across his wife's novel.

If Leonard's fiction had reacted against the social and novelistic conventions of the day with impatience, Virginia's ambition was to master them and subdue them to her purposes. Her friend Katherine Mansfield had been shocked and disappointed with the result – 'a novel in the tradition of the English novel . . . we had never thought to look upon its like again!'[11] – and her complaint persuaded Woolf to dismiss *Night and Day* as somehow outside the main line of her development. Yet in her early years her imagination had been so steeped in the traditions of English fiction that she quite naturally began by reworking its characteristic vein of social comedy. Ultimately derived from Jane Austen, this had recently been refurbished by E. M. Forster in, for example, *A Room with a View* (1908) and *Howard's End* (1910). Novels of this kind tended to focus on the experiences of a young woman within a specific social group, often (though not invariably) culminating in marriage. Woolf's first novel, *The Voyage Out* (1915) had already interrupted the reader's expectations by substituting Rachel's sudden death for her marriage and it had further explored the nature of those expectations by presenting Rachel's response to her reading, both alone and in conversations with others, as well as by introducing an aspiring novelist in a leading role: Terence Hewet shares his author's impatience with ready-made answers and clear-cut distinctions – ' I want to write a novel about Silence . . . the things people don't say' (VO, 204), he explains, anticipating Woolf's account of *Night and Day* as concerned with 'the things one doesn't say' (*Letters* ii, 400). Woolf thought that traditional fiction failed to attend sufficiently to the inner voice, and her novel *The Waves* (1931) might be regarded as the ultimate fulfilment of Terence's project. Katharine's speaking silences in *Night and Day* may be another variation on this theme.

In formal respects, and particularly in terms of plot structure, *Night and Day* is both more disciplined and more conventional than its predecessor. For Woolf, its mastery of form was a step forwards even while it increased her frustration with its constraints: 'the form . . . must sit tight, and perhaps . . . sits too tight; as it was too loose in The Voyage Out' (*Letters* ii, 400). For the same reason critics with a professional interest in technique (among them Mansfield and Forster) regarded it as a step backwards. *Night and Day* sticks closely to the dance routine of romantic comedy as the wrongly matched partners recognise their mistakes in the nick of time and the beloved dreamers, Katharine and Ralph, recognise their true affinities. Instead of disrupting the formality of the dance, however, Woolf endows it with the self-consciousness of Shakespearian comedy or Mozartian opera, so that the comic unwinding draws attention to its own artifice. Cassandra steps out, pat, from behind a curtain, having overheard a crucial conversation about herself (ND, 352) and conveniently misses her train back to Lincoln; Mrs Hilbery returns from Shakespeare's tomb bearing garlands that acknowledge Woolf's debt to the evergreen comic tradition, and she effects reconciliations by a kind of delicate foolery. As she had told Katharine earlier, they could all play Shakespeare characters: 'You'd be Rosalind . . . your father's Hamlet, come to years of discretion; and I'm – well, I'm a bit of them all: I'm quite a large bit of the fool, but the fools in Shakespeare say all the clever things' (ND, 260).

Several accounts of the novel have focused on its genre as the crucial factor in determining its effect and meaning, interpreting its comic mode as integrative rather than disruptive or destructive; they are responding to the novel's humour and to a poised and ironic style that invites comparison with the classically comic modes and structures of Shakespeare, Mozart or Jane Austen.[12] Yet although these elements are clearly important, often sign-posted in the text by specific echoes or allusions, such interpretations overlook the novel's continuous process of self-interrogation, its questioning of the traditional hierarchies of public and private, external and internal, male and female experience, and of the value system idealising love and marriage which underpins the formal structure and endorses the traditional closure of marriage. Like much post-romantic writing, the novel questions whether daily life can ever assimilate or be made adequate to the idealism of dreams (or of literature), and finds that endowing both its lovers with full subjectivity creates a potential for division and disharmony that carries with it tragic implications. An examination of these unresolved debates would suggest that this is a darker and more serious novel than its form might indicate.

By the time Woolf had completed her novel, she was fully aware of the limitations that her chosen form imposed and had realised that, while parody and subversion could contribute their own critique, the choice of fictional form to a large extent determined the view of life or 'reality' being put forward. Both in her essays and in her novels Woolf continually sought to question assumptions about the nature of 'reality' as it was generally accepted in contemporary fictional writing. Her unease with her form, even as she mastered it, is written into *Night and Day*, but she also set out its lesson in more theoretical terms in a key essay – almost a manifesto – published in April 1919 and originally entitled 'Modern Novels' (it was later revised for *The Common Reader* as 'Modern Fiction'). Here she criticised the well-ordered novel of tradition that she had been wrestling with, for its artifice, its failure to correspond to the actual experience of living:

> . . . the question suggests itself whether life is like this after all? Is it not possible that the accent falls a little differently, that the moment of importance came before or after, that, if one were free and could set down what one chose, there would be no plot, little probability, and a vague general confusion in which the clear-cut features of the tragic, the comic, the passionate, and the lyrical were dissolved beyond the possibility of separate recognition? ('Modern Novels', *Essays* iii, 33)

This essay turns from a critique of H. G. Wells, Arnold Bennett and John Galsworthy to a celebration of the Russians, not merely as moderns but as writers of incomparable profundity and humanity whose truthfulness is evidence by their very inconclusiveness: 'It is the sense that there is no answer, that if honestly examined life presents question after question which must be left to sound on and on after the story is over' (*Essays* iii, 36). For Woolf, the Russians, and in particular Dostoevsky – 'the greatest writer ever born' (*Letters* ii, 5) – revealed the full potential of the novel to question accepted hierarchies, whether social, cultural or literary.[13]

The challenge of Dostoevsky is actually thrown down within the novel itself as Katharine (who claims to hate books) passes Ralph without seeing him in the street because she is preoccupied with a sentence from *The Idiot*: 'It's life that matters, nothing but life – the process of discovering, the everlasting and perpetual process, not the discovery itself at all' (ND, 106, 111). The sentence comes from part III, chapter V, where Ippolit insists upon reading aloud his testament, the 'necessary explanation' of his philosophy – that of a man about to die. Ippolit's assertion that life should be a continual voyage of discovery proposes a cultivation of open-ended experience that challenges *Night and Day*'s acceptance of either work or marriage as the paths to self-fulfilment; but it also challenges the novel's form, acting as a reminder that novels need not be strained through the net of tradition, but could instead dispense with the rules in favour of a vision of unifying intensity such as Dostoevsky's. Woolf had been reading *The Idiot* in 1915, when she started writing her second novel (*Diary* i, 10, 23), but the novel also figures in Leonard's *The Wise Virgins* where Harry give Gwen a copy in the hope of widening her horizons. And this precise quotation involves a further allusion, since E. M Forster had used it in the course of reviewing *The Voyage Out*.[14]

Woolf's essay on 'Modern Novels' reveals the extent that she had come to feel trapped within the traditional novel form even as she mastered it. That she experienced it as essentially masculine in its concerns and outlook is suggested by one of the additions she made to the essay in rewriting it for inclusion in *The Common Reader*. Here a male figure of authority imposes the plot of the conventional novel on the resisting novelist. 'The writer seems constrained, not by his own free will but by some powerful and unscrupulous tyrant who has him in thrall, to provide a plot . . . The tyrant is obeyed; the novel is done to a turn' ('Modern Fiction', *Essays* iv, 160). Woolf's later fiction would deliberately reject conventional plots and, in particular, the type of love story that ends with a gifted young woman gladly giving herself up to the servitude of marriage. *Night and Day* comes closest to using this plot. While the ending attempts to keep its options open, readers often assume that Katharine will agree either to a private wedding in a registry office or a grand marriage in Westminster Abbey – as if the novel consistently conforms to the conventions it employs and fulfils the expectations of romance unquestioningly.[15]

Woolf's unease with her form was so great that she displaced it onto her heroine Katharine whose fears of entrapment within a masculine narrative recapitulate her author's. Like Woolf, she finds herself uneasily participating in a patriarchal plot, or, more precisely, within a series of them, each of which demands that she play a different role. She experiences the imposition of these roles that she has not chosen and cannot reconcile with one another as a loss of self, a loss that she associates with books and words as the source of imposed or inauthentic 'feelings' that she cannot readily accept or internalise. Her resulting sense of alienation from language pervades the book and does not find a resolution.

Katharine recognises the need not only to escape her own image as perceived by others, but also to possess a territory of her own. She flies from the nets of language cast about her into a world of pure signs – of mathematics and the inexorable laws that govern heavenly or earthly movement. Here at last is a world free of gender distinctions and therefore of the single greatest source of confusion in life, 'the dense crossings and entanglements of men and women' (ND, 86). As a subject for study, mathematics is 'unwomanly', reflecting Katharine's desire to transcend her destination as a woman and to work in the world of abstract thought that had traditionally been reserved for men.

For Katharine, 'the star-like impersonality of figures' is contrasted with 'the confusion, agitation, and vagueness of the finest prose' (ND, 34), and for a moment the world of literature is feminised by this contrast (and linked to Mrs Hilbery who shares these attributes). For Katharine, literature is concerned with feelings, and thus associated with all the accident and slippage attendant on desire and the body. She distrusts the subjectivity and the arbitrariness of language, accepting that 'everyone tells lies' (ND, 73) or makes up 'stories to suit their own version' (ND, 101). Just as Plato had dismissed the poets from his ideal republic because they did not deal in truth, so Katharine would dismiss literature, the occupation of her parents and the passion of her fiancé, which enshrines and encloses women in its alienating plots: 'Yes, I do hate books' . . . [she confides to Ralph] 'Why do you want to be for ever talking about your feelings? That's what I can't make out. And poetry's all about feelings – novels are all about feelings' (ND, 120).

The Hilberys' house in Cheyne Walk signifies the beauty, order and claustrophobia of the Victorian literary tradition. Woolf had been taken by her father on more than one occasion to visit Carlyle's house close by,[16] while Dante Gabriel Rossetti, George Eliot and Henry James (who makes a walk-on appearance in the novel as Mr Fortescue) had all lived in Cheyne Walk. Katharine inhabits a household filled with books and dominated by the worship of her grandfather Richard Alardyce, buried in Westminster Abbey in Poet's Corner. Both her parents are absorbed in the cult of dead poets, since her father spends his time working out minor details of the biographies of Byron and Shelley (perhaps a comically reductive version of Leslie Stephen's work as editor of the *Dictionary of National Biography*), while for the last ten years her mother has been writing the biography of Richard Alardyce. Katharine plays vestal virgin at the poet's shrine, taking visitors to see the relics in his study and sitting down each morning to help her mother with the biography she is unable to finish, in part because traditional biography cannot accommodate the many irregularities of the poet's life. Mrs Hilbery's problems with her biography caricature Woolf's difficulties with the form of the traditional novel, and both of them labour beneath the burden of the discourses of the past: 'no one can escape the power of language . . . Even Katharine was slightly affected against her better judgement' (ND, 258).

Katharine has reacted against her family's obsession with the words of great men by preferring silence, but this does not release her from domestic servitude: instead, she has acquired 'the reputation which nothing in her manner contradicted, of being the most practical of people' (ND, 32), with the result that she is left to cope with the day-to-day running of the household, leaving her parents to enjoy a certain childlike irresponsibility. She is obliged to be dependable in order to license their literary games. She resents her role as her mother's secretary, and also the efficiency expected of her: ' "I should have thought that you never forgot anything, " William remarked . . . "That's part of the myth about me, I know, " Katharine replied' (ND, 113).

If Katharine's parents have cast her as the devoted and practical daughter who pours the tea and protects them from the dreary routines of household management, William Rodney focuses on her potential as another Victorian fiction, 'the angel in the house'. Rodney believes that it is marriage that validates women's existence: ' "Why, you're nothing at all without it, you're only half alive, using half your faculties; you must feel that for yourself " ' (ND, 532). Any indication of Katharine's independence threatens him and he believes she ought to give up her present 'odious, self-centred' life (ND, 56), give up being a subject and become an object, the object of his sonnet, the wife who will complete his sense of himself. Rodney forces his image of Katharine into a dream of bourgeois marriage. His rival, Ralph, also appropriates her image, deliberately incorporating it into his day-dreams – 'Yes, Katharine Hilbery'll do' (ND, 16) – though for him she is an altogether less domestic muse.

William Rodney's ideal of marriage is shared by a powerful ally in Mrs Hilbery who combines two types of female creativity that Woolf would later see as distinctive, and even mutually exclusive. These types can be identified with the originating figures of Anny Thackeray Ritchie and Julia Stephen, with the mother as writer and the mother as guardian of the family. In *To the Lighthouse*, they are figured as the painter Lily Briscoe and Mrs Ramsay who prompts divided feelings in Woolf, being at once the long-lost nurturing mother and the imprisoned and imprisoning 'angel in the house', the self-sacrificing wife and mother that Woolf felt she must destroy within herself in order to become a writer: 'had I not killed her she would have killed me. She would have plucked the heart out of my writing' ('Professions for Women', CE ii, 286). Mrs Hilbery shares Mrs Ramsay's penchant for matchmaking and general conciliation. She defuses her husband's anger against the misbehaving couples with practised ease, coaxing him back into the safe and soothing world of literary speculation with a question about the date of *Hamlet* (ND, 425).

Yet Mrs Hilbery is also associated with the power of literature and the strong appeal that women's writing itself can make on behalf of love and marriage. It is she who urges Katharine when she marries to be 'quite, quite sure you love your husband' (ND, 83) and who argues for the beauty of the traditional wedding ceremony. By linking her with literary myths of love and marriage, Woolf finds a way of personifying their compelling power within the book. Katharine, on the other hand, is convinced that romance and marriage can never be combined since they belong to two different and opposing orders of experience, to be confused only at one's peril. Her separation of 'the passion and the prose' is linked with her rejection of words and literature, as well as of her mother's 'sentiment' and the coercive designs on her of Ralph and William Rodney.

Katharine's reluctance to simplify marriage into an inevitable outcome, either for herself or the novel, is linked to her doubts about her parents' relationship: 'after all, she considered, thinking of her father and mother, what is love?' (ND, 86). The most painful instance in the book of a failed marriage is that of Richard Alardyce: after a brief idyll, his marriage had turned sour and his wife had sought consolation elsewhere. The question Mrs Hilbery asks, whether anyone can expect more than three months' happiness (ND, 96), is also the question that troubles Katharine. Can romantic love and marriage ever be satisfactorily combined? One person who has already decided that they can't be is Katharine's cousin Cyril, the black sheep of the family who teaches (as Woolf had once done) at a working men's college and refuses to get married on principle; he lives with his mistress and children in a shabby suburb off the Kennington Road (ND, 85, 98).

But even when marriage works, how compatible is it with full selfhood? If women are to enjoy as rich a life as men (and Katharine is endowed with a busy family life and a intense inner being), how will they cope with the subordination of themselves and their desires that William Rodney and many others consider essential for marriage? Lady Otway declares 'I really don't advise a woman who wants to have things her own way to get married' (ND, 177). Up to this point, Katharine has seen marriage as offering her a chance of escaping from the pressures and obligations of family life, and conferring greater personal freedom. She agrees to become engaged to William Rodney because he is relatively undemanding. Not being in love with him, she expects to remain effectively in control of herself and the situation. She pictures married life as allowing her to maintain her distance while providing greater opportunities to follow her own interests, go to lectures and work at her mathematics (ND, 113). Lady Otway's words force Katharine to reconsider her engagement, since they expose marriage as promising not self-discovery but self-subordination.

Katharine's desire for power and independence remains largely unrecognised, operating at a subliminal level, but it is vicariously fulfilled through the figure of Mary Datchet. Mary's presence in the novel as an exemplary 'New Woman' opens up the possibility of work as an alternative to marriage. While her resolve is severely tested, she finally chooses singleness and self-dedication to a political cause, and in the last chapter the light from her room shines out as 'a sign of triumph . . . not to be extinguished this side of the grave' (ND, 431). Mary has not been to college, lives in rooms of her own above the Strand, and finds fulfilment in her work. While the novel reveals significant differences between men's work, which is respected and properly paid, and Mary's, which is minimally rewarded, it nevertheless confers on her a sustaining sense of her own value. Her active pleasure in 'winding-up the world' (ND, 62) is contrasted with the boredom and monotony that William Rodney and Ralph Denham experience at work. Rodney compensates by living an intense cultural life outside office hours, while Ralph indulges in fantasies of escaping to a country cottage to write a history of England. If work is a burden for men, for women it is an aspiration and a privilege. Ralph's sister Joan and Mary Datchet both have jobs and even the dreamy Cassandra is trying to build up a silk-manufacturing industry within the narrow confines of her bedroom. When it comes to working, women are disadvantaged by their lack of education and opportunities.

Before the First World War, women's access to education and rewarding work had been strictly limited, but the situation was gradually changing and *Night and Day* reflects some of these changes as they were taking place. Mary initially works for a society dedicated to 'general suffrage'. Early in 1918 the vote was granted to women over thirty – 'I don't feel much more important – perhaps slightly so', Woolf observed (*Diary* i, 104). *Night and Day* was not yet finished, and this may be one reason Mary moves on from the 'S.G.S.' to work for a society with a wider socialist programme and the need for a properly paid secretary. Ibsen and Shaw had recorded the advent of the 'New Woman' who demanded a vote and independence, and had slammed the domestic door behind her. Both in their very different ways had warned of the impact such demands would have on the traditional structure of marriage, though their accounts were sometimes misread as propaganda. In *Night and Day* it is cousin Cyril who invokes Ibsen and Samuel Butler by way of self-justification (ND, 89).

Woolf had touched on these writers in *The Voyage Out* where Rachel reads Ibsen and acts out his heroines (VO, 112), but *Night and Day* is her first full-scale attempt to record the complex reactions and interactions of books on fantasy life, and of fantasy life on social practice in a period of rapid social change. Inevitably at this stage of her career her reach outstretched her grasp. *The Years* makes a second attempt at mastering the same sort of material, at relating being to non-being, and the life of the imagination to that of history. Planning *The Years*, she wrote in her diary, 'I want to give the whole of present society – nothing less: facts, as well as the vision. And to combine them both. I mean, The waves going on simultaneously with Night & Day. Is this possible?' (*Diary* iv, 151–2). In both novels, the scale of her conception drove her on to write at uncharacteristic length, and both came to seem 'interminable' to her. She felt defeated by the technical problems they posed, problems for which an honest novelist could find no satisfactory solution.

Discussing her novel in progress with the social reformer Beatrice Webb, Woolf explained that she wished 'to discover what aims drive people on, & whether these are illusory or not' (*Diary* i, 196). *Night and Day* makes its own spiritual quest from a version of Victorian positivism that identifies self-fulfilment with family life or work for social ideals, through the more playful interlude of literature associated with the Hilberys, to a concern with something beyond either – to 'the things one doesn't say . . . the dive underground . . . the reality of any feeling' (*Letters* ii, 400). This transcendent state is articulated mainly through dreams, and the two dreamers, Ralph and Katharine, must find and recognise each other, rejecting more worldly claims on them. But in the process of mutual discovery and learning to trust inner promptings, they are forced to acknowledge that 'There may be nothing else. Nothing but what we imagine' (ND, 324). 'Life, the process of discovering' may itself be no more than an illusion.

Day-dreams play a crucial role in the novel: co-existing with, yet transfiguring, everyday life, they provide the chief means of representing inner being. They also constitute an interesting development from *The Voyage Out* where the surface of life, as well as the form of the novel, had been punctuated by the heroine's delirium, dreams and nightmares. The shift from night-dreams to day-dreams in her second novel is paralleled by Woolf's exertion of a firmer control over her plot as well as over her fictional world as a whole, so that there is altogether less 'accident', less of the involuntary and the inexplicable in *Night and Day* – though, paradoxically, this had the effect of making it look less experimental to its critics.

Katharine's day-dreams are characterised by an idealism that finds all human life falling short of the world within: 'There dwelt the things one must have felt had there been cause; the perfect happiness of which here we taste the fragment; the beauty seen here in flying glimpses only' (ND, 116). Everyday life belongs to 'another world, a world antecedent to her world, a world that was the prelude, the antechamber to reality' (ND, 299). Looking out of the window, she even associates her enclosure in domestic life with lights and fires, as if she was specifically thinking of that classic contrast of the ideal and the real, Plato's parable of the caves, in which the firelight deceives the cave dwellers into thinking that it is the sun.

While the inhuman beauty of her dreams relates them to the abstractions of numbers and the stars, they also include narratives that suggest that she has absorbed more of literature than she cares to admit: episodes in which she is taming wild ponies or steering a ship in a hurricane (ND, 34) are clearly shaped by a reading of adventure stories (and may, incidentally, provide an indirect source of information about Woolf's own early reading). As the narrative observes, their furniture 'was drawn directly from the past and even from the England of the Elizabethan age' (ND, 116). Despite Katharine's rejection of them, books provide the main elements of her fantasy life, and within that life she acquires masculine attributes of power and mastery, controlling horses or ships. Sometimes a 'magnanimous hero' may accompany her on a wild ride, but he is significantly anonymous, a companion rather than a master. Katharine thus enters the predominantly masculine world of adventure stories by reinventing herself as a man. The 'furniture' of her dreams and their easy crossing of gender boundaries anticipate the early episodes of Woolf's fantasy biography, *Orlando* (1928).

The rich fulfilment of her inner life deters her from looking beyond it for satisfaction; she recognises her dreams of waterfalls, seashores and forests as antithetical to daily existence. They afford 'an image of love . . . which naturally dwarfed any examples that came her way', and on one occasion an image of sexual abandonment that also involves abandonment to the power of the imagination:

> Splendid as the waters that drop with resounding thunder from high ledges of rock, and plunge downwards into the blue depths of night, was the presence of love she dreamt, drawing into it every drop of the force of life, and dashing

them all asunder in the superb catastrophe in which everything was surrendered, and nothing might be reclaimed. (ND, 87)

For Katharine, this image of the waterfall is exceptional, reversing the taming and steering imagery to suggest the loss of all control. The traditional construction of sexual desire in terms of feminine self-surrender may be more threatening to the sense of self than the social convention of marriage that can be subject to conscious negotiation. In her fantasy, physical passion is figured as an elemental force whose power she cannot resist. Yet, unknown to her, she shares this view of it with Ralph who, in a memorable and resonant image, sees himself simultaneously as a lighthouse and as the helpless sea bird dashed by the storm against its windows (ND, 334, 337). Ralph also shares Katharine's propensity to dream, but she is what he dreams about. His dreams recognise the freedom and independence she aspires to, transforming her into a goddess who can confer recognition on him (as she had signally failed to do at their first encounter). Although his dreams thus complement hers, she strongly resents being their object, finding them falsifying and potentially coercive.

Beside the visionary intensity of her dream world, Katharine's fiancé William Rodney appears comic and absurd. Since she regards her inner and outer lives as mutually exclusive, she is never tempted to conflate the two, as so many tragic heroines had done. On the contrary, she sees marriage not as the fulfilment of fantasies of romance, but as an unavoidable step from which only limited gains can be expected. Viewed in this light, one match is as suitable as another and 'she was able to contemplate a perfectly loveless marriage, as the thing one did actually in real life, for possibly the people who dream thus are those who do the most prosaic things' (ND, 87). Her agreement to marry William is a practical arrangement, leaving her free to continue her fantasy life unhindered. But it is also a gesture of resignation or despair, paralleled by Ralph's proposal to Mary Datchet. Like him, she accepts that she cannot construct a meaningful relation between her inner and outer life.

Katharine's fantasies reveal her longing for a degree of power and control more often achieved by men, largely withheld from women, and quite at odds with her society's conception of marriage. She cannot reconcile her hidden desire for domination with being a woman, her idealism with everyday life, or her inner passions with love or marriage. These unbridgeable gaps are the source of her silences which the novel articulates as dreams, 'the things one doesn't say'; yet the most obvious sense of this phrase connects it with the crude and unspeakable life of the body that participates in the world of dreams through sexuality. And sexuality is precisely the novel's own point of silence, as Lytton Strachey (typically) pointed out to Woolf. 'I take your point about the tupping and had meant to introduce a little in that line, but somehow it seemed out of the picture', she replied (*Letters* ii, 394).[17] Its absence is the more noticeable by contrast with the novels written before and after, *The Voyage Out* and *Jacob's Room*, both of which treat desire with comparative directness while acknowledging its disturbing or disruptive nature, and the difficulty of accommodating it within social rules and familial relationships.

The lovers in *Night and Day*, on the other hand, seem scarcely conscious of each other's bodies. Mary Datchet recognises that she is in love with Ralph when she looks at the head of Ulysses in the British Museum (ND, 65–6), while Ralph evokes Katharine's image by looking at photographs of Greek statues, at 'the head of a goddess, if the lower part were concealed' (ND, 327). There is a stronger physical awareness and intimacy between Katharine and Mary, as Mary pats Katharine's knee affectionately (ND, 145) or fingers the fur on the hem of her skirt (ND, 232, 235). But the exigencies of form demand that desire be introduced in order that the lovers may fall in love and thus renew the possibilities of love and marriage, but above all to negotiate the gap between dream and reality.

Kew Gardens provides a setting in which desire can bring reconciliation and a symbolic re-entry into Eden. 'Doesn't one always think of the past, in a garden with men and women lying under the trees?' asks Eleanor in Woolf's dazzling short story 'Kew Gardens', published in 1919, but written in 1917 (CSF, 91). At Kew the separate strands of experience are brought together. Katharine delights in the laws of plant life that Ralph expounds for her, while realising that plants (unlike numbers or stars) are gendered; they are 'living things endowed with sex' (ND, 281). They combine within themselves the abstract and the actual, releasing Katharine from the isolation of her mind to an awareness of her body. Outer and inner worlds touch as the couple enter the Orchid House, where plants 'peer and gape . . . from striped hoods and fleshy throats . . . In defiance of the rules she stretched her ungloved hand and touched one' (ND, 282). And with this gesture of conciliation towards the desires of the body, Katharine glimpses for the first time the possibility of bringing together

> the thought and the action . . . the life of solitude and the life of society, this astonishing precipice on one side of which the soul was active and in broad daylight, on the other side of which it was contemplative and dark as night. (ND, 288)

But the novel does not end here, nor can the concept of 'falling in love' be unproblematic, since it has been transferred from the world of literature and fantasy into the world of daylight yet cannot be rooted in any bodily experience apart from desire itself – intangible, elusive and subject to the vagaries of the imagination. For Woolf, the whole experience of falling in love is characterised by a continuous lurching backwards and forwards between 'dreams and realities' (the novel's provisional title in the manuscript draft). 'Dreams and realities, dreams and realities, dreams and realities', intones the novelist Terence Hewet in *The Voyage Out* as he turns away from eavesdropping on Rachel and Helen, wondering whether he is in love with them (VO, 172). Ralph waiting for Katharine in the drawing room 'scarcely knew whether [his eyes] beheld dreams or realities' (ND, 120).[18] The interlocking uncertainties of dream and desire come together in the lovers' final walk by the river when 'She felt his arm stiffen beneath her hand, and knew by this token that they had entered the enchanted region' (ND, 432).

In a new definition of the 'night and day' theme, the final pages are darkened by the lovers' apparently uncontrollable fluctuations between mutual joy and a distancing that they refer to as their 'lapses' (ND, 402–3). While these reflect something of the irrational currents of desire, they also reflect Katharine's emotional independence and her resentment of Ralph's alienating fantasies about her. Similar tensions are apparent towards the end of *The Voyage Out* where Rachel demands 'Is it true or is it a dream?', the lovers quarrel, consider breaking off their engagement and at moments 'almost dislike each other' (VO, 261, 285–6, 293).

Being in love is essentially an act of imagination, a willed suspension of disbelief, so that when that fails the relationship collapses. Katharine confides to her mother her fear that love is

> 'an illusion – as if when we think we're in love we make it up – we imagine what doesn't exist. That's why it's impossible that we should ever marry. Always to be finding the other an illusion, and going off and forgetting about them, never to be certain that you cared, or that he wasn't caring for some one not you at all, the horror of changing from one state to the other, being happy one moment and miserable the next – that's the reason why we can't possibly marry. At the same time . . . we can't live without each other, because –' (ND, 412)

Mrs Hilbery replies 'We have to have faith in our vision', but her words only highlight the extent that the lovers' happiness depends on their capacity for believing in it. The slightest change around them can unbalance that state and produce one of their 'lapses'. Worst of all is the suspicion that love itself is no more than an illusion, a conspiracy between society and the individual to reconcile us to the irrepressible needs of the animals. The harmony induced by Kew Gardens is dissipated by a visit to the zoo.

Walking beside the river again on 26 March 1919, Leonard once more reverted to the subject of 'the illusory nature of all pleasures & pains;

from which he concludes that mankind is a wretched tribe of animals'. In her diary the next day Woolf partly attributed this Swiftian mood 'to Night & Day which L. has spent the past 2 mornings & evenings in reading'. Unlike more recent critics, he found it a dark book:

> L. finds the philosophy very melancholy. It too much agrees with what he was saying yesterday. Yet, if one is to deal with people on a large scale & say what one thinks, how can one avoid melancholy? I don't admit to being hopeless though – only the spectacle is a profoundly strange one; & as the current answers don't do, one has to grope for new ones; & the process of discarding the old, when one is by no means certain what to put in their place, is a sad one. Still, if you think of it, what answers do Arnold Bennett or Thackeray, for instance, suggest? Happy ones – satisfactory solutions – answers one would accept, if one had the least respect for one's soul? (*Diary* i, 259)

For Woolf, mastering the traditional novel had only exposed its limitations. Its naturalistic surface and closure in marriage had not resolved any of her artistic problems. The neat formulations of classical realism could no longer close the gap between nineteenth-century narrative confidence and twentieth-century doubt, and the sadness of that recognition is reflected in this diary entry which provided the seed for her essay on 'Modern Novels', written a day or two later and published in the *Times Literary Supplement* on 10 April 1919. And with that essay she stepped decisively away from the self-questioning induced by *Night and Day*. She was no nearer separating what was real from what was illusory – that question would haunt her for the rest of her life – but she now knew that however they were defined in the future, it could no longer be on the old terms or in the old form.

## Notes

1. 'All rivers at night are melancholy, sentimental, sad, like emblems of the mystery and unreality of human things. Under their spell we seem to see things larger than our own small selves', Leonard Woolf, *The Wise Virgins: A Story of Words, Opinions and a Few Emotions* (1914; London: Persephone Books, 2003), p. 87.
2. *The Critical Writing of Katherine Mansfield*, ed. Clare Hanson (London: Macmillan, 1987), letter to J. M. Murry, p. 59; 'A Ship Comes into the Harbour' (*Athenaeum*, 21 Nov. 1919), pp. 57, 59.
3. Woolf's first novel *The Voyage Out* (1915) had introduced the Dreadnoughts, and Mrs Thornbury had observed that flying 'would be quite necessary in time of war, and in England we were terribly behindhand' (VO, 60, 122).
4. Woolf's letter to Smyth compares writing the novel to attending the antique class at art school (as her sister Vanessa had done), reworking the imagery of classicism that E. M. Forster had used to describe *Night and Day* in his

essay, 'The Early Novels of Virginia Woolf' (1925), where he calls it 'a deliberate exercise in classicism. It contains all that has characterised English fiction for good or evil during the last hundred and fifty years – faith in personal relations, recourse to humorous sideshows, insistence on petty social differences', *Abinger Harvest* (1936; London: Penguin, 1974), p. 122.

5. As Elizabeth Heine observed (in *Virginia Woolf Miscellany* no. 9, Winter 1977, p. 10), at one point in the surviving MS (on the 22nd leaf), Effie's name appears, crossed out and corrected to 'Katharine', and in a diary entry for 18 January 1915 Woolf wrote 'I want to see what can be said *against* all forms of activity & thus dissuade L[eonard] from his work, speaking really not in my own character but in Effie's' (*Diary* i, p. 22). Woolf took the name 'Katharine' (spelt with two 'a's, as in its Greek root) from her husband's novel, *The Wise Virgins*, where it belongs to the character based on Vanessa. The name 'Effie' may have been suggested by that of Effie Stillman, a sculptor and friend of the Stephens. Her sister Lisa, a portrait painter, was a role model for Vanessa (*A Passionate Apprentice*, 20, 39).
6. The MS of *Night and Day* is in the Berg Collection of the New York Public Library.
7. 'I've been writing about you all morning, and have made you wear a blue dress: you've got to be immensely mysterious and romantic, which of course you are; yes, but it's the combination that's so enthralling.' For the pressure on Vanessa 'to be what people call "practical "', see 'Reminiscences' (MB, 3).
8. 'The Enchanted Organ', *Essays* iii, pp. 400–1; see also Henrietta Garnett, *Anny: A Life of Anne Isabella Thackeray Ritchie* (London: Chatto and Windus, 2004).
9. See Leslie Stephen's *Mausoleum Book*, pp. 12–15, 41–5, 82.
10. Mark Hussey also considers the impact of *The Wise Virgins* on *Night and Day* in 'Refractions of Desire: The Early Fictions of Leonard and Virginia Woolf', *Modern Fiction Studies*, 38:1 (Spring 1992), 127–46.
11. 'A Ship Comes into the Harbour', *The Critical Writings of Katherine Mansfield*, p. 59.
12. See, for example, the chapter on *Night and Day* in Avrom Fleishman, *Virginia Woolf: A Critical Reading* (Baltimore, MD: Johns Hopkins University Press, 1975); Margaret Comstock, ' "The Current Answers Don't Do": The Comic Form of *Night and Day*', *Women's Studies*, 4 (1977), pp. 153–71; Jane Marcus, 'Enchanted Organ, Magic Bells: *Night and Day* as a Comic Opera', in *Virginia Woolf and the Languages of Patriarchy* (Bloomington: Indiana University Press, 1987).
13. In 1921 Woolf began Russian lessons with S. S. Koteliansky ('Kot') and she later worked with him on his translation of 'Stavrogin's Confession', the suppressed chapter of Dostoevsky's *The Possessed* (published by the Hogarth Press as their joint translation in 1922) – see Natalya Reinhold, 'Virginia Woolf's Russian Voyage Out', *Woolf Studies Annual*, vol. 9 (New York: Pace University Press, 2003), pp. 1–27.
14. F. Dostoevsky, *The Idiot*, trans. Richard Pevear and Larissa Volokhonsky (London: Granta Books, 2003), p. 394 (Woolf would have used Constance Garnett's translation); *The Wise Virgins*, pp. 84, 90; E. M. Forster's review of *The Voyage Out* was published on 8 April 1915 in the *Daily News and Leader* (p. 7), reprinted in *Virginia Woolf: The Critical Heritage*, ed. Robin

Majumdar and Allen McLaurin (London and Boston: Routledge and Kegan Paul, 1975), p. 54.

15. As, for example, Rachel Blau du Plessis assumes in *Writing Beyond the Ending: Narrative Structures of Twentieth-Century Writers* (Bloomington: Indiana University Press, 1985), p. 58.
16. Carlyle had lived at 24 Cheyne Row. Virginia visited his house with her father on 29 Jan. 1897, (*A Passionate Apprentice*, p. 24), and again on 29 March 1898 with Vanessa and Hester Ritchie (Aunt Anny's daughter), when they signed the Visitors' Book.
17. Strachey's letter on *Night and Day* is unfortunately missing – see *Virginia Woolf and Lytton Strachey: Letters*, ed. Leonard Woolf and James Strachey (London: Hogarth Press, 1956), p. 115.
18. Woolf used 'Dreams and Realities' as the title of her review of Walter de la Mare's *Motley and Other Poems* (1918), published on 30 May 1918 in the *TLS* (*Essays* ii, 252–5). It was also the title of an essay of 1878 by her father, later reprinted in his *An Agnostic's Apology and Other Essays* (London: Smith, Elder, 1893).

Essay 4

# Reading People, Reading Texts: 'Byron and Mr Briggs'

> We know that our lives are shaped like stories . . . we read *life* as well as *books*, and the activity of reading is really a matter of working through signs and texts in order to comprehend fully and powerfully not only whatever may be presented therein but also our own situations, both in their particularity and historicity and in their more durable and inevitable dimensions.[1]

In their various ways, all Woolf's works – novels, short stories and essays – contribute to an ongoing debate about the nature and the purpose of writing; but she was equally preoccupied with the nature of reading, and especially so between the publication of *Night and Day* in the autumn of 1919 and that of *Mrs Dalloway* and *The Common Reader* in the spring of 1925. Struggling to come to terms with an older literary tradition associated with her father and to let go of the dead leaves of the past, she began to search for new and more open ways to practise reading as well as writing. She wanted to understand how reading worked and how it related to the wider interpretation of signs.

Woolf had always loved and needed reading: she wrote essays on 'Hours in a Library' (the title of her father's best-known book), 'Reading', 'On Re-reading Novels', 'How It Strikes a Contemporary' (the title of a Robert Browning poem), 'How Should One Read a Book?' and 'All About Books' (*Essays* ii, 55; iii, 141, 336; 353; iv, 388; CE ii, 263). She discussed it in her fiction, diaries and letters, and kept careful records of what she read. At least twenty-six notebooks are devoted to her reading, and many other documents include further notes on it.[2] She reviewed books regularly, believing that it contributed to her professional development, and her earliest and steadiest earnings derived from reviewing rather than from fiction. If she was a great writer, she was also a great reader, and her experience as a reader played an important part in her journey to modernism. In 1923, she wrote

> It encourages me to feel that all this reading has an end in view. In five years, I shall have fagged out a good book from it, I hope; a rough, but vigorous statue testifying before I die to the great fun & pleasure my habit of reading has given me. (*Diary* ii, 259)

Modernism altered its readers' relation to what they read, for they confronted more difficult texts and had to contribute more to activate their meaning. Woolf's interest in what happens during the process of reading led her to explore some of its side effects and to pursue analogies between the process of 'reading people' and reading texts. As she did so, Lord Byron became a touchstone, a controversial figure whose writings provoked extraneous judgements on his character and way of life.

Byron bothered Woolf because, like many before her, she responded to his personality – or to the myth of his personality – as much as to his writings themselves. This is partly because his work conveys his personality so strongly, or rather because different works convey different aspects of his personality strongly – for there is Byron the romantic poet, author of *Childe Harold's Pilgrimage* and the love lyrics; Byron the satirist of *The Vision of Judgement* and *English Bards and Scotch Reviewers*; and Byron the cynic and man of the world, the author of *Don Juan*. As a popular poet, the romantic Byron stood second only to Sir Walter Scott (reprints of the Cantos of *Childe Harold* ran into hundreds of thousands of copies), but as the author of *Don Juan* he shocked and alarmed many of his former fans. Respectable circulating libraries either refused to buy it, or issued it tactfully under 'D' as ___ ____, while Subscription Clubs that had dined together for years suddenly broke up over whether to acquire it or not. And there was also the prose Byron, author of the *Letters*, which Woolf particularly admired: 'There are people who would exchange all Byron's poems for half his letters' ('Swinburne Letters', *Essays* ii, 258). *Don Juan* she considered a masterpiece, finding it 'difficult to rank [it] much lower than the Prelude' ('Byron and Mr Briggs', *Essays* iii. 481). With it, Byron had 'pointed the way; he showed how flexible an instrument poetry might become, but none has followed his example to put his tool to further use' ('Poetry, Fiction and the Future', *Essays* iv, 434). The narrative energy of *Don Juan* and the immediacy of his *Letters* encouraged Woolf to see him as a novelist in the making.

In February 1930, having just finished André Maurois's two-volume biography, Woolf took up Byron again. She concluded that there was

> much that is spurious, vapid, yet very changeable, & then rich & with greater range than the other poets, could he have got the whole into order. A novelist, he might have been . . . The truth may be that if you are charged at such high voltage, you cant fit any of the ordinary human feelings; must pose; must

> rhapsodise; don't fit in. He wrote in the Inn Album that his age was 100. And this is true, measuring life by feeling. (*Diary* iii, 288)[3]

Byron's disruptiveness, his failure to get 'the whole into order . . . [to] fit in' were, she felt, key aspects. He remained a test of readers, and even of reading, a poet whose work and personality had become inextricably confused.

Woolf was by no means the first writer to use Byron as a literary touchstone for exploring connections between reading and life, between books and their readers. In the eleventh chapter of Jane Austen's *Persuasion*, Anne Elliott and Captain Benwick discuss the relative merits of 'the *Giaour* and *The Bride of Abydos*; and moreover, how the *Giaour* was to be pronounced'.[4] Links between Byron and unrestrained feeling anticipate Louisa Musgrove's accident on the Cobb in the following chapter. Jane Austen's type of English social comedy (and *Persuasion* in particular, with its unexpected choice of marriage partner) is strongly evoked in Woolf's second novel, *Night and Day* (1919), where the heroine's cousin is named Cassandra, like Jane Austen's beloved sister. In a striking passage from this novel, Byron appears first as an unidentified volume, then as a familiar and instantly recognisable book of poetry, and finally offers a perspective on its hero, Ralph Denham.

> 'No, you're right,' [Ralph] said. 'I don't know you. I've never known you.'
>
> 'Yet perhaps you know me better than anyone else,' [Katharine] mused.
>
> Some detached instinct made her aware that she was gazing at a book which belonged by right to some other part of the house. She walked over to the shelf, took it down, and returned to her seat, placing the book on the table between them. Ralph opened it and looked at the portrait of a man with a voluminous white shirt collar which formed the frontispiece.
>
> 'I say I do know you, Katharine,' he affirmed, shutting the book. 'It's only for moments that I go mad.' (ND, 358)

During the conversation that follows, Mrs Hilbery, Katharine's mother, comes in.

> [Mrs Hilbery] seemed, as usual, bound on some quest of her own which was interrupted pleasantly but strangely by running into one of those queer, unnecessary ceremonies that other people thought fit to indulge in.
>
> 'Please don't let me interrupt you. Mr – ' she was at a loss, as usual, for the name, and Katharine thought that she did not recognise him. 'I hope you've found something nice to read,' she added, pointing to the book upon the table. 'Byron – ah, Byron. I've known people who knew Lord Byron,' she said.
>
> Katharine, who had risen in some confusion, could not help smiling at the thought that her mother found it perfectly natural and desirable that her daughter should be reading Byron in the dining room late at night alone with a strange young man. She blessed a disposition that was so convenient, and

felt tenderly towards her mother and her mother's eccentricities. But Ralph observed that although Mrs Hilbery held the book so close to her eyes she was not reading a word. . . .

I'm sure I should like your poetry better than I like Lord Byron's,' said Mrs Hilbery, addressing Ralph Denham.

'Mr Denham doesn't write poetry; he has written articles for father, for the Review,' Katharine said, as if prompting her memory.

'Oh dear! How dull!' Mrs Hilbery exclaimed, with a sudden laugh that rather puzzled her daughter.

Ralph found that she had turned upon him a gaze that was at once very vague and very penetrating.

'But I'm sure you read poetry at night. I always judge by the expression of the eyes,' Mrs Hilbery continued. . . . 'I don't know much about the law . . . But I think I do know a little about poetry,' she added. 'And all the things that aren't written down, but – but – ' She waved her hand, as if to indicate the wealth of unwritten poetry all about them. 'The night and the stars, the dawn coming up, the barges swimming past, the sun setting . . . Ah dear,' she sighed, 'well, the sunset is very lovely too. I sometimes think that poetry isn't so much what we write as what we feel, Mr Denham.' (ND, 361–2)

Similarities and contrasts are drawn between people and books. For the lovers, Katharine and Ralph, the book that lies between them lacks any significance, other than that it is 'out of place'. Mrs Hilbery, on the other hand, does not need to pick it up to identify it: 'Byron – ah, Byron. I've known people who knew Lord Byron', she says immediately. Several lines later, she implicitly compares Ralph with Byron when she reassures him, 'I'm sure I should like your poetry better than I like Lord Byron's.' As Katharine points out, her mother's assumption that Ralph writes poetry is wrong: he is in fact a lawyer. Mrs Hilbery was also wrong in assuming that she was interrupting a romantic scene in which the lovers were reading Byron's love poetry together. In fact, they had not even identified the volume, let alone read it. Her suppositions are actually misreadings.

Yet, as always, Mrs Hilbery speaks more wisely than she knows: what Ralph shares with the volume of Byron is that he too is 'out of place'; whenever he is inside the Hilberys' house, he is conscious that he does not 'fit in'. He had felt more at home waiting in the street below their window, in the storm and wind, than in their formal Victorian dining room. And while Ralph fails to correspond to Byron in that he does not write poetry, at another level he *does* correspond to him, since he too is a misfit, full of passionate and stormy feelings that cannot be easily contained or analysed. As Mrs Hilbery observes, 'poetry isn't so much what we write as what we feel'. This passage offers a series of reconsiderations as to how people and books invite our judgement, and the ways readings and misreadings may correct one another. Through it, the narrative advances, though not directly, and not to any single or simple revelation.

Relationships have been suggested, contradicted and re-described. For Woolf, the process of reading, whether people or texts, had no natural terminus; it was one of continuous invitation, progression, correction and re-correction that lasted as long as life itself.

Reading people and reading texts are often thought of as antithetical processes. John Dryden praised Shakespeare for being 'naturally learn'd: he needed not the spectacles of books to read Nature'.[5] In an early short story, 'Memoirs of a Novelist', Woolf contrasted the verbal clichés of a bad Victorian biography with the sudden revelation of character provided by a photograph facing the text (see above, pp. 32–3). A rather different contrast, this time between reading people and reciting poetry, occurs in the opening scene of her first novel, *The Voyage Out*, where Helen Ambrose 'knew how to read the people who were passing her', while her husband Ridley, embarrassed by her tears, strides along reciting Macaulay's *Lays of Ancient Rome* (VO, 5). Women in Woolf's texts are often more interested in and more adept at 'reading people' than men are, but they are also readers of texts, though they may read in different ways from men, as the scene of the Ramsays reading together at the end of the first part of *To the Lighthouse* suggests.[6]

Woolf recognised the power of reading and knew that its impact could be as strong as that of any actual experience, and that, like any powerful force, it could be felt as threatening as well as inviting, coercive as well as seductive. In *The Voyage Out*, both the Dalloways attempt to leave their mark on its unformed heroine Rachel, Clarissa by giving her *Persuasion* to read and Richard by forcing a kiss on her (VO, 53–4, 66). Rachel, struggling to come to terms with the adult world, is using books to help her do so. The men and women around her encourage her by presenting her with different books, from Jane Austen's *Persuasion* to Gibbon's *Decline and Fall of the Roman Empire* – books that reflect their hopes for her future, rather than her own. Rachel discovers for herself some books that promise greater self-determination – proto-feminist texts such as Meredith's *Diana of the Crossways* and Ibsen's *A Doll's House*, which she acts out in the privacy of her room (VO, 112). At the same time, she is haunted by a cheap novel of social criticism that describes the terrible fate of a woman who has been forced into prostitution by poverty, and who dies in a sordid lodging-house, nameless and alone:

> She looked grudgingly at the novel which had once caused her perhaps an hour's discomfort, so that she had never opened it again, but kept it on her table, and looked at it occasionally, as some medieval monk kept a skull, or a crucifix to remind him of the frailty of the body.
>
> 'Is it true, Terence,' she demanded, 'that women die with bugs crawling across their faces?' (VO, 284)

Woolf's first novel suggests that reading books and reading people can pose comparable problems, and both may threaten a young woman searching for an independent self. Her second novel, *Night and Day*, plays out a more obvious conflict between lived experience on the one hand, and the world of books and the traditional values they embody, on the other. Those values are endorsed by Katharine's parents, her family and her bookish fiancé, who writes her poems while planning to domesticate her. Katharine shares her author's impatience with the legacy of Victorian fiction, characterised in 'Modern Fiction' as a 'powerful and unscrupulous tyrant' who holds the writer 'in thrall' (*Essays* iv, 160). In *Night and Day*, literary tradition is felt as a pressure and a weight, at once endorsing the authority of the father, and the mother's seductive faith in the power of love and marriage. Katharine rebels against both of them. Like her author, she has outgrown the master-narrative she inherited, the story of a young woman entering the adult world and finding romance. Marriage, the novel's usual catastrophe technically speaking, now only too often becomes an actual catastrophe in the more familiar sense of the word (Sally Seton and the young Clarissa Dalloway 'spoke of marriage always as a catastrophe' – MD, 37). Committed to upholding duty, heterosexual love and marriage, Victorian values could be as much of a burden on the reader as on the writer. Woolf spoke for both in feeling 'a momentary doubt, a spasm of rebellion, as the pages fill themselves in the customary way. Is life like this? Must novels be like this?' (*Essays* iv, 160).

A tension remained between the empowerment afforded by reading, and the threat to selfhood that it might pose. Reading potentially confers self-affirmation (as Rachel's readings of proto-feminist texts were intended to do), yet the specific nature of its address system could exclude outsiders – women, the uneducated, or anyone of different ethnicity – from a discourse conducted in first-person plurals, 'we', 'us' – or it could impose a conformity that a reader might resist. One such reader is Julia Hedge, the feminist in *Jacob's Room*, who resents the names of male authors inscribed in gilt letters round the dome of the British Museum Reading Room (J's R, 91). Other coercive aspects of literature are exposed when Jacob presents the women in his life with some uncomfortably inappropriate books, bullying the orphaned Fanny Elmer into reading *Tom Jones* (the history of a foundling) and giving the trivial and heartless Sandra Wentworth-Williams the poems of John Donne (J's R, 106–8, 140–2).

The power of books to encourage particular ways of interpreting experience was another troubling factor, and one that was evidently on Woolf's mind in January 1920 when she wrote 'An Unwritten Novel',[7] the story of a misreading occasioned by previous readings – and, incidentally, the first of a series of railway scenarios in which the life of an unknown woman in a railway carriage is reconstructed. The narrator, travelling from London to Eastbourne, spins a fantasy around the woman opposite her, imagining her as a downtrodden and embittered spinster, tormented by guilt that she feels as an incurable itch between her shoulder blades – the result of a childhood trauma: 'A crime . . . They would say she kept her sorrow, suppressed her secret – her sex, they'd say – the scientific people' (CSF, 115). Woolf had in mind a type of novel that she identified as 'Freudian Fiction' in a review for the *TLS*, written a month or two later (25 March 1920, *Essays* iii, 195–7). The woman, designated 'Minnie Marsh', is imagined as living out her life in just such a scrupulously lower-middle-class setting – 'a matter of crusts and cruets, frills and ferns' – as Arnold Bennett or H. G. Wells might have given her (CSF, 118). When the train reaches Eastbourne, the woman's son is there to meet her and the narrator's condescending and book-shaped fantasy collapses, but her deflation turns to exhilaration as she contemplates the endless new narrative prospects that his intervention has opened up:

> Mysterious figures! Mother and son. Who are you? . . . Wherever I go, mysterious figures, I see you, turning the corner, mothers and sons . . . it's you, unknown figures, you I adore; if I open my arms, it's you I embrace, you I draw to me – adorable world! (CSF, 121)

'An Unwritten Novel' parodies the kinds of fiction that Woolf could not take seriously, and perhaps criticises its power to influence the way we think about the lives of other people. Yet her story also celebrates the flexibility of the imagination as it continuously reorganises our experiences, as well as the vividness of its enactments.[8] Although the tale of Minnie Marsh takes place only in the narrator's head, what the narrator imagines is as vivid to the reader as the naturalistic 'railway carriage' frame. Despite being cancelled by its own title, as well as by emerging 'facts', 'An Unwritten Novel' has actually been written and stands as a testament to the power of imaginative acts. From another point of view, it is a text within a text, and Woolf continued to be fascinated by these: witness Mrs Hilbery's unfinished biography of her father, Orlando's poem 'The Oak Tree', Bernard's writing in *The Waves*, Miss La Trobe's pageant in *Between the Acts*, and, if we extend this category into another medium, Lily Briscoe's portrait of Mrs Ramsay and James – itself a further version of the mysterious 'Mother and Son' theme with which 'An Unwritten Novel' ends. The process of 'reading', that is, of imagining 'Minnie Marsh', thus dissolves into that of writing about her. As Robert Scholes puts it, 'What we read is the past. What we write is the future.'[9]

The 'Mysterious figures! Mother and son' with which Woolf's short story ended were evidently prophetic, for in mid-April 1920, she began work on *Jacob's Room*, a novel that begins and ends with Mrs Flanders in search of her lost son. By May, she had reached chapter III, which rewrites the railway carriage scenario from a different perspective.[10] This time a woman traveller is contemplating a mysterious young man. The object of her gaze is Jacob: here, as elsewhere in the novel, he becomes a text under scrutiny. Mrs Norman's misreading may have been suggested by her 'novel from Mudie's' (a popular lending library). At any rate, she permits herself a moment of imagined melodrama:

> The train did not stop before it reached Cambridge, and here she was shut up alone, in a railway carriage, with a young man . . . She would throw the scent-bottle with her right hand, she decided, and tug the communication cord with her left. She was fifty years of age, and had a son at college. Nevertheless, it is a fact that men are dangerous. (J's R, 23)

Jacob ignores her and begins to light his pipe although, as Mrs Norman points out, it is a non-smoking carriage. She examines his socks, his tie and finally his expression, deciding that, after all, her fears were unjustified:

> – as for knocking one down! No, no, no! . . .
>
> Nobody sees any one as he is, let alone an elderly lady sitting opposite a strange young man in a railway carriage. They see a whole – they see all sorts of things – they see themselves . . . One must do the best one can with her report. Anyhow, this was Jacob Flanders, aged nineteen. It is no use trying to sum people up. One must follow hints, not exactly what is said, nor yet entirely what is done . . .
>
> 'Who . . .' said the lady, meeting her son; but as there was a great crowd on the platform and Jacob had already gone, she did not finish her sentence. (J's R, 23–4)

The scene ends, as 'An Unwritten Novel' had done, with Mrs Norman's son arriving to meet her. Her misreading of Jacob as a sexual threat replays contemporary narratives that warned women against travelling alone in closed railway compartments with unknown men. Here, her misreading is attributable to gender difference, and corresponds to the novel's pervasive sense of the mystery of the opposite sex. *Jacob's Room* sets out to read the character of Jacob from his various enigmatic appearances, and from the social and literal spaces he occupies. In doing so, it recalls E. M. Forster's *The Longest Journey* (1907) which Woolf had reviewed: there, Ricky's room at Cambridge had held a key to the mystery of his birth, although his fiancée Agnes had signally failed to read it aright. Aspects of Ralph Denham's character, in *Night and Day*, could similarly be read from his room in Highgate.

Jacob himself, educated at Rugby and Trinity College, Cambridge, is at home in the world of books, and in a tradition of educated historical debate derived from the classics, from Macaulay and Carlyle. But the novel also includes the dissenting voice of Julia Hedge the feminist, as well as of several other young women lacking in self-confidence, financial security and social roots. The inadequacy of the literary tradition to provide for such readers is criticised in the text, as it had been in *The Voyage Out* and *Night and Day*, but in *Jacob's Room* that critique is integrated into the structure of the narrative itself: it is disjunctive and episodic, frequently changes voices and viewpoints, and ends, not with Jacob's marriage nor even with his death, but with his mother's unanswered question and gesture, ' "What am I to do with these, Mr. Bonamy?" She held out a pair of Jacob's old shoes'. (J's R, 155)

By opening up her text to uncertainties, Woolf revised the role of the reader within it, so that the reader now resembled the observer in the railway carriage, acting as witness to a series of signs and events whose ultimate significance remains unknown. The reader's position is at once destabilised and reinforced: she is not obliged to adopt any pre-determined position, yet a more active participation and a more positive effort to 'make a whole' of the text is also required of her.

In May 1921, Woolf began 'wondering how to shape my Reading book' (Diary ii, 120): she was thinking about a book that would reprint a selection from her articles and reviews, along with new material – the book that eventually became *The Common Reader* (1925). It would provide an account of the reading process while unobtrusively introducing its readers to a wider canon, rather as Roger Fry had done in his collection of essays *Vision and Design* (1920). It would find room for those genres that arise from or lie close to life, such as diaries and letters, till then usually omitted from serious critical discussion, and would investigate neglected minor writers and eccentrics such as Margaret Cavendish, Duchess of Newcastle. It would correct the unexamined assumptions of the literary world by setting marginal or forgotten voices closer to the centre. No one, she reminded scholars, can truly claim to read Greek, because we cannot tell what the words meant to their original readers. All knowledge of the past is reconstructed, mediated and thus distorted – it constantly needs to be re-examined. She cast about for a form that would encourage the reader to participate in the discussion, and even considered embedding them within family conversations, to make them seem less dogmatic and opinionated.[11]

In late February or March 1922, as she was finishing *Jacob's Room*, Woolf began to draft an introduction to her 'Reading' book, stimulated by a distinction she perceived between serious criticism and mere reviewing, and by the publication of a new edition of Byron's Correspondence. She began it 'with the usual fabulous zest. I have never enjoyed any writing more' (*Diary* ii, 168, 169, 172). What she wrote survives in the form of an essay of thirty-eight pages, entitled 'Byron and Mr Briggs', in a heavily corrected longhand draft that was never completed and was only transcribed and published posthumously. 'Byron and Mr Briggs' is rambling and loosely organised, yet, like other unfinished work, it displays a freedom and spontaneity that can be lost in the transition to publication. But in this case, no more than a few phrases were salvaged for the single-page introduction to *The Common Reader*. There, she would quote from Dr Johnson's definition:

> The common reader, as Dr Johnson implies, differs from the critic and the scholar. He is worse educated, and nature has not gifted him so generously. He reads for his own pleasure rather than to impart knowledge or correct the opinions of others. Above all, he is guided by an instinct to create for himself, out of whatever odds and ends he can come by, some kind of a whole – a portrait of a man, a sketch of an age, a theory of the art of writing. He never ceases, as he reads, to run up some rickety and ramshackle fabric . . . (*Essays* iv, 17)

The common reader pursues signs and attempts to knit them into a larger fabric, a whole – to create from them a meaningful structure through an effort of the imagination.

Though never ultimately defined, the impulse to complete an experience, to create 'some kind of a whole', provides the unifying theme of 'Byron and Mr Briggs'. One possible source for this concept is G. E. Moore's idea of organic unity in which different elements conjoin to make something more than the sum of their individual parts. Moore discussed his concept of an 'organic whole' in the context of aesthetics, and 'the consciousness of a beautiful thing'.[12] Woolf would have recognised the significance of this discussion when she first read Moore's *Principia Ethica* in the summer of 1908, for this was the book that had shaped the thinking of a generation of Cambridge undergraduates that included Woolf's brother Thoby, her husband Leonard, Lytton Strachey, Maynard Keynes and Roger Fry. In 'Byron and Mr Briggs' Woolf compared the process of reading and trying to create 'some kind of a whole' to the exercise of the imagination in the railway carriage. Section 8 begins,

> To make a whole – it is that which we have in common. Our reading is always urged on by instinct to complete what we read, which is, for some reason, one of the most universal and profound of our instincts. You may see it at work any night among the passengers in a third class railway carriage. Is he related to the woman opposite? No they work in the same office. In love then? No; she wears a wedding ring. Going home then to the same suburb? Ah, yes . . .

Everyone plays this familiar game. Everyone feels the desire to add to a single impression the others that go to complete it. (*Essays* iii, 482)[13]

Even as Woolf reaches out towards her definition, she proceeds via a series of questions, mistaken assumptions and self-corrections. As in the scene from *Night and Day* quoted earlier, in 'An Unwritten Novel' and in chapter III of *Jacob's Room*, the imaginative misreading of scenes and people itself becomes creative.

This must have been the kind of reading that Helen Ambrose had practised on passers-by in the opening pages of *The Voyage Out* – making up a whole, creating living people; yet Woolf also defined it as a game and, according to Nigel Nicolson, it was one she played with him on one occasion.[14] Its virtue was that it was 'perpetually interrupted by life'. This game 'that we play in railway carriages with people who leave us at Putney' was a potent image for Woolf since it brought together the activities of reading, imagining and writing (*Essays* iii, 485). The process of projecting imaginative life onto passers-by parallels the process of reading and reconstructing texts. And, on occasion, a text can be quite as mysterious and uncommunicative as any train passenger. Discussion of 'the railway carriage game' is succeeded by an account of a beautiful but laconic lyric, which Woolf had found in her favourite bedside reading, Quiller-Couch's *Oxford Book of English Verse*:

Western Wind, when will thou blow
The small rain down can rain?
Christ, if my love were in my arms
And I in my bed again! (*Essays* iii, 486)[15]

The traveller in the third-class railway carriage from Waterloo to Richmond via Putney is another version of Woolf's common reader,[16] though the common reader need not be confined to the modern age. In an effort to endow him with historical specificity, Woolf invents an ancestral common reader, Tom Briggs (1795–1859), a contemporary of Byron and a maker of spectacles, who lived in Cornhill. His name could have been taken from any nineteenth-century subscription list, though it probably derives from a character invented by the artist 'Leech' whom the young Stephens came across in their old bound copies of *Punch*. The making of spectacles suggests modes of perception and, by extension, of reading (Shakespeare, according to Dryden, 'needed not the spectacles of books'). When Woolf declared in her essay on 'Modern Fiction' that 'Life is not a series of gig-lamps symmetrically arranged' (*Essays* iv, 160),[17] she may have pictured Tom Briggs's shop window, with its spectacles 'symmetrically arranged' on trays, quite as much as – or even instead of – rows of carriage lamps. The first example of 'gig lamps' meaning spectacles was recorded in 1853, according to the *Oxford English Dictionary*.

Tom Briggs reads Coleridge on Shakespeare, but dismisses Keats's latest poems as trash *(Essays* iii, 478–9). His opinions are unreliable but his own, for he is free of the scholar's duty to be accurate or the critic's to be judicious. He has a hearty literary appetite, and his reading is governed by the pleasure principle. The freshness of his reactions compensates for their carelessness; what bias he has is personal, and so arbitrary and random. As an outsider, an uneducated man who doesn't know much but knows what he likes, Tom Briggs enjoys a further freedom that anticipates that of the woman narrator in *A Room of One's Own* who, when turned away from Trinity College Library, thought 'how unpleasant it is to be locked out; and . . . how it is worse perhaps to be locked in' (ROO, 21). Woolf endorses Tom Briggs's judgement, drawing on Dr Johnson's definition of the common reader to do so: he rejoiced 'to concur with the common reader; for by the common sense of readers, uncorrupted with literary prejudice, after all the refinements of subtilty and the dogmatism of learning, must be finally decided all claim to poetical honours' (*Essays* iii, 477).[18]

Tom Briggs is also a generic figure, endowed with a large family of descendants, all of whom are avid readers: there is Briggs the Colonel who died somewhere in the Empire, his Shakespeare beside him; Briggs the stockbroker who 'read Darwin; and burnt Swinburne'; there is old MacCallum Briggs; and last but not least there is Mrs Briggs '(a Grant from Dundee) [who] knew the Waverley novels by heart but she could never abide George Eliot' (*Essays* iii, 479). The common reader can also be a woman, as Woolf observes in the course of discussing a reading of Byron's *Letters* by 'a spiritual descendant of Tom Briggs'. The reading caricatures him as the 'big boy who limped off the field in a rage because he had been clean bowled for two or three runs'. It hurries over Byron's love life, but pauses over Shelley's and the observation, 'But Mary loved him' reveals the reader's true gender: ' "He", do we say? But it is obvious from the shape of each sentence, from the tilt of the whole that he is a woman. "But Mary loved him". The cat is out of the bag' (*Essays* iii, 480–2).[19] Here the woman writer betrays herself not so much by her syntax as by her sentiments.

In 'Byron and Mr Briggs', Byron's *Letters* provide a central example, in part because he wrote to his men and women friends so differently, but mainly because they elicited such different responses from male and female readers. Towards the end of Woolf's essay, the narrator is replaced by an after-dinner conversation between characters from her novels – Mr Pepper, Clarissa Dalloway and Terence Hewet from *The Voyage Out*, and Julia Hedge and Rose Shaw from *Jacob's Room*. Rose, charming in hydrangea-coloured silk, declares that 'Byron was an extremely fascinating man' and she can well understand the source of his appeal: 'his vitality, his cloak, and then the desire to redeem him. Every woman would think it was left for her to do that' (*Essays* iii, 494) – a view that Woolf later made fun of in an essay for *Vogue* in which she inverted the traditional cliché that women readers always fell in love with Byron:

> No woman ever loved Byron; they bowed to convention; did what they were told to do; ran mad to order. Intolerably condescending, ineffably vain, a barber's block to look at, compound of bully and lap-dog, now hectoring, now swimming in vapours of sentimental twaddle, tedious, egotistical, melodramatic, the character of Byron is the least attractive in the history of letters. But no wonder that every man was in love with him. In their company he must have been irresistible . . . ('Indiscretions', *Essays* iii, 461)

'Byron and Mr Briggs' reflects Woolf's efforts to define what happens in the process of reading, but, as is the nature of work in progress, it is difficult to follow: images engender new arguments rather than illustrating the unfolding lines of thought, so that they are often powerful rather than conclusive. The most memorable is that of 'the railway carriage game', its chief purpose to illustrate the impulse to 'make [fragmentary experience into] a whole', but it also suggests resemblances between reading people and reading texts, validating misreading as an inevitable feature of the game, since life keeps interrupting: with each new snatch of conversation, each new departure or arrival, another misapprehension is corrected, making the process of reassessment continuous. Reading thus imitates the workings of thought itself as it steadily digests information, restructuring itself in response to continual adjustments, corrections and alterations. In allowing for misreading, 'the railway carriage game' resembles the energetic if inaccurate reconstruction of texts made by the common reader and both break with the very different tradition of sign-reading exemplified by Sherlock Holmes in which the detective shows himself to be infallible. Holmes reads character and circumstance from arbitrary signs but, unlike Woolf's observers, he is never mistaken and his deductions are always confirmed, however unlikely they may seem at first. The realist mode associated with the Sherlock Holmes stories left no room for the doubts and uncertainties that Woolf found so generative.[20]

For Woolf, 'the railway carriage game' was as much about writing as reading, and this becomes evident when she re-uses it once more in 'Mr Bennett and Mrs Brown'. Written in December 1923, this essay responded to Arnold Bennett's criticism that 'the characters [of *Jacob's Room*] do not vitally survive in the mind'.[21] In it, she pointed out that Bennett and his fellow Edwardians had failed to recognise that the creative process must be open, rather than closed, and that it must include reading as well as writing if it is to remain a living process. In the extended argument of 'Character in Fiction' (or 'Mr Bennett and Mrs Brown', mark 2[22]), she established Mrs Brown in the corner of the railway carriage as the object that the writer must learn to read and understand, a symbol for the elusive nature of experience that the writer must recapture: 'she is, of course, the spirit we live by, life itself' (*Essays* iii, 436). Bennett aspired to a Holmesian infallibility; believing that he knew everything that could be known of Mrs Brown's material circumstances, he had apprehended nothing of her essential mystery. Where 'An Unwritten Novel' had parodied Bennett's lower-middle-class settings and situations, this essay criticises his naturalistic writing technique more generally, and finds it reductive. An adequate reading procedure must allow for the fragmentary or provisional nature of the signs we encounter and, beyond that, for the radical discontinuity of character itself – something that Bennett refused to acknowledge.

Though Bennett had failed to see it, the structure of *Jacob's Room* freed the reader from some of the more coercive features of older literary traditions, while allowing Woolf to voice her own distrust of writing without reading, without looking at the way that experience continuously adjusts or corrects the tidy narratives we compose. For writers typically construct narratives and meanings, and like them to be tidy, like them to 'come down beautifully with all their feet on the ground' (W, 183); whereas Woolf, like Bernard in the final section of *The Waves*, knew that life was not like that, and that the novel should not be like that. Experience was not always coherent or meaningful, and even when it was there were always dissenting voices:

> But it is a mistake, this extreme precision, this orderly and military progress; a convenience, a lie. There is always deep below it, even when we arrive punctually at the appointed time with our white waistcoats and polite formalities, a rushing stream of broken dreams, nursery rhymes, street cries, half-finished sentences and sights . . . (W, 196)

Bernard had once pictured himself as Byron, as a poet and an outsider, in the manner of Ralph Denham in *Night and Day*, or even of Jacob Flanders. Jacob's affinities with Byron are suggested early in the book when he asks Mr Floyd to give him 'the works of Byron in one volume', whereas his brothers Archer and John had chosen a paper-knife and a kitten (J's R, 16). Jacob also resembles Byron in his rebelliousness and scepticism, his various love affairs, his travels in Italy and Greece, but above all in his early death, and in the enigma of his life. Looking back,

Bernard in *The Waves* recalls how, when young, he had once thought it his part 'to stride into rooms and fling gloves and coat on the back of chairs, scowling slightly', to dash off Byronic letters ('the rhythm is the main thing in writing') and to mourn for lost love beneath 'Byron's tree'. Even spilling his tea and mopping it up with his pocket-handkerchief could be seen as 'Byronic untidiness' (W, 192, 58, 62, 67). For Bernard, living, reading and writing are seamless activities, as they were for his creator.

Byron's disruptive presence, so often figured as a volume of his works, still haunted Woolf in her final novel, *Between the Acts* – indeed he appears on the second page. Although Giles Oliver is this novel's Byronic hero, it is his father Bart who remembers that 'over sixty years ago . . . his mother had given him the works of Byron in that very room', and goes on to quote 'She walks in beauty like the night' and 'So we'll go no more a-roving by the light of the moon', lines full of magic for him, though they no longer speak to a younger generation (BA, 6). As she finished *Between the Acts*, Woolf turned back once more to the account of reading that she had never managed to write. This time she would call it 'Reading at Random or Turning the Page'. The first essay, 'Anon', was more or less finished when she died, but the second, 'The Reader', was only just begun.[23]

## Notes

1. Robert Scholes, *Protocols of Reading* (New Haven, CT, and London: Yale University Press, 1989), p. 18, cited by Susan Stanford Friedman, 'Virginia Woolf's Pedagogical Scenes of Reading: *The Voyage Out*, *The Common Reader* and her "Common Readers" ', *Modern Fiction Studies*, 38:1 (Spring 1992), p. 106.
2. See Brenda R. Silver, *Virginia Woolf's Reading Notebooks* (Princeton, NJ.: Princeton University Press, 1983).
3. Compare 'Byron was a novelist – that is to say he came at his conception through his observation of actual life; whereas a poet thinks of life in general, or so intensely of his own in particular as to include the general life' ('Byron and Mr Briggs', *Essays* iii, 481).
4. Jane Austen, *Persuasion*, ed. D. W. Harding (1818; London: Penguin, 1965), p. 121 (at the end of chapter 11; Louisa falls off the Cobb in chapter 12, p. 129).
5. John Dryden, *An Essay of Dramatic Poesy* (1688).
6. TTL, 129–32, discussed above, p. 10 and n. 8, p. 22.
7. Woolf writes of it as if it were finished on 26 January 1920 (*Diary* ii, 13).
8. The theme of 'Sympathy' (CSF, 108–11) – see discussion above, p. 34.
9. Scholes, *Protocols of Reading*, p. 6. A woman in a railway carriage labelled 'M.M.' (later identified as 'Milly Masters') appears in the frame material added to 'The Shooting Party' (CSF, 254) – see essay 12, p. 183.

10. Woolf began drafting *Jacob's Room* on 16 April 1920, probably when the printing of Hope Mirrlees's poem *Paris* had been completed (see chapter 5 below). By page 56, she was writing chapter VI, recording on a verso page of her notebook, '28th May 6 weeks' – see Virginia Woolf's *Jacob's Room: The Holograph Draft*, ed. Edward L. Bishop (New York: Pace University Press, 1998), pp. 2, 34.
11. 'The brilliant idea has just come to me of embedding [the essays] in Otway conversation. The main advantage would be that I could then comment, & add what I had had to leave out, or failed to get in . . . I should mitigate the pomposity & sweep in all sorts of trifles. I think I should feel more at my ease' (*Diary* ii, 261). The Otways were the large and talkative family of Katharine's cousins in *Night and Day*, inspired by the Stracheys.
12. G. E. Moore, *Principia Ethica* (1903; Cambridge: Cambridge University Press, 1993), chapter I, D, 20–22, pp. 82–7.
13. In discussing 'Byron and Mr Briggs', I have referred, for the sake of convenience, to Andrew McNeillie's edition, appendix II of the third volume of his *Essays of Virginia Woolf*. McNeillie's records Woolf's many corrections, so for the sake of clarity, I have drawn on an earlier and simpler transcription by Edward A. Hungerford, 'Byron and Mr. Briggs', *Yale Review*, vol. lxviii no. 3, (March 1979), pp. 321–49, section 8 at pp. 333–4.
14. 'Once I travelled alone with her to London and she whispered to me as the train drew out of the station, "See that man over there?" "Yes." "Well, he's a bus-conductor from Leeds. He's been visiting his uncle who has an apple farm at Marden." "But, Virginia, how can you possibly know that? You've never seen him before." "No question about it," and then, for as long as the journey lasted, she told me the man's life story, while he sat in his corner, smoking his pipe, unaware that he was the subject of her impromptu novel', Nigel Nicolson, *Long Life* (London: Weidenfeld and Nicolson, 1997), p. 39, also recalled in Nicolson's *Virginia Woolf* (London: Weidenfeld and Nicolson, 2000), p. 118.
15. A. T. Quiller-Couch, *The Oxford Book of English Verse* (Oxford: Clarendon Press, 1908), p. 53 (it is this anthology that Mrs Ramsay is reading in *To the Lighthouse*, 129–32). Woolf commented, 'Yet there again with the poem, as with Byron's letters, the mind is trying to make a whole' (*Essays* iii, 487). Woolf reconsidered this lyric in the revised version of 'How Should One Read a Book?' (CE ii, 6), and it haunts Louis in *The Waves* (W, 153–6).
16. Rachel Bowlby links him with 'the standardised "man on the Clapham omnibus"' in an extended discussion of Woolf's railway carriage imagery, *Feminist Destinations and Further Essays on Virginia Woolf* (Edinburgh: Edinburgh University Press, 1997), p. 5.
17. As this passage does not appear in an earlier version of the essay, 'Modern Novels', published in 1919, it must have been added when Woolf revised the essay for publication in *The Common Reader*, so was almost certainly written after 'Byron and Mr Briggs'.
18. The quotation is from Johnson's Life of Gray, and refers to his 'Elegy Written in a Country Churchyard'. Woolf quoted more accurately from it in the brief preface to *The Common Reader* (*Essays* iv, 19).
19. This passage is so heavily revised that this is only one of several possible readings, though the general sense is clear enough. Desmond MacCarthy

had used the phrase, 'He lets one cat out of the bag' to refer to Arnold Bennett's assertion 'that women are inferior to men in intellectual power', in a review in the *New Statesman*, 2 October 1920, that Woolf attacked. Thereafter she used the phrase in the context of gender issues – compare *Three Guineas*: 'There can be no doubt of the odour now. The cat is out of the bag; and it is a Tom' (TG, 174).

20. Catherine Belsey deconstructs the Sherlock Holmes stories as examples of 'classic realism' in *Critical Practice* (London and New York: Methuen, 1980), pp. 109–17.
21. Arnold Bennett, 'Is the Novel Decaying?' *Cassell's Weekly*, 28 March 1923, p. 47, reprinted in *Virginia Woolf: The Critical Heritage*, ed. Robin Majumdar and Allen McLaurin (London and Boston: Routledge and Kegan Paul, 1975), p. 113.
22. In May 1924, Woolf rewrote her original article as a lecture and then as an article for the *Criterion* entitled 'Character in Fiction', but the revised version is still regularly reprinted as 'Mr Bennett and Mrs Brown', because the Hogarth Press issued it as a pamphlet under that title, later in 1924.
23. '"Anon" and "The Reader": Virginia Woolf's Last Essays', ed. Brenda R. Silver, *Twentieth Century Literature* 25 (1979), pp. 356–441.

Essay 5

# 'Modernism's Lost Hope': Virginia Woolf, Hope Mirrlees and the Printing of *Paris*

As Eleanor Pargiter walks through Bloomsbury, glancing automatically into the basements, she notices

> . . . a man in an apron . . . working at a case of type. She watched him . . . fascinated by the way he flicked type into a great box with many compartments; there, there, there; rapidly, expertly; until, becoming conscious of her gaze, he looked up over his spectacles and smiled at her. She smiled back. Then he went on, making his quick half-conscious movements. (Y, appendix, 390)

Can the man who smiles back at her be Leonard, in a uniquely frame-breaking moment? In the first draft of this scene, Eleanor had glanced into a carpenter's shop. Woolf had deliberately changed this to a printing shop, although it is uncertain whether Leonard's trembling hand would have allowed him to 'diss' (distribute) type.[1] This moment occurs in the '1921' sequence, one of the 'two enormous chunks' that Woolf cut from *The Years* before publication. The passage is exceptional in several ways, not least in being one of the rare references to printing in Woolf's writings; yet, though she seldom discussed it, the impact of the Hogarth Press on her sense of what writing might be, as well as on her material practice of it, is widely acknowledged. Moreover, the Press introduced her to several key modernist writers, notably Katherine Mansfield and T. S. Eliot: their work was among the first to be published by the Woolfs. To their names we must add that of Hope Mirrlees, author of an extraordinary poem, *Paris*, dated 1919 but published by the Hogarth Press in May 1920 – a poem about the city simultaneously mourning its dead and celebrating 'the Peace Carnival' (*Paris*, 12[2]) as the world's most powerful statesmen arrived to attend the post-war Peace Conference.

When or where Hope Mirrlees first met the Woolfs remains uncertain, though it was probably through Hope's close college friend Karin Costelloe, the daughter of Mary Berenson, who married Adrian Stephen, Virginia's younger brother, in 1914. Through Karin, Hope also came to know the Stracheys, Duncan Grant and Ottoline Morrell. Hope is first mentioned in Virginia's diary in August 1918, when Karin compared her with Hope (to Virginia's annoyance – *Diary* i, 186). In September, there were further conversations about Hope, one with David Garnett who recalled an encounter with her in Paris three years earlier and another with Pernel Strachey (then Vice Principal of Newnham College, where Jane Harrison taught and Hope had studied), 'Partly about Hope Mirrlees, whom we've asked to write us a story' (*Diary* i, 188, 191).[3] An undated letter from Hope to Virginia responds to the request Virginia had mentioned to Pernel: 'I have nothing at all that is short & suitable to your Press – otherwise I should so much have liked to publish something with you'; she goes on to praise Woolf's short story 'The Mark on the Wall' as 'an exquisite thing'.[4] Evidently she was flattered to have been asked, and must have kept the request in mind. On 25 October 1918, Hope wrote to Virginia to thank her for advice on how to get her first novel, *Madeleine, One of Love's Jansenists*, published. She told Virginia that it had finally been accepted by Putnam's (they must later have changed their mind since Collins published it, along with her two other novels).

By January 1919, Woolf was listing Hope as the 'latest of all' of her friends (*Diary* i, 235, 326). Six months after, Hope had promised the Woolfs the manuscript of *Paris* (*Diary* i, 282) – she may still have been working on it since the poem refers to events of the previous month (for example, the General Strike on 1 May (*Paris*, 13–14). On 8 August, Hope spent a weekend with the Woolfs at Asheham (*Diary* i, 295), and she may have taken the manuscript – or some version of it – with her. Soon afterwards Virginia described to a friend how carefully she had dressed for dinner, with stockings matching a wreath in her hair, how she wore powder and scent, and knew 'Greek and Russian better than I do French; is Jane Harrison's favourite pupil, and has a written a very obscure, indecent and brilliant poem, which we are going to print' (*Letters* ii, 385).

If Hope actually left a manuscript of *Paris* with the Woolfs, she would have been following in the footsteps of Katherine Mansfield who had delivered the manuscript of *Prelude* to the Woolfs on a similar weekend visit to Asheham two years earlier (*Diary* i, 43–4). There were in any case a number of parallels between Woolf's friendship with Mirrlees and that with Mansfield – indeed, back in February 1919, Woolf had imagined that she had quarrelled with both of them, but it turned out that 'my literary ladies are faithful, though intermittent' (*Diary* i, 244). Her friendship with Mansfield is well documented, but that with Mirrlees played a larger part than has previously been suspected in Woolf's turn to modernism. With Mansfield, Woolf explored the nature of women's sensibilities and how they might be used to achieve new forms of writing. Mirrlees was more interested in 'high' modernism and those avant-garde experiments with poetry and painting, with Cubism and Simultaneism that were taking place in Paris among the poets who frequented Adrienne Monnier's bookshop and who published in Albert-Birot's review *SIC* or Reverdy's *Nord-Sud*.

In March 1919, after lunch at the '17 Club', Virginia asked Hope to write to her, to which she replied, 'Oh no. I cant write to people' – Woolf was later to tease her about this (*Diary* i, 258; *Letters* iii, 4). Yet among the small number of their surviving letters, several suggest that they discussed contemporary writing, including their own. A letter from Virginia replies to a (missing) letter from Hope, praising her short story 'Solid Objects', published in the *Athenaeum* on 22 October 1920: 'it was written too quick, but I thought it had some points as a way of telling a story'. She went on to invite Hope to stay for a weekend so that

> we can discuss Miss Rose Macaulay, Miss Sitwell, Faith Henderson, and Virginia Woolf . . . Miss Sitwell I haven't read, but I would if you would lend her to me. Are you writing? I ask as a publisher . . . Do send us something: verse or prose – (*Letters* vi, 497)

Woolf's feelings about Hope remained a complicated mixture of admiration tinged, perhaps, with envy for her intimacy with the venerable Jane Harrison. Five years younger than herself, Hope was 'a very self-conscious, wilful, prickly & perverse young woman, rather conspicuously well-dressed & pretty' (*Diary* i, 258). She was 'her own heroine [i.e. Madeleine] – capricious, exacting, exquisite, very learned, and beautifully dressed', 'a spoilt prodigy', endowed with money and good looks, at home in languages and literature. 'I like her very much, but also find her as indeed I find her writing so full of affectations and precocities that I lose my temper' (*Letters* iii, 200–1).

Woolf felt obliged to tiptoe carefully around these difficulties in reviewing *Madeleine, One of Love's Jansenists*, for the *TLS* in October 1919. While she evidently considered it clumsily constructed, she sympathised with Hope's conviction that 'It is the inner world that matters' and she praised the preface, but by implication condemned what followed: it showed its author

> unusually aware both of the difficulties and of the possibilities of the art of fiction. That is at once something gained; to be aware of a difficulty may not mean that you solve it, but it does imply an intelligent choice. (*Essays* iii, 108)

Woolf never liked Mirrlees's novels and told Jacques Raverat, 'I cant get an ounce of joy from them' (*Letters* iii. 164). *Madeleine*, set in the seventeenth century, describes its heroine's unrequited passion for the *précieuse* Mme de Scudéry, represented as the Sappho of her day. Struggling with her review of the novel, Woolf had assumed it 'all sapphism so far as I've got – Jane and herself' (*Letters* ii, 391),[5] but later in the novel Jane Harrison appears quite recognisably, not as the churlish Mme de Scudéry, but as the wise and benevolent Abbess of Port Royal, the Jansenist convent that Sainte-Beuve had celebrated in his classic account. Mme de Scudéry is probably a lightly disguised portrait of Nathalie Barney, the Sappho of her day; she may well have snubbed Hope as Mme de Scudéry snubs Madeleine.

We do not know how much of *Paris* was completed or what form it took when Hope first showed it to the Woolfs in August 1919 (as Woolf's letter suggests she did). If she handed it over to them then, why did they postpone printing it until the beginning of February 1920 when Virginia first mentions that they are 'printing a poem' (*Letters* ii, 420)? Early in 1919 they had hand-set and printed T. S. Eliot's *Poems* which they published with Murry's *The Critic in Judgment* that summer, but *Paris*, their next hand-printed book, did not appear until May 1920. Were they too busy with other tasks to begin in the autumn of 1919, or was Hope still at work on it? It is certainly a work of great density, and she was still making alterations to the poem even at proof stage.

*Paris* was the single most difficult task Woolf ever undertook as a printer (though Nancy Cunard's *Parallax* of 1925 was to pose comparable problems). By 1920, she had typeset two volumes of poetry. The first consisted of the poems of her brother-in-law, Cecil Woolf, killed during the Great War, a task attended by 'all sorts of accidents' (*Diary* i, 124). The second, the *Poems* of T. S. Eliot, was 'our best work so far by a long way, owing to the quality of the ink' (*Diary* i, 257). Eliot's *Poems*, written in quatrains and couplets, were comparatively straightforward to set, and later, when Virginia came to work on *The Waste Land* in 1923, it had already been published in the *Criterion*, making her task significantly easier. Mirrlees's *Paris*, on the other hand, was not merely written in free verse – it actively employed typography and spacing as part of its system of representation.

By a lucky chance, three pages have survived in proof. On these, Hope made some corrections and one substantive textual change, but she also gave instructions for adjustments to the typesetting ('slightly larger spaces between the words') that could not be carried out because there was not enough room on the page.[6] She evidently 'saw' her poem quite as vividly as she 'heard' it. She was familiar with 'shape' poems from such seventeenth-century English poets as George Herbert and Henry Vaughan, but the most important model for her own times was

Mallarmé's meditation on the nature of art, *Un coup de dés jamais n'abolira le hasard* ('A throw of the dice will never abolish chance'), first published in 1897, and reprinted in 1914 in accordance with Mallarmé's own sketches. In his preface to this foundational work of modernism, Mallarmé explains that he is using the page as the basic unit and that the poem's novelty lies in the way the reading process is spread out ('un espacement de la lecture'), while 'the white spaces acquire a special significance, and are immediately striking. They were always needed for poetry, creating a surrounding silence' ('Les "blancs" en effet, assument l'importance, frappent d'abord; la versification en exigea, comme silence alentour, ordinairement').[7] Mallarmé varied the spaces between words and letters, and their sizes and fonts, ranging them across the page like the constellations scattered across the sky.[8] Guillaume Apollinaire's *Calligrammes* (1918) took this development a stage further, creating pictorial shapes out of the words of his poems.

From these examples, and those of Jean Cocteau and Pierre Reverdy, Mirrlees learned that the placing of a line of poetry itself constituted a form of punctuation, and that the spaces on the page form a crucial part of the rhythm of writing. She later acknowledged Cocteau's sequence of poems *Le Cap de Bonne-Espérance* as a key influence on *Paris*, and she was probably present when he read it at Adrienne Monnier's bookshop in the rue de l'Odéon in February 1919, or perhaps on a later occasion. Monnier herself observed that Cocteau had taken Mallarmé's poem as his model for his leap into modernism.[9]

Working from Hope's manuscript (as it probably was), Woolf had to select the appropriate size and font of type indicated, and the typographical problems it posed are reflected in the exceptional number of mistakes she made. Most of these occur in French words and could well have been present in Hope's original, but some occur in familiar English words (for example 'carryl ong' for 'carry long', and 'leisuerly', *Paris*, 17, 19). By 24 April 1920, with the printing completed and the book bound, Woolf spent an annoying afternoon making two further corrections by hand in each of 160 copies (*Diary* ii, 33) – they apparently printed 175 altogether.

*Paris* is written in the language of international modernism, the narrative mainly in English but with many French headlines, advertisements and refrains. Its eccentric typographical features are only the most obvious aspect of its exploration of space and vision – an exploration that takes the form of a journey across Paris and through the day, from morning to night, observing its posters, street signs, paintings, statues, monuments and architectural features. It further extends its gaze to what is imagined or seen with the inner eye, in trance or dream states. The poem employs a variety of sign systems – not only using several languages, but also roman and italic type in upper and lower case to represent the numerous signs to be seen in the city. Words are bordered with black, as on the votive tablets placed in churches, or set out as memorial plaques to the famous dead, and there are capitalised brand names, announcements and instructions, eight bars of music, and even a star sign. Three lines of type represent the Tuileries by imitating Le Nôtre's layout of the gardens, three lines represent queuing taxis, and on 1 May 1919, when daily life was interrupted by a general strike, the horizontal lines of print become vertical, representing the marching defile of strikers – or, perhaps, the slender stems of lily-of-the-valley, normally sold in the street on 1 May, but not available that year (*Paris*, 4; 21; 13–4).

The poem begins (as it will end), by invoking Hope's muse and close friend, Jane Ellen Harrison, a classical scholar known for her research into ancient Greek ritual and its relation to art, and the powers of its female deities. 'I want a holophrase' (*Paris*, 3) announces the search for a single word that might encompass the complex range of experiences the poem comprehends (in *Themis*, Harrison had defined the holophrase as a primitive stage of language in which long words expressed complex relationships more fully and less analytically than in more developed languages[10]). From here, the narrator descends into the 'Nord-Sud' metro line (now line 12) which carries her from 'Rue du Bac' on the Left Bank, underneath the Seine, to the place de la 'Concorde' (its name suggesting the Peace Conference). This section reworks the classical descent into the underworld (as the chorus from Aristophanes' play *The Frogs* indicates), establishing the poem as an elegy for the war dead. The Nord-Sud metro line running from Montmartre to Montparnasse reflected the recent cultural shift that had brought artists and writers from the north to the south of Paris (and thus suggested the title of Pierre Reverdy's avant-garde review of 1917–18).

The posters in the metro introduce themes of French imperialism and 'négritude': ZIG ZAG was (and is) a cigarette paper advertised by the head of a Zouave (French Algerian) soldier who supposedly rolled the first ever cigarette; LION NOIR was a make of black shoe polish; CACAO BLOOKER was a Dutch drinking chocolate. Their reds and blacks suggest 'black-figured vases in Etruscan tombs', linked with death and burial. A poster for 'Byrrh' (an aperitif) shows a shouting drummer girl dressed in scarlet who is identified with the Scarlet Woman from the Book of Revelation. St John appears as the witness of war and destruction and of the 'logos', another version of the 'holophrase', the all-embracing word (*Paris*, 3).[11]

Characterising Hope's outlook in the spring of 1919, Woolf noted her 'aristocratic & conservative tendency in opinion, & a corresponding taste for the beautiful & elaborate in literature' (*Diary* i, 258). True enough as far as it goes, yet such an account fails to do justice to Hope's concern with contemporary politics and culture, her subversive irony at the expense of the Church and the middle classes, and the various innovative features of her poem. *Paris* overthrows traditional boundaries, not only between different languages and literatures, but also between different kinds of discourse and different levels of culture, so that it segues from metro posters to the paintings in the Louvre (rehung in February 1919, having been stored underground during the war years). These included the 'Pietà' of Avignon (whose Virgin mourning her Son also refers to the bereaved mothers of France) and Manet's 'Olympia', one of several buried allusions to the old tiger, Georges Clemenceau, Prime Minister and Chairman of the Peace Conference: in 1907 he had spearheaded a campaign for the painting to be displayed in the Louvre (*Paris*, 8[12]).

In addition to actual paintings, the poem envisages a series of possible paintings as part of an extended meditation on the nature of art and its capacity to transform the pain and violence of history into beauty and stillness:

> Whatever happens, some day it will look beautiful:
> Clio is a great French painter (*Paris*, 15)

As first drafted (the Toronto proof-pages reveal), Mirrlees had recorded her sequence of revolutionary scenes thus:

> Cézanne's *Quatorze Juillet*,
> David's *Prise de la Bastille*,
> Poussin's *Fronde*,
>
> Hang in a quiet gallery.

Whether 'Cézanne's *Quatorze Juillet*' was supposed to show the later celebration of Bastille day or the actual taking of the Bastille itself is uncertain, but it was too close to the '*Prise de la Bastille*', so Mirrlees altered it on the proof to 'Manet's *Massacres des Jours de Juin*', thus creating a historical sequence of acts of French political resistance, that extended from the strike of 1 May 1919, through 'les journées de Juin' of 1848 (when the army rounded up and disarmed protesters, and then shot them) and the Revolution of 1789, to the popular rising of the Fronde in 1652. Manet was also a more plausible choice than Cézanne to represent the events of 1848, since he had painted *The Execution of Maximilian* in 1867 and that of the communards in May 1871. Paris itself is also recreated as a series of pictures: the Eiffel Tower, with its 'cross-hatched' lines, becomes an etching, while the soldiers in the Tuileries waiting to be demobbed seem to be part of a drawing in coloured chalks, to be printed and sold to tourists 'in the rue des Pyramides at 10 francs a copy' (*Paris*, 15).

As it proceeds, the poem's intermittent 'tranced' states become rising dreams, first knee-deep and then, as the atmosphere grows heavier, waist-deep (*Paris*, 16, 19). They are linked with the figure of the river Seine, signifying both the underworld and the unconscious:

> If through his sluggish watery sleep come dreams
>     They are the blue ghosts of king-fishers. (*Paris*, 14)

Finally, from behind the 'ramparts of the Louvre', holding the river of the unconscious at bay, the great analyst of dreams appears, perhaps making his début in an English poem:

> Freud has dredged the river, and grinning horribly,
> waves his garbage in a glare of electricity. (*Paris*, 21)

Paris has become a city of dreams, as Baudelaire saw it in 'Les sept Vieillards':

> Fourmillante cité, cité pleine de rêves,
> Où le spectre en plein jour raccroche le passant!

The 'famous dead of Paris' pass one other invisibly on the Pont Neuf. But such hallucinatory moments may be drug-induced – the poem twice refers to Algerian tobacco, while the Duchess of Alba, in Goya's painting of 1795, is 'Long, long as the Eiffel Tower/ Fathoms deep in haschich' (*Paris*, 5). Mirrlees's fantasy novel *Lud-in-the-Mist* (1926) would relate the story of a town near the borders of Fairyland whose magic fruits were washed downriver, where they drove the respectable citizens of Lud into ecstatic frenzies – *Lud* at once looks back to Rossetti's *Goblin Market* and forward to its current status as a cult novel about drug-taking. But the poem's culminating 'tranced moment' may be that of its conception:

> From the top floor of an old Hotel,
>         Tranced,
> I gaze down on the narrow rue de Beaune. (*Paris*, 17)

The 'old Hotel' (in the traditional sense of a substantial town house) is also a modern hotel, the Hotel de l'Elysée where Hope and Jane Harrison regularly stayed when they were in Paris (its address, '3 Rue de Beaune', appears at the end of the poem). It stands on the corner of the Quai de Voltaire, and from its high windows the poet may have been able to look downstream and see the sun 'sinking behind le Petit-Palais' and the crowds crossing the Solférino bridge, silhouetted like flies against the apricot evening sky (*Paris*, 20). If not through an actual window, Hope also saw them in her mind's eye, and this 'tranced' moment, exceptional in its use of the first person, may represent the genesis of the entire poem (elsewhere, the narrator remains impersonal and transparent, present only as an observer or commentator).

As if anticipating Joyce's Nighttown, *Paris* ends in the realm of the unconscious as the narrator travels up to Montmartre, finding a floor show for Americans, black jazz musicians and alternative sexualities: *'I don't like the gurls of the night-club – they love women'* (*Paris*, 21). As the night wears on, Verlaine and Rimbaud sit up late, smoking and drinking 'Absynthe', whereas the President of the Republic (Raymond Poincaré) is respectably in bed with his wife, and at the maternity hospital at Port-Royal 'babies are being born' (*Paris*, 22). Such contrasts re-enact the ritual conflict between the Virgin, associated with the disciplined and structured worlds of art and religion, and 'the wicked April moon' that stands for the chaos, contingency and nonconformity of life (*Paris*, 14 – and see the poem's own note on this, on p. 23 ).[13] The poem closes, as it had opened, with a salutation to the city of Paris as 'Notre-Dame', Our Lady of Grace, echoing the prayer 'Ave Maria . . . ':

> JE VOUS SALUE PARIS PLEIN DE GRACE (*Paris*, 22)

But the final line is wordless: it is the star sign for the constellation of the Great Bear, Ursa Major, dedicating the poem to Jane Harrison, and was part of a private code that the two women shared. At the same time, the Great Bear – the seven stars of the Book of Revelation, perpetually pointing towards the Pole Star at the highest point of the night sky – also stands for art's aspiration to permanence – its significance in Mallarmé's poem *Un coup de dés*. As *Paris* draws to a close, its typographical and semantic games bring together personal and political meanings, and popular and classical traditions.

The star sign of the Great Bear also appears as the epigraph to Hope's three novels, and written in reverse (that is, with the square on the left, rather than on the right), Jane Harrison used it to sign off postcards to Hope. Privately, they wrote to each other as the Elder and Younger Walrus, or else as the two wives of 'the Old One', Jane Harrison's ancient and totemic teddy bear, endowed with an imaginary *mana*. Bears had always held a special enchantment for Harrison, and she believed that a small stone bear she had once found on the Acropolis was sacred to

'Artemis Brauronia', to whom young Athenian girls dedicated themselves in a ceremony of confirmation:

> Always these well-born, well-bred little Athenian girls must, to the end of their days, have thought reverently of the Great She-bear. Among the Apaches today, we are told, only ill-bred Americans or Europeans who have never had any 'raising' would think of speaking of the Bear without his reverential prefix of 'Ostin', meaning 'Old One', the equivalent of the Roman senator.[14]

If the Great She-bear stood for an ancient matriarchal deity, she also represented all things Russian (in Harrison's letters, all Russians became 'Bears', while Frenchmen were 'Frogs'). Jane Harrison felt that in her later years she had fallen in love with the Russian language, as she had once fallen in love with Greek. She was deeply and romantically attracted to Russia, believing that 'The Russian stands for the complexity and concreteness of life – felt whole, unanalysed, unjudged'.[15] Hope (who shared her mentor's capacity for learning new languages) also learned Russian, and in October 1914 both of them enrolled on a Russian course at the École des Langues Orientales, around the corner from the Hotel de l'Elysée. They returned to Paris in 1915, when Jane sent Gilbert Murray a postcard showing herself and Hope, who is holding the teddy bear; and again between April and June 1919, while Hope completed her diploma in Russian and began work on her poem *Paris* (which included numerous topical references).

In 1922, at the age of seventy-two, Jane Harrison finally decided to leave Cambridge for good. She was bitterly disappointed with the University's refusal to give women degrees and horrified at the attack on Newnham that had followed the vote. She burned most of her correspondence and followed Hope to Paris where they shared rooms at the American Women's Club and cultivated a circle of French intellectuals and Russian émigrés. Woolf visited them there in April 1923 and was amused at Jane's impatience with the Cambridge vogue for Catholic conversion (*Letters* iii, 58–9). That Christmas, Jane sent Virginia a copy of her book *Ancient Art and Ritual*.[16] The following year, the Hogarth Press published *The Life of the Archpriest Avvạkum by Himself*, a seventeenth-century Russian classic, jointly translated by Jane and Hope, dedicated to Alexey Remizov and introduced by their friend Prince Mirsky; Hope also published her second novel, *The Counterplot*.[17] Jane Harrison was compiling her *Reminiscences of a Student's Life*, written initially for the *Nation*, where Leonard Woolf was the literary editor, and later published by the Hogarth Press in 1925. That year, they lost their rooms at the Club, and so moved back to London, to a narrow house at 11 Mecklenburgh Street on the edge of Bloomsbury. In 1926, Hope brought out her third novel, *Lud-in-the-Mist*, and they jointly translated and published a collection of Russian folk-tales, *The Book of the Bear*. It was illustrated by Ray Garnett (David Garnett's wife) and dedicated, of course, 'To the GREAT Bear'.

In February 1928, Virginia Woolf visited Jane Harrison for the last time. She found her 'raised in bed, with her old white head lifted up, on pillows, very aged & rather exalted' (*Diary* iii, 176). She died two months later, as Virginia learned on meeting Hope, completely distraught, in St George's Gardens (*Diary* iii, 179–80). The Woolfs attended the funeral, where Leonard (who had been particularly fond of Jane) 'almost cried', but Virginia found the traditional Christian service an obstacle, wondering 'Who is "God" & what the Grace of Christ? & what did they mean to Jane?' (*Diary* iii, 180, 181) That autumn, Woolf paid her own homage to Jane Harrison for her proto-feminist approach to anthropology and classical studies, and her concern with the role of women in early Greek religion and society. Towards the end of the first chapter of *A Room of One's Own* (1929), Woolf celebrated the community of women that Harrison had loved and the constant self-renewal that characterises university life, as the autumn evening of her actual visit to Newnham is magically transformed into spring and the garden is suddenly alive with blossom and young women:

> and then on the terrace, as if popping out to breathe the air, to glance at the garden, came a bent figure, formidable yet humble, with her great forehead and her shabby dress – could it be the famous scholar, could it be J—H— herself? All was dim, yet intense too, as if the scarf which the dusk had flung over the garden were torn asunder by star or sword – the flash of some terrible reality leaping, as its way is, out of the heart of the spring. (ROO, 15)[18]

Hope also longed to memorialise her friend, and spent many years assembling material and attempting to write Jane's biography, but something had broken in her when Jane died. As Woolf noticed in 1929, she had changed both outwardly and inwardly, for the shock had affected her thyroid gland:

> It is said that Hope has become a Roman Catholic on the sly. Certainly she has grown very fat – too fat for a woman in middle age who uses her brains, & so I suspect the rumour is true. She has sat herself down under the shade. It is strange to see beauty – she had something elegant & individual – go out, like a candle flame. (*Diary* iii, 268)

Hope's conversion repudiated Jane's Victorian unbelief (and her own Scottish upbringing). In its wake, she moved to Thurloe Place, to be close to the Brompton Oratory, and as far as her poem *Paris* was concerned she now connived at its oblivion, refusing to allow Leonard to reprint it because of its satire at the expense of the Church. When, at the end of her life, she did agree to its reprinting, she excised a series of passages referring to Holy Communion, to the nuns droning out masses, and to the Virgin Mary.[19] In later years, she became a devoted friend of T. S. Eliot, who helped her publish the first part of her projected biography of Sir Robert Cotton (*A Fly in Amber*, 1962). The older Hope did indeed display that 'aristocratic & conservative tendency in opinion' that Woolf had noted in her younger self, while the former poet – bold, subversive and startlingly original – had disappeared for ever.

Yet *Paris* did not altogether disappear. It was not widely reviewed and the *TLS* dismissed it uncomprehendingly, but a more sophisticated account in the *Athenaeum* identified the influence of a generation of 'younger French poets' (particularly Salmon, Cendrars and Drieu La Rochelle), describing it as 'immensely literary and immensely accomplished. One reads it with pleasure and interest, admiring the author's learning and wit, and the skill with which the verse is handled.'[20] Later in 1920, T. S. Eliot began work on a long and ambitious poem about the dead returning to the city, its structure underpinned by recent anthropological thought (that of Jessie L. Weston, as well as Jane Harrison), and employing notes on a larger scale than Hope had done at the end of her poem, to help the reader negotiate its difficulties.

Woolf, too, was to learn from its lessons. Where her first two novels had been conventional in structure, her third, *Jacob's Room*, sought out a form that corresponded more closely to its content. As the production of *Paris* drew to a close in mid-April 1920, Woolf began a new notebook with an idea for 'a work of fiction, to be called, perhaps, Jacob's Room'. On 20 April, most copies of *Paris* were bound in a harlequin paper of small red, gold and blue diamonds. A few were bound with the same design printed in red, gold and green, and Woolf used this paper to bind the notebook in which she began writing *Jacob's Room*. She continued, 'I think the main point is that it should be free./ Yet what about form?/ . . . To change style at will.'[21] She had learned from *Paris* how to be free, how 'to change style at will'. Her next novel would abandon the traditional thirty-two-chapter structure and instead use the layout of the page to create silences and meaningful pauses in the text, expressing these as gaps of varied line lengths, in a prose variation on Mallarmé's 'blanks', his white spaces. *Jacob's Room* is a novel about the blank moments of life, about how little we know of other people, and how much of experience consists of 'fissures, ruptures, gaps, and chasms'. As Edward L. Bishop has observed in a study of its typographical gaps, 'the intent of the novel is not just to tell the story of Jacob but to make us aware of these spaces.'[22]

*Jacob's Room* is the novel that most clearly reflects the impact of Hope's poem, so it is not, perhaps, surprising that Hope should have read it with passionate enthusiasm, once she had got past what she thought was a dull opening:

> I have admired all your writings enormously but never has any of them swept me off my feet as this has . . . I suppose the 'libido' of writing has always been a morbid craving to swallow the round green world and all its contents like a pill & to possess it, and I believe you are the first person that has been able to glut that appetite – it is a book which must give *complete* satisfaction to writer & reader alike.
>
> Then, as well, in it you solve for the first time the dilemma of modern literature, by colonising the shadowy New World *imperially* so that it falls into line with and forms an ongoing whole with the old world of tradition.
>
> It is astonishing how certain pages are *exactly* like Matisse, the same seductive virtuosity, the tip of pen or brush the antenna through which one feels the world – & then other pages are infinitely greater than Matisse, as great writing must be greater than great painting.

Woolf replied to Hope's tribute,

> I wish we could talk the matter over, instead of writing. I don't feel satisfied that I have brought it off. Writing without the old banisters, one makes jumps and jerks that are not necessary; but I go on saying that next time I shall achieve it . . . I grow more and more dissatisfied with my contemporaries. None of them seems to be able to carry the thing through – for the most part because they will not or cannot write I think. But this won't apply to you. (*Letters* iii, 3)

## Notes

1. The eight manuscript notebooks of *The Years* are in the Henry W. and Albert A. Berg Collection of the New York Public Library; this scene occurs in Notebook 6, p. 13. For the significance of glancing into basements, see 'A Sketch of the Past' where Woolf refers to the brief experiences (or 'seeds') that a writer makes use of, 'the germs of what might have been, had one's life been different. I pigeonhole "fishing" thus with other momentary glimpses; like those rapid glances, for example, that I cast into basements when I walk in London streets' (MB, 139).
2. All page references are to *Paris, A Poem* by Hope Mirrlees (London: Hogarth Press, 1919, though it was actually published in May 1920). Woolf herself, writing of London in June 1920, two months after typesetting the poem, noted, 'Nowadays I'm often overcome by London; even think of the dead who have walked the city' (*Diary* ii, 47); see also T. S. Eliot's *The Waste Land*.
3. David Garnett recalled meeting Jane Harrison and Hope Mirrlees when they were staying at the Hotel de l'Elysée and learning Russian at the nearby

École des Langues Orientales in 1915 – see vol. 2 of his autobiography, *The Golden Echo: The Flowers of the Forest* (London: Chatto and Windus, 1955), pp. 97–8.

4. Woolf later recounted something of Hope's difficulties in getting *Madeleine* published to her friend Lady Robert Cecil (*Letters* iii, 200). The correspondence between Woolf and Mirrlees survives only intermittently: before 1928, Woolf's published letters include four to Mirrlees, dated 30 July [1919] (*Letters* ii, 381, inviting her to stay at Asheham); [end Oct. 1920] (*Letters* vi, 497); 6 Jan. 1923 (*Letters* iii, 3, concerning *Jacob's Room* and responding to Hope's letter dated 12 Dec. 1922); 17 April 1928 (*Letters* iii, 484, a condolence note for Jane Harrison's death, but see also Hermione Lee, *Virginia Woolf* (London: Chatto and Windus, 1996), p. 574). The Monk's House Papers at the University of Sussex Library include seven unpublished letters from Mirrlees to Woolf. These are an undated letter, probably written in September 1918, but any date between July 1917 (the publication of 'The Mark on the Wall') and the late spring of 1919 (the conception of *Paris*) is possible; 25 Oct. 1918 (about the publication of *Madeleine*); 12 Dec. 1922 (to which Woolf's of 6 Jan. 1923 responds – see the end of this essay); 10 June 1923; 27 June 1923 (here Mirrlees thanks Woolf for recommending *The Counterplot* to her US publisher Donald Brace – see n. 17 below); 18 Oct. 1925 (when Jane and Hope were staying at Cavalaire in the Midi); 17 Oct. 1928, congratulating Woolf on her 'exquisite romantic Orlando', and in particular for having in it 'solved the problem of the "historical novel"': 'It would be just like Mozart, if Mozart had had irony – and now I come to think of it I believe he had'.
5. As Mary Beard notes, Woolf liked to represent the relationship between Hope and Jane as 'sapphic', that is, lesbian. She cites Woolf's letter to Molly MacCarthy on her impending visit to Paris of 1923: 'There I shall stay a few days & meet Jane Harrison & Hope Mirrlees who have a Sapphic flat somewhere, while Leonard returns' (*Letters* iii, 30). Beard adds the phrase 'who have a Sapphic flat somewhere', omitted in Nicolson's edition of the *Letters* – see *The Invention of Jane Harrison*, (Cambridge, MA, and London: Harvard University Press, 2000), pp. 154, 213, n. 77; and compare Woolf's letter to Jacques Raverat of early 1925, 'we like seeing [Hope] and Jane billing and cooing together' (*Letters* iii, 164).
6. The proofs are in the E. J. Pratt Library, Victoria University, Toronto, and provided the starting point for my study of the poem. They reflect how strongly Mirrlees visualised her poem on the page.
7. Stéphane Mallarmé, *Collected Poems*, translated and with a commentary by Henry Weinfield (Berkeley, Los Angeles, London: University of California Press, 1994), pp. 124–45; preface, p. 121 (but I have used my own translation).
8. For the influence of *Un coup de dés*, see Johanna Drucker, *The Visible Word: Experimental Typography and Modern Art, 1909–1923* (Chicago and London: University of Chicago Press, 1994), pp. 50–9.
9. According to Suzanne Henig 'Miss Mirrlees feels *Paris* was "liberated, so to speak, came to life, owing to a poem by Cocteau called *Le Cap de Bonne-Espérance*"', Henig, 'Queen of Lud: Hope Mirrlees', *Virginia Woolf Quarterly* (Cherry Hill, NJ), vol. i, no. 1 (Fall 1972), p. 13. For Cocteau's

reading, and Monnier's response to his poem, see *The Very Rich Hours of Adrienne Monnier*, translated by Richard McDougall (New York: Charles Scribner's Sons, 1976), pp. 90–3, 456–7.

10. Jane Ellen Harrison, *Themis: A Study of the Social Origins of Greek Religion* (1912; London, Merlin Press, 1989) pp. 473–5.
11. 'Byrrh' also appears in Cocteau's poem, as does St John (with whom the poet named Jean identifies), Cocteau, *Le Cap de Bonne-Espérance*, Préface de Jacques Brosse (Paris: Gallimard, 1967), pp. 87, 70.
12. Other allusions refer to Gambetta's announcement of the Third Republic in September 1870, an event at which Clemenceau was present, and to his attempted murder by Emile Cottin on 19 February 1919 (*Paris*, 4, 10).
13. The Preface to Mirrlees's novel *Madeleine* draws a similar contrast: 'Life is like a blind and limitless expanse of sky, for ever dividing into tiny drops of circumstances that rain down, thick and fast, on the just and the unjust alike. Art is like the dauntless plastic force that builds up stubborn, amorphous substance cell by cell, into the frail geometry of a shell' (*Madeleine*, London: Collins Sons, 1919), p. vii.
14. Jane Harrison, *Reminiscences of a Student's Life* (London: Hogarth Press, 1925), p. 71. Accounts of this private bear cult are given by Mary Beard, *The Invention of Jane Harrison*, pp. 135–8; Sandra J. Peacock, *Jane Ellen Harrison: The Mask and the Self* (New Haven, CT: Yale University Press, 1988), pp. 109–15; Annabel Robinson, *The Life and Work of Jane Ellen Harrison* (Oxford: Oxford University Press, 2002), pp. 238–42.
15. Harrison, *Aspects, Aorists and the Classical Tripos* (Cambridge: Cambridge University Press, 1919), p. 5.
16. *Catalogue of Books from the Library of Leonard and Virginia Woolf* (Brighton: Holleyman and Treacher, 1975), v/s section II, p. 3.
17. *The Counterplot* (1924) was dedicated to Jane Harrison and translated into French as *Le choc en retour*, with an afterword by Charles Du Bos. It may have originated in the form of its inset play (Woolf wrote to Hope in January 1923, 'Don't forget your play for the Hogarth Press', *Letters* iii, 4). A letter of 24 August 1924 to Pernel Strachey indicates that Woolf had read *The Counterplot* (*Letters* iii, 127), and the previous September she had enquired of Donald Brace whether he would be interested in publishing it in America – her unpublished letter to Donald Brace, 18 Sept. 1923, is transcribed in Edward L. Bishop, 'Mind the Gap: The Spaces in *Jacob's Room*', p. 45 – for further details, see n. 22 below.
18. The identity of Newnham and Jane Harrison are confirmed by Woolf's draft version of this scene, *Women & Fiction: The Manuscript Versions of 'A Room of One's Own'*, ed. S. P. Rosenbaum (Oxford: Blackwell, Shakespeare Head 1992), pp. 23–4.
19. HM to Leonard Woolf, 12 March 1946, asserted 'I definitely do not wish any of *Paris* to be reprinted' (letter in the Hogarth Press Archive at the University of Reading Library). *Paris* was introduced by Suzanne Henig and reprinted with cuts in the *Virginia Woolf Quarterly*, vol. i, no. 2 (Winter 1973), pp. 4–17.
20. *Athenaeum*, 21 May 1920, p. 686.
21. Quotations from the opening page (dated 'Thursday, April 15th 1920') of the first notebook of three containing the MS of *Jacob's Room*, in the Berg

Collection of the New York Public Library, in *Jacob's Room: The Holograph Draft*, transcribed and edited by Edward L. Bishop (New York: Pace University Press, 1998), p. 1. The full significance of the binding shared with *Paris* is explained by David H. Porter in *Virginia Woolf and the Hogarth Press: 'Riding a Great Horse'* (London: Cecil Woolf, Bloomsbury Heritage Series, 2004), p. 16. Some copies of E. M. Forster's *The Story of the Siren*, also hand-set and published in July 1920, were bound in the same diamond-patterned paper, this time turned round to run horizontally, rather than vertically, as used for *Paris* and the first *Jacob's Room* notebook.

22. Edward L. Bishop, 'Mind the Gap: The Spaces in *Jacob's Room*', *Woolf Studies Annual*, vol. 10 (New York: Pace University Press, 2004), p. 41. In an article on 'Virginia Woolf and the Hogarth Press', Laura Marcus argued that 'The experience of laying out Eliot's poetry on the page influenced Woolf's decision to use white spaces in *Jacob's Room*' (*Modernist Writers and the Marketplace*, ed. Ian Willison, Warwick Gould and Warren Chernaik (London: Macmillan, 1996), p. 132). But as this essay demonstrates, those gaps were not the result of setting Eliot's *Poems* (1919), written in quatrains and couplets, or of setting *The Waste Land*, which she did in 1923 after *Jacob's Room* was finished, but derived from her experience of laying out Hope Mirrlees's *Paris*.

Essay 6

# The Search for Form (i): Fry, Formalism and Fiction

> In England the atmosphere is naturally aqueous, and as if there weren't enough outside, we drench ourselves with tea and coffee at least four times a day. It's atmosphere that makes English literature unlike any other – clouds, sunsets, fogs, exhalations, miasmas . . . the element of water is supplied chiefly by the memoir writers. Look what great swollen books they are! . . . Dropiscal.

observes Ann, in 'A Talk About Memoirs' that Woolf wrote for the *New Statesman* in the spring of 1920 (*Essays* iii, 181). Weather, that topic so popular with the inhabitants of a damp northern island (or so it is said), leads directly into a wider aesthetic question: to what extent does climate determine art? More than thirty years later, the critic and art historian Nikolaus Pevsner would address that question in the course of considering *The Englishness of English Art* (1956). His book was partly a belated response to Roger Fry's dismissive *Reflections on English Painting*, published in 1934 (the year of his death). Pevsner was a European who had chosen to be English. Fry was an Englishman who had chosen to be European, and in chapter seven of her biography of Roger Fry, Woolf recalled his impatience with the inhabitants of 'Birds Custard Island', with their narrow views and misplaced enthusiasm for their weather:

> How much they missed – how little they allowed themselves to enjoy life. It was the English passion for morality, he supposed, and also the English climate. The light, he pointed out, was full of vapour. Nothing was clear. There was no structure in the hills, no meaning in the lines of the landscape; all was smug, pretty and small. Of course the English were incurably literary. They liked the association of things, not things in themselves. (RF, 131)

It is only a short step from Fry's critique of Englishness to the opening of chapter five of *Orlando*, where a great cloud hangs over nineteenth-century England, rain falls incessantly and the damp produces a proliferating fecundity – in the family, the garden, the henhouse, but, most distressingly of all, in the inkpot (O, 157–9).

Fry's view of the English – that they are incurably literary, and that they like the associations of things more than the things themselves, both amused and alarmed Woolf. Christopher Reed has pointed out that

> in its first phase, between 1909 and 1917, formalism explicitly opposed itself to literature. Even the term 'literary' applied to art signified an unhealthy emphasis on illusion at the expense of such formal values identified by Fry as rhythm of line, mass, proportion, light and shade, colour and perspective. In 1914, Clive Bell's *Art* , a summary of formalist principles developed primarily by Fry in journalistic essays published over the previous few years, concluded that because art is sullied by any reference outside itself, 'Literature is never pure art . . . Most of it is concerned to some extent, with facts and ideas'. At about the same time, Roger Fry was writing, 'I think literature is usually very little to do with art.'[1]

Reed goes on to quote from Woolf as she describes Fry's impatience with literature at this stage of his thinking:

> He laid sacrilegious hands upon the classics. He found glaring examples in Shakespeare, in Shelley, of the writer's vice of distorting reality, of importing impure associations, of contaminating the stream with adjectives and metaphors. Literature was suffering from a plethora of old clothes. Cézanne and Picasso had shown the way; writers should fling representation to the winds and follow suit. (RF, 138–9)

Narrative was dubious as a source of aesthetic value because, like narrative painting, it was too often guilty of 'suggesting emotion and conveying ideas'.[2] Part of the superiority of the visual arts lay in the direct way they revealed their underlying structure to an analytical eye. The view that literature was inferior as a medium to the plastic arts (a view at one time shared by Fry and Virginia's sister Vanessa), posed a special threat, not only because this was the art Woolf herself practised, but also because it devalued her talent in relation to Vanessa's. At the same time, she felt unable to dismiss such views out of hand: she held Fry's opinions in the greatest respect and wanted to integrate them into her own artistic practice and adapt them to her own developing theories of aesthetics. But how were such views to be reconciled with her own literary aims?

Literature employed 'impure' (in the sense of non-aesthetic) associations because of the very nature of its medium: language operates through a web of associations and significations – 'every word has an aura', as Fry noted in conversation with Woolf and Clive Bell over dinner in November 1917 (*Diary* i, 80). It operates by stimulating the imagination, rather than requiring a response to an object set before our eyes. Fry's accusation that the English liked 'the association of things, not things in themselves' was bound up with his sense that they were a literary rather than a painterly nation and could not distinguish between form and content. He illustrated their difference in his essay, 'The Artist and Psychoanalysis', taking as his example the first six notes of the tune 'God Save the King'. Played in sequence, they had acquired strong emotional overtones, had become 'symbolic of numerous other things with which [they had] become associated' (he explained), but the emotions they prompted were quite distinct from – and quite irrelevant to – the purely aesthetic effect that that particular sequence of notes might have. In conscious reaction against Ruskin and his school of criticism, Fry rejected 'symbolism in works of art', and the people who were always looking for it.[3] *The Artist and Psychoanalysis* was published as a pamphlet by the Hogarth Press in November 1924, but Woolf had read it two months earlier. She responded by trying to redefine form in a way that would be more constructive for her own art of literature. Her letter to Fry tells him that he had stirred up 'all sorts of bats and tadpoles – ideas, I mean', and that she was

> puzzling, in my weak witted way, over some of your problems: about 'form' in literature. I've been . . . trying to make out what I mean by form in fiction. I say it is emotion put into the right relations; and has nothing to do with form as used of painting. But this you must tidy up for me when we meet (*Letters* iii, 132–3).

Woolf's letters to Fry often strike a note of self-deprecation, at once serious and self-mocking. In fact, she had already shown herself more than capable of understanding the implications of his position when, five years earlier she had reviewed the 1919 Royal Academy Summer Exhibition for the *Athenaeum*. Her account shows how well she had grasped his arguments about the difference between form and content, and his critique of gratuitous emotion that has little to do with the aesthetic effect of a given work of art. And just as Fry would later instance the emotions produced by 'God Save the King', Woolf here focused on the blatant appeal to patriotism, and the clichéd emotions that underpinned so much of that particular (immediately post-war) Exhibition: 'the flag of England – sweet chimes of home – a woman's honour – an Englishman's word – only a scrap of paper – for your sake, Alice – God Save the King – and all the rest of it' (*Essays* iii, 89).

Woolf's illustrations of how these emotions were reflected in the paintings on exhibition anticipated Fry's argument in *The Artist and Psychoanalysis*. She too condemned the symbolism that the paintings depended on, the idealised representations of English gardens or village life where each was 'a perfect specimen . . . not only the saddest, sweetest, quaintest, most picturesque, tenderest, jolliest of its kind, but has a symbolical meaning much to the credit of England' (*Essays* iii, 92). At the end of her review, she effectively submitted it for Fry's approval by observing that she would leave it to him 'to decide whether the emotions here recorded are the proper result of one thousand six hundred and seventy-four works of art' (*Essays* iii, 93). Her account shows that she had accepted Fry's argument that bad art evokes inappropriate emotions, emotions irrelevant to questions of aesthetic value or judgement. She was probably familiar with Fry's ideas about form from an early stage since her brother-in-law Clive Bell apparently discussed them with her at Fitzroy Square, her home from 1907 to 1911.[4]

Woolf's 1919 critique of the Royal Academy's Summer Exhibition commented not only on the populist appeal of its paintings, but also on their 'narrative quality'. They belonged to the mode of Victorian genre painting in which every picture told a story. Fry was uninterested in this aspect of British painting but he did observe at the end of *Reflections on British Painting* that one identifiable source of weakness among British painters was their sense that 'they must be poets at all costs';[5] and though he never said it in so many words, he implied that Britain's 'sublime achievements in literature' were not unconnected with the inadequacy of its tradition of painting, a 'British art . . . not altogether worthy of that civilization'. Fry's opening sentence had already cleared the way for such a judgement by arguing that, 'However valuable patriotism may be in certain fields of human activity, there are others from which it should be rigorously excluded. And assuredly one of those is art-history and the critical appreciation of works of art.'[6] Bart Oliver in *Between the Acts* was to make a similar point when he asked William Dodge, 'Since you're so interested in pictures . . . why, tell me, are we, as a race, so incurious, irresponsive and insensitive . . . to that noble art, whereas Mrs Manresa . . .has her Shakespeare by heart?' (BA, 35).

Fry's opinions on the unacceptable emotions so often evoked by inferior works of art confronted Woolf with a challenge. Her initial introduction to modernism with its emphasis on form had come through painting and its theorisation by Bell and Fry, yet their ideas presented her with problems. Was it really the case that the very elements from which literature was made – the suggestive and associative nature of language and the operation of symbolism – somehow detracted from it, or was this merely the result of differences in terminology? Dining with the two of them in November 1917, Woolf became sharply conscious of the difficulties of translating terms from one art form into another: 'Roger asked me if I founded my writing upon texture or upon structure; I connected structure with plot, & therefore said "texture". Then we discussed the meaning of structure & texture in painting & in writing' (*Diary* i, 80). Connecting structure with plot, and plot with the unacceptable and unspoken term 'narrative', may have encouraged Woolf to choose 'texture', but from a formalist point of view 'structure' could have been the 'right' answer (if there was indeed a right answer). At any rate, it was the structural aspect of form to which she now turned her attention.

Fry, meanwhile, had moved on. By 1920 he had discovered Mallarmé's poetry and was beginning to translate it. He was also reading Proust's novels, which he found 'a source of endless joy', though he had little patience with English novels, regarding them as on a par with William Frith's popular painting, 'Derby Day' – a convenient emblem of all that he despised in British painting (RF, 192–4). Through Bell and Fry, Woolf acquired a distaste for conventional 'realist' narrative, yet what was to be put in its place? The structural values that Fry celebrated were difficult to achieve in fiction without resort to other associative systems, such as symbolism (also mistrusted in his system of aesthetics). While Fry was never, as Woolf delicately put it, 'a safe guide' on the subject of literature, it could also be argued that 'many of his theories held good for both arts' (RF, 194). The characteristic that distinguished fiction from the plastic arts most sharply was that it operated within the dimension of time, rather than space – both the time taken to read it, and the time represented within it – and the novelist had somehow to accommodate time within any notion of literary form. In the event, time and rhythm (a concept of great importance for Fry) would become crucial terms for Woolf too: 'Design, rhythm, texture – there they were again in Flaubert as in Cézanne' (RF, 194). From 1917, she began consciously to integrate these features into her own artistic practice and to think of form as an essential element in fiction – and one that might have a visual or spatial, even a 'plastic' dimension. The rest of this essay explores some of the ways in which her concept of form evolved, focusing particularly on 'Kew Gardens' and the sequence of novels, *To the Lighthouse* (1927), *Orlando* (1928) and *The Waves* (1931).

Woolf's first conscious exercises in modernist form were written in response to the arrival of the printing press at Hogarth House in April 1917. The two short stories she wrote for the press that summer, while utterly different from one another, both abandoned traditional narrative and struck out in new directions. The first, 'The Mark on the Wall', created a flowing fantasia of thought, a richly feminine reverie interrupted by a male speaker who brings with him the concerns of the wider world – the War, a newspaper. While 'The Mark on the Wall' spins a web of associations, her second story,' 'Kew Gardens', concentrates upon appearances; it experiments with the painter's eye and the novelist's ear, and its narrative voice is detached and impersonal. It is an attempt at writing 'post-impressionism' (a term coined by Fry), at evoking its flashing colours and reiterated forms. The Gardens are presented as sequences of primary colour: a repeated 'red, blue and yellow', later modulated to 'green-blue . . . Yellow and black, pink and snow white'; they are filled with the suggestively animal forms of 'heart-shaped and tongue-shaped leaves' (CSF, 90–5). These sequences of colour and shape occur within a highly formal design constructed from the alternation of binary opposites.

'Kew Gardens', like 'The Mark on the Wall', was written to be hand-printed on the Woolfs' newly acquired printing press which now sat on their dining-room table (according to Hope Mirrlees, it was 'not much bigger than a radio'[7]). On it, they hand-printed their books in folio – that is to say, their books were made up from single sheets of paper folded down the middle to form four pages (so that the page numbering rose by multiples of four). Virginia would begin by setting the type (that is, placing the individual metal letters line by line on the printing stick to make up the page) for the first three pages. The second and third page were then locked into the inner forme and were printed first on the inner fold of the sheet. Leonard could not begin printing until Virginia had typeset three of the four pages of that sheet. While he was printing the inner forme, she would set the fourth page. The half-printed sheets would then be turned over and the outer forme – pages 1 and 4 – would be printed on the reverse. While Leonard was doing this, Virginia would 'diss' – that is, redistribute – the metal letters she had used for the inner forme – to their respective boxes so that the whole process could begin again for the next sequence of four pages. 'Kew Gardens' was made up of sixteen pages (four lots of four sheets, folded and sewn together, one after another) and it included woodcuts by Vanessa in addition to Woolf's printed text. I have explained this process at some length, because it seems likely that the process of folio printing – the folding of a single sheet of paper to make two, and the further transformation of these into the outer pages 1 and 4, and the inner pages 2 and 3 – provided a model for Woolf's first experiment in formalism.

'Kew Gardens' is made up of binary opposites – not only colours against shapes, but also the opposition between the human and the non-human world – the contrast that will separate 'Time Passes' from the first and third parts of *To the Lighthouse* and the interludes from the monologues of *The Waves*. The story narrates a series of minute events taking place on the floor of a flowerbed among insects and snails, and these alternate with four human conversations whose complex arrangement suggests that of the printing process. In this series of dialogues, the first and fourth are spoken by a man and a woman: the first couple are married and accompanied by a son and a daughter, and they recall earlier experiences of love, while the fourth couple are still courting. In between, there are conversations between two men, and two women – the men focusing upon the spiritual and the women on the economic consequences of the War.

The four couples are distinguished not only according to gender, but also according to the subjects they talk about: the first two couples discuss metaphysical ideas, while the second two discuss food. These divisions correspond to those created in the process of folio printing: the first and fourth couples being mixed (and so corresponding to pages 1 and 4, the outer forme of the sheet), while the same-sex conversations correspond to pages 2 and 3 (the inner forme). But a second level of distinctions, that of the content of their dialogues, produces a different arrangement, so that the first and second conversations are now compared (they are back to back, like pages 1 and 2), as are the third and fourth (like pages 3 and 4). Woolf may have incorporated the technique of its reproduction into her story deliberately – rather like the painters who let their brush strokes show. And just as, at a further level, 'Kew Gardens' draws attention to its painterly use of colour and design (it includes a covert reference to Renoir's *Les Parapluies*), so it also draws attention to its sequence of binary divisions by contrasting homosexual and heterosexual erotic feeling, madness and sanity, outside (the gardens) and inside (the palm house, a tea-room), creating a series of boxes within boxes, or wheels within wheels, as the last lines explicitly acknowledge: 'But there was no silence; all the time the motor omnibuses were turning their wheels and changing their gear; like a vast nest of Chinese boxes all of wrought steel turning ceaselessly one within another the city murmured' (CSF, 95).

For Leonard, 'Kew Gardens' was 'in its own small way and within its own limits perfect; in its rhythms, movement, imagery, method, it could have been written by no one but Virginia. It is a microcosm of all her then unwritten novels, from *Jacob's Room* to *Between the Acts*'.[8] If 'Kew Gardens' was Woolf's first formalist fiction, the novel that would engage most fully with Roger Fry's painterly aesthetic and his concept of underlying form was *To the Lighthouse* (1927). Here Lily Briscoe envisages her painting both in terms of its immediate appeal to the eye and its deep underlying structure. Thinking about it, '[s]he saw the colour burning on a framework of steel: the light of a butterfly's wing lying upon the arches of a cathedral' (TTL, 54), and when she begins the painting again, ten years later, 'Beautiful and bright it should be on the surface, feathery and evanescent, one colour melting into another like the colours on a butterfly's wing; but beneath the fabric must be clamped together with bolts of iron' (TTL,186). That contrast recalls Woolf's early memory of going to Paddington Station to meet her brother Thoby immediately after their mother's death – 'the great glass dome at the end of the station was blazing with light. It was glowing yellow and red and the iron girders made a pattern across it' (MB, 103). That scene had conferred a sudden sense of insight, a feeling that 'matches what I have sometimes felt when I write' (MB, 103). The paradox of Lily's vision also provides an answer to Clive Bell's notorious question in *Art*: 'Everyone . . . has called a butterfly or a flower beautiful. Does anyone feel the same kind of emotion for a butterfly or a flower that he feels for a cathedral or a picture?'[9] Lily, passionately engaged in her painting, links Fry the painter to Woolf the writer. And for Lily, as for Fry, the act of painting was more important than the ultimate fate of the work. When Fry's paintings failed to sell, he decided to 'go on painting, and when the canvases are dry, I will roll them up' (RF, 191).

At the centre of *To the Lighthouse* stands the painter and her portrait, a portrait whose structure epitomises that of the novel itself with its central stroke that is also the lighthouse – or, from a different perspective, the 'Time Passes' section. When Fry wrote to congratulate Woolf on the novel ('the best thing you've done'), he also wondered what arriving at the Lighthouse had meant. Mindful of his strictures against the associations of things and his distrust of symbolism, she explained it in terms of its form: 'I meant *nothing* by The Lighthouse. One has to have a central line down the middle of the book to hold the design together' – a comment that identifies Lily's painting with the structure of the book itself, while emphasising its author's use of a painterly aesthetic. In the same letter, Woolf also told Fry that she had originally intended to dedicate the novel to him, but had then lost her nerve, feeling that it was somehow inadequate in comparison with his own achievements: '[r]eally therefore the not-dedication is a greater compliment than the dedication would have been' (*Letters* iii, 385).

That dedication would have been entirely appropriate, for *To the Lighthouse* is a novel about how an artist struggles to achieve (a modernist and a painterly) form, while at the same time actually embodying that form. In a notebook dated March 1925, Woolf had pictured the novel as 'Two blocks joined by a corridor', drawing a shape like a solid 'H'[10] – two long episodes separated by ten years, and joined by a short corridor, the central stroke of the 'Time Passes' section, at right angles to the rest. The novel's three parts also correspond to two days separated by a single night, since 'Time Passes' records not only the events of the natural world but also those of the mind or the unconscious in sleep. The first part, 'The Window', ends with the family going to bed, while the third, 'The Lighthouse', begins as they get up, though in fact ten years has passed rather than a single night, effectively creating a sense of two time schemes operating at once (Woolf could have found a model for this in Shakespeare). Woolf's 'H' figure corresponds not only to the novel's three-part structure, but also to the three beams of the lighthouse – long, short, long. Mrs Ramsay feels that 'the long steady stroke, the last of the three . . . was her stroke' (TTL, 70), though in terms of the actual structure of the novel, the longest part (which is also Mrs Ramsay's part), comes first, rather than last.

A closer examination of *To the Lighthouse* reveals a more complex and elaborate design, and a concern with form, proportion and even numerical significance that invites comparison with the work of James Joyce or T. S. Eliot, and reflects how deeply Woolf had absorbed a modernist sense of form. Clive Bell had perceived a kinship between art and mathematics:

> I wonder, sometimes, whether the appreciators of art and of mathematical solutions are not even more closely allied. Before we feel an aesthetic emotion for a combination of forms, do we not perceive intellectually the rightness and necessity of the combination?[11]

In *To the Lighthouse*, Woolf sees such creativity as a form of selfless love: the love that Mr Bankes feels for Mrs Ramsay, 'that never attempted to clutch its object; but, like the love which mathematicians bear their symbols, or poets their phrases, was meant to be spread over the world and become part of the human gain' (TTL, 53).

The structure of *To the Lighthouse* initially seems to resemble that of 'Kew Gardens' in being based on binary opposition, for it is delicately poised between male and female viewpoints, between father and mother, between Mr Ramsay and Mrs Ramsay (in Woolf's diary entries, she saw it as focused first on her father and later on her mother). From the beginning, she had pictured it in three parts, but those parts were then further subdivided into numbered sections. At first these sections seem to alternate between female and male points of view (rather as the early sections of *Mrs Dalloway* had done). Sections 1, 3 and 5 begin with Mrs Ramsay consoling and reassuring James, 'Yes, of course, if it's fine to-morrow'; 'Perhaps you will wake up and find the sun shining and the birds singing'; 'And even if it isn't fine to-morrow . . . it will be another day' (TTL, 7, 19, 31). The even-numbered sections open with the male speakers, Charles Tansley and Mr Ramsay, who insist upon 'fact' and reason at the expense of the child's feelings. The very short second section begins with Tansley taunting James with the words 'No going to the Lighthouse, James', to Mrs Ramsay's annoyance (TTL, 19). Mrs Ramsay's words begin and end 'The Window', the first part of *To the Lighthouse*, and her completeness and desire to unify her family link her with the odd-numbered sections, while her husband's divisiveness associates him with the even numbers.

Woolf's linking of the unity of women with the number one, with odd numbers, and possibly prime numbers more generally, and of men with the doubleness and divisiveness of two shows that she was evolving her own numerical system rather than drawing on existing numerological tradition in which the male principle is unitary and the female divisible, in which 'it is the odd that is male, and the even female'.[12] Woolf's numbering of individual sections is echoed in that of the novel's three parts: the first belongs to Mrs Ramsay and the third to Lily Briscoe. But the second section, 'Time Passes', is dedicated not to the world of male rationality but to its equivalent and antithesis, the irrational violence of the Great War and the alternative state of mind represented by the unconscious and the rich yet alien world of nature.

The third part, 'The Lighthouse', gave Woolf the greatest difficulty: 'The problem is how to bring Lily & Mr R[amsay]. together & make a combination of interest at the end.' There were to be two endings – Mr Ramsay's arrival at the lighthouse and the completion of Lily's picture, and she wanted to make them happen simultaneously: 'Could I do it in a parenthesis? so that one had the sense of reading the two things at the same time?' (*Diary* iii, 106) she wondered, but in the end she used the parenthesis to isolate the novel's sudden deaths and retained the pattern of alternation she had established earlier, so that there are two final scenes, rather than one. Instead, she found a different solution, that of bringing Lily and Mr Ramsay together at the structural centre of the third part. Just as the first part had initially alternated between the soothing voice of the mother and the harsh male voices of 'fact', so the third part alternates between Lily on the lawn, searching for her vision, and Mr Ramsay in the boat, sailing towards the lighthouse, so that Lily's search for creative form is counterpointed with Mr Ramsay's single-minded journey towards his goal. And, as in the first part, the whole sequence begins and ends with the female principle, the principle of life and creativity which alternates with the even-numbered sections describing the sail to the lighthouse. Exactly half-way through, in the seventh of the thirteen sections (in the manuscript, it is the fifth of nine sections) Lily, having summoned Mrs Ramsay in vain, is suddenly rewarded with a vision of her: 'for this was Mrs. Ramsay in all her beauty . . . stepping with her usual quickness across fields' (TTL, 196–7). And when Lily looks out across the water, she sees a 'brown spot in the middle of the bay' that is Mr Ramsay's boat, 'now half-way across' (TTL, 197), just as the reader is half-way through the third part. This was how Woolf solved the problem of bringing Lily and Mr Ramsay together, a solution that silently includes the reader as well (as a figure for the progress of a narrative, the voyage is as old as the *Odyssey*).

In the published text, the sections of *To the Lighthouse* are numbered nineteen in part one ('The Window'), ten in part two ('Time Passes'), and Woolf intended there to be thirteen in part three ('The Lighthouse'), but the first British edition mis-numbered section two as section three, so that the rest of the numbering was thrown out accordingly; the American first edition correctly provided thirteen sections. Oddly, given Woolf's concern with the numbering of the sections, the mistake in the British edition went unnoticed until 1943, two years after her death. The sections in the first and third parts consist of prime numbers (19, 13), and added to the ten sections of 'Time Passes', they total forty-two, a number that was evidently on Woolf's mind as she worked on the third part, since the later pages of her manuscript include two separate sums adding up to forty-two. Although neither of these is precisely the 19 + 10 + 13 scheme that she finally adopted, the second, '10 + 20 + 12 = 42', is not far off, though the figures occur in a different order.[13] But why did Woolf deliberately aim for forty-two sections? One explanation lies in the close connections between Mrs Ramsay and Virginia's mother, Julia Stephen.

*To the Lighthouse* was published on 5 May 1927, the day of Julia Stephen's death thirty-two years earlier in 1895. The 19 plus 13 sections of the novel add up to 32 (as do the 20 + 12 in her marginal sum), held apart by the ten years (and ten sections) of 'Time Passes'. There could be no precise fit between the chronology of the novel and Woolf's personal history since the novel represents the deaths of Mrs Ramsay, Prue and Andrew as falling in the ten years that divide the past from the present, the years that include and correspond to the Great War, whereas the equivalent losses in Woolf's own life had taken place much earlier – in 1895, 1897 and 1906. It may or may not be an accident that the nineteen sections of the first part correspond to the nineteen years from her mother's death in 1895 to 1914, while the thirteen sections correspond to the thirteen years from 1914 to the book's publication in 1927.

A further possible significance of forty-two is that it was Woolf's age in October 1924, when she had her first glimpse of the next book ('I see already The Old Man', *Diary* ii, 317), though most of it was actually written in 1926 when she was forty-four – the age she wrote into the book as Lily's in the third section: 'Here was Lily, at forty-four, wasting her time, unable to do a thing, standing there, playing at painting, playing at the one thing one did not play at, and it was all Mrs. Ramsay's fault', and again, 'One can't waste one's time at forty-four, she thought' (TTL, 163–4). When, many years later, Woolf described the process of writing the novel, she recorded her age as forty-four, although the moment of conception that she remembered had taken place between March and May 1925. She saw its writing as an act of exorcism:

> It is perfectly true that [my mother] obsessed me, in spite of the fact that she died when I was thirteen, until I was forty-four. Then one day walking round Tavistock Square I made up, as I sometimes make up my books, *To the Lighthouse* . . . Why then? I have no notion. But I wrote the book very quickly; and when it was written, I ceased to be obsessed by my mother. I no longer hear her voice; I do not see her. (MB, 92–3)

If the publication date of *To the Lighthouse* held a special significance for Woolf, that of her next novel, *Orlando*, was actually written into the book itself, as Orlando awakes from a reverie to a sudden sense of being 'violently struck on the head. Ten times she was struck. In fact it was ten o'clock in the morning. It was the eleventh of October. It was 1928. It was the present moment' (O, 206). Such self-conscious, self-reflexive writing, aware of the reader reading as the writer writes, looks back to that moment in *To the Lighthouse*, when Lily sees Macalister's boat, half-way across the bay, just as the reader is half-way through the third part. A comparable moment occurs earlier in the same chapter: Orlando's pregnancy apparently (and surely significantly) had originated in Kew Gardens in October, but it lasts for only six months instead of nine, so that she is delivered on March 20th – precisely the date that Virginia wrote to Vita to tell her that she had finished the book which, like Orlando's pregnancy, had begun the previous October (O, 202–4).[14] Analogies between the art (or should it be the act?) of creation and the sexual act would later be suggested in the sixth chapter of her next book, *A Room of One's Own*, where the writer is required to lie back and be receptive. *A Room*, written immediately after *Orlando*, is stucturally closely linked with it:[15] each has six chapters and *A Room's* Judith Shakespeare is the tragic female double of the Elizabethan Orlando (see essay 1).

The writing of 'Time Passes', the central sequence of *To the Lighthouse*, gave Woolf a great deal of trouble: it was to be 'eyeless',[16] by which she meant, among other things, that there was to be no single point of view, whether of character or narrator. Like the fifth section of *Mrs Dalloway*, it is concerned with the unconscious, the dreaming mind as it floats through the house or along the beach, envisaging tidal waves or houses tumbling to destruction. Woolf sent a typescript of an early version of it to Charles Mauron, the friend of Roger Fry, for translation. At this stage it was divided into nine sections rather than ten, and is closer to the manuscript version than to the published text. Preparing it for independent publication influenced its development, as did its subsequent re-integration into the novel (at this point, Lily and Mr Carmichael reappear in a new tenth section). There may be some relation between the original nine sections of 'Time Passes' and the nine chapters of *The Waves*, the novel that took up the challenge thrown down by 'Time Passes' to write of 'the world seen without a self' (W, 221) and of the mysterious place beyond selfhood which we share, and from whose 'dark materials' spring both creation and destruction. 'Time Passes' brings together the human unconscious and the natural world, the world of the interludes of *The Waves*, the world of nature beyond the human, with its slow procession of sunlight and starlight, the breaking of the waves on the shore, the cries of birds and the life of insects and small creatures creeping along the earth – the mysterious life that had alternated with human conversation in 'Kew Gardens'.

*The Waves* has a deep and complex structure, arrived at slowly and intuitively. Yet it could be seen as playing variations on the sixes and sevens that make up the total of forty-two sections used in *To the Lighthouse*, for it has six 'speaking' characters and a silent seventh in the doomed figure of Percival. The six are divided into three men and three women who are then paired off in further ways, perhaps with an echo of the pairings in 'Kew Gardens': Susan and Bernard are linked by their different forms of creativity; Neville and Jinny by their focus on sexual love (both homo- and heterosexual), and Louis and Rhoda share a sense of public inadequacy and private pressure from their inner lives. Percival is the silent hero whose death at the centre of the novel takes place at noon when the sun is at its zenith. He is Jane Harrison's 'Spirit of the Year' whose permanently re-enacted life and death reconcile the human community to the renewal and decay of the natural world.[17] That reconciliation is primarily effected through the Last Supper, as described in the Gospels or the sacred feast and mourning described in Jane Harrison's *Themis*, enacted in the novel as the dinner shared with Percival and the later dinner at Hampton Court. Jane Harrison had shown how ancient rites were transformed into Greek drama in her book *Ancient Art and Ritual* (1913) – she had gaven Woolf a copy of it at the end of 1923. During the two suppers in *The Waves*, the individual voices briefly join one another as choruses in a conscious if covert allusion to the structure of Greek drama with its echoes of the death of the year-hero.

*To the Lighthouse* (1927), *Orlando* (1928) and *A Room of One's Own* (1929) were all composed at high speed; by contrast, the writing of *The Waves* (1931) seemed peculiarly slow. Ultimately, the soliloquies of its six characters were separated into nine unnumbered chapters by a series of interludes evoking the passage of time in the natural world, its cyclical changes corresponding to the gradual aging process of the six characters.

The novel went through two complete drafts, and a further set of typescript revisions that have not survived, but can be reconstructed by observing the differences between the later manuscript and the published text. In the process of moving on from manuscript to typescript, Woolf identified and developed another pattern within her form. She rewrote it so that the nine unnumbered chapters (separated by ten italicised interludes) themselves create the shape of a pyramid, or rather of the wave whose rhythm and sound permeate the novel. At this late stage, she brought chapters 1 and 8 into close correspondence, emphasising their shared theme of being, alone and together. Similarly chapters 2 and 7 were reworked to bring out the theme of time, while 3 and 6 focus in different ways upon language and self-awareness. Chapters 4 and 5 represent the summit of the wave at noon, followed by its relapse:

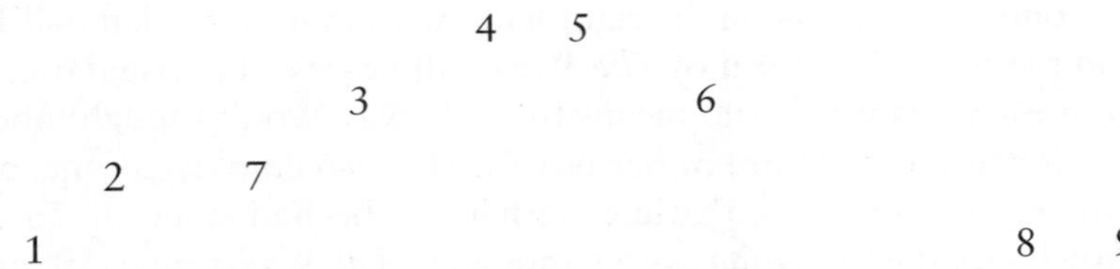


While each chapter constitutes an individual unit, taken together they form the shape of a wave, echoing the book's title as well as its allusions to contemporary debates in physics.[18]

Chapter nine, Bernard's final soliloquy, remains outside this wave figure, being at once a 'summing-up' of everything that has happened and a critique of the structural principles from which narrative fiction was traditionally constructed. And just as the six characters' lives are all coloured by the silent presence of a seventh who must die, so the eight chapters that form the wave, continually in motion, are interrupted and changed by the ninth which, on the one hand signifies a further ending, the death of Bernard and the breaking of the wave upon the shore, yet on the other establishes a new rhythm and a different dynamic. Though Bernard begins by offering to explain 'the meaning of my life', his attempt at doing so reveals that it cannot be done, bringing only a profound exhaustion with existing forms of order: 'How tired I am of stories . . . how I distrust neat designs of life' (W, 183). Bernard's rejection of language and the narratives embedded in it might recall Fry's early impatience with literature, were it not for the fact that Bernard also rejects design and the aesthetic ambitions of 'beautiful phrases' in favour of a complete surrender to contingency and the chaos and indifference of the natural world. He undergoes a deeper loss of self that drains away meaning as the eclipse drains away light, in a premonition of approaching death. The ninth chapter explores the meaning of Woolf's own moment of despair in the summer of 1926, figured for her as a fin 'passing far out' in the waste of waters, though whether she regarded the fin itself as a threat or as an emerging direction amid the waters remains uncertain (W, 218; *Diary* iii, 113).

Woolf's final reworking of *The Waves* reflects her translation of Fry's concept of underlying form – expressed in terms such as volume and mass, depth and recession – into a structure that, though built out of words, nevertheless made a shape and possessed a visual, perhaps even a spatial dimension. The folded pages or alternating sequences of 'Kew Gardens', Jacob's 'room which will hold it together', the 'H' structure with which *To the Lighthouse* had begun and its subsequent development into a shape corresponding to Lily's painting ('It was a question . . . how to connect this mass on the right hand with that on the left' – TTL, 60), and the pyramidal form of *The Waves* all possess this visual dimension, although this was by no means the only way Woolf thought about and developed the structure of her novels. She also employed time, and the numbers associated with time, rather as she had done in *To the Lighthouse* (see the following essay), though in *The Waves* time is treated less as a system of numbers than as a larger and more permanent framework, its great cycles epitomised within the lives of men and women. At the very last stage of revision, she ensured that all but one of the italicised interludes recorded the arc of the sun across the sky and the sequence of the seasons,[19] thus drawing explicit analogies between the ages of man and the cycles of the day and the year (as Shakespeare had done in sonnet 73, 'That time of year thou mayst in me behold'). The structure of *The Waves* enacts the complex interplay between the natural and the human world as we celebrate and mourn the relentless numbers of time. The sun's hourly progress across the sky, the earth's yearly orbit, the monthly cycles of moon and tides constitute the primal rhythms of life on earth. The search for form in art is part of a wider need to find meaning in our circumstances, as we negotiate our way through time and space and the determining conditions of our existence.

## Notes

1. Christopher Reed, 'Through Formalism: Feminism and Virginia Woolf's Relation to Bloomsbury Aesthetics', *The Multiple Muses of Virginia Woolf*, ed. Diane F. Gillespie (Columbia and London: University of Missouri Press, 1993), p. 13. I am indebted to Reed's excellent account of Fry's impact on

Woolf, and also to Allen McLaurin, *Virginia Woolf: The Echoes Enslaved* (Cambridge: Cambridge University Press, 1973).

2. Clive Bell, *Art* (1914; London: Chatto and Windus, 1923), p. 18, while discussing a popular Victorian painting, William Frith's *Paddington Station*.
3. 'The Artist and Psychoanalysis', *A Roger Fry Reader*, ed. Christopher Reed (Chicago and London: University of Chicago Press, 1996), pp. 355, 362.
4. In the course of dedicating his book *Civilization* to Woolf, Clive Bell told her that the Great War was the cause of 'the difference between this essay and the book about which I used to chatter in your workroom in Fitzroy Square', *Civilization: An Essay* (1928; London: Chatto and Windus, 1932), p. vi.
5. Roger Fry, *Reflections on British Painting* (London: Faber and Faber, 1934), p. 148.
6. Ibid., pp. 23, 21.
7. Quoted by Donna Rhein, *The Handprinted Books of Leonard and Virginia Woolf at the Hogarth Press, 1917–1932* (Ann Arbor, MI: UMI Research Press, 1985), p. 42.
8. Leonard Woolf, *An Autobiography*, vol. II, 1911–69 (Oxford: Oxford University Press, 1980), p. 229.
9. Clive Bell, *Art*, pp. 12–13. In *Brideshead Revisited*, Sebastian Flyte also responds to Clive Bell's question by answering, 'Yes. *I* do', and thus transforms Charles Ryder's vision by his answer – Evelyn Waugh, *Brideshead Revisited* (1945; London: Penguin, 1962), p. 30 (noted by McLaurin, p. 23).
10. Virginia Woolf, *To the Lighthouse: The Original Holograph Draft*, ed. Susan Dick (London: Hogarth Press, 1983), Appendix A, p. 48.
11. Clive Bell, *Art*, pp. 25–6. Woolf may have had this passage in mind when she portrayed Vanessa as the mathematician Katharine Hilbery in *Night and Day*.
12. Christopher Butler, *Number Symbolism*, (London: Routledge and Kegan Paul, 1970), p. 22; see also his article on 'Numerological Thought' in *Silent Poetry: Essays in Numerological Analysis*, ed. Alastair Fowler (London: Routledge and Kegan Paul, 1970), where 2 is defined as 'the first female number, and 3 the first masculine one', p. 7.
13. The first sum (facing what would become section 4 of the third part) runs 25 + 17 = 42, with the words 'the stagnant past' or 'part', written beside it; the second sum is written on the back of a sequence not finally used, but located in section 11, *To the Lighthouse: The Original Holograph Draft*, pp. 265 verso, 335 verso. Forty-two is an interesting number: the computer Deep Thought in Douglas Adams's *The Hitchhiker's Guide to the Galaxy* (1979) gave 'forty-two' as the answer to the (unformulated) Great Question 'Of Life, the Universe and Everything'.
14. *Letters* iii, 473; *Diary* iii, 177, Thursday 22 March, though in the novel, the date is given as 'Thursday, March the 20th' (O, 204).
15. ROO, 94; 'act' is the US variant (see p. lix). 'Different as they are in form, the two books are complementary', noted Winifred Holtby, *Virginia Woolf: A Critical Memoir* (London: Wishart, 1932), p. 161.
16. It was 'the most difficult abstract piece of writing – I have to give an empty house, no people's characters, the passage of time, all eyeless & featureless with nothing to cling to' (*Diary* iii, 76).

17. Jane Harrison, *Themis: A Study of the Social Origins of Greek Religion* (1912; London: Merlin Press, 1989), esp. pp. xvii, xix.
18. See, for example, Gillian Beer, 'Physics, Sound, and Substance: Later Woolf', *Virginia Woolf: The Common Ground* (Edinburgh: Edinburgh University Press, 1996), pp. 112–24; Michael Whitworth, *Virginia Woolf: Authors in Context* (Oxford: Oxford University Press, 2005), pp. 180–2.
19. J. W. Graham, ed., *The Waves: The Two Holograph Drafts* (Toronto and Buffalo: University of Toronto Press, 1976), introduction, pp. 35–6.

Essay 7

# The Search for Form (ii): Revision and the Numbers of Time

Thanks to the synoptic edition of *Ulysses*, various studies of Yeats's revisions, Valerie Eliot's edition of *The Waste Land* manuscript and the transcription and publication of many of Virginia Woolf's manuscripts, we now read modernist texts with some awareness of the complex processes by which they came into being.[1] Typically, these include a formalising or tightening of structure at some stage, sometimes along musical lines. Such processes could even be seen in terms of a 'call to order', after what Woolf (in the course of a discussion of Joyce) described as 'the usual smash and splinters' (*Letters* ii, 598). T. S. Eliot entitled the long poems he wrote between 1935 and 1941 *The Four Quartets*, yet their structural model was not so much the classical quartet (which usually consists of four parts, played by four instruments), although there *were* four poems, but rather the work which had established his reputation – the five-part structure, with a divided second section and a short lyrical fourth section that was *The Waste Land*. Yet, as its manuscript notoriously reveals, that structure was in turn the outcome of Pound's judicious editing of Eliot's original drafts.[2] Though from one point of view accidentally arrived at, this five-part structure became the model for *The Four Quartets* – part of the process of building an 'oeuvre' as if it were an architectural monument that Mallarmé had proposed. Comparable processes of revision or restructuring can be identified in the work of Yeats and Joyce who opened up new layers of meaning and significance as they worked (though Auden's rewriting or suppression of earlier poems in the light of his own changing convictions involves a rather different conception of the relationship between the artist and his work).

As revisers, Eliot and Yeats proceeded very differently; while both recognised the effect of context each manipulated it in a different way. Eliot's compositional process characteristically involved re-using and rearranging sequences, so that the opening of *Burnt Norton* was initially written as a chorus for *Murder in the Cathedral*. Eliot originally composed the 'Phlebas' lyric in French to provide the conclusion to his poem 'Dans le restaurant', then he translated it into English, setting it at the end of the sequence 'Death by Water'. Not until *The Waste Land* was published did it stand alone, as the fourth section. Yeats, on the other hand, revised individual poems, re-ordering them within individual collections. The novelists Joyce and Woolf revised towards the point of publication, and made comparatively few changes thereafter. Both structured their material according to a formalist aesthetic, seeking to elicit further designs and meanings from it. Woolf's process of revision, I shall argue, sometimes included a 'formalist' phase as a novel neared completion, a phase in which the underlying form was made more explicit. Prose fiction's central concern with the nature of time, lived or remembered, and its regularly repeated rhythms contributed significantly to the structures produced at this stage.[3]

Many of the manuscripts of Woolf's novels have been transcribed and published, the exceptions being *Night and Day* (of which too little survives), *Flush*, and all but the '1880' section of *The Years*. Yet despite the intense scholarly focus on her work over the last thirty years and more, there has been comparatively little research into her processes of revision, even though Woolf preserved much of the material needed for such a study in the form of the holograph drafts of her novels (which she usually kept, recognising their future importance); her diary and to a lesser extent her letters also comment on the progress of her work. She increasingly used her diary to analyse and reflect upon her writing. At the beginning of *The Waves*, she noted 'I want to watch & see how the idea at first occurs. I want to trace my own process' (*Diary* iii, 113). In this instance, her diary account is so invitingly full that Leonard himself at one stage planned to write a study of Woolf's method of composition based on her diary entries and the novel's two surviving manuscripts. He told Vita Sackville-West,

> I should like to compare her first draft with the final draft and also with what she says in her diaries at the moment about writing them. It happens that the last part of *The Waves* is extraordinarily interesting from this point of view as she gives a description in her diary of the actual writing of it.[4]

Two complete drafts of *The Waves* have survived, and many pages of Woolf's diary describe the problems she encountered in the course of writing it; yet, inevitably, as much again has been lost. Though the second draft closely resembles the published text in terms of structure and sequence, it differs substantially in terms of the actual words on the page. In fact, as her diary records, Woolf carried out two further revisions between completing the second draft and publishing the final text, first retyping the whole thing since she could 'see no other way to make all the corrections, & keep the lilt, & join up, & expand & do all the other final processes. It is like sweeping over an entire canvas with a wet brush' (*Diary* iv, 25). This revision took from 1 (or perhaps 5) May to 22 June 1931, and when it had been retyped by 'Mabel', her professional typist, she made a further set of changes, revising the interludes and the Hampton Court scene, between 28 June and 17 or 18 July:

> And yesterday, 22nd June . . . I finished my re-typing of The Waves. Not that it is finished – oh dear no. For then I must correct the re- re- typing. This work I began on May 5th, & no one can say I have been hasty or careless this time. (*Diary* iv, 30; see also 35–6)

But the intervening typescripts on which she worked have not survived.

There are comparatively few extant typescripts of Woolf's work, and these are mainly from the later years of her life, although it seems to have been her practice to type up after lunch her morning's work in longhand, and later to have the whole text professionally retyped for Leonard to read before sending it on to her printers, R. & R. Clark in Edinburgh. One exception to this pattern occurs in the case of the 'Time Passes' episode of *To the Lighthouse*, which Charles Mauron translated into French and published in the Winter 1926 issue of *Commerce*, before the novel's publication on 5 May 1927.[5] In this case, the surviving typescript from which he worked represents an intermediate stage of revision between the manuscript and the published text. A further stage in the history of the writing of *To the Lighthouse* is recorded on the American proofs, where a long passage about the 'unhappy years' after Mrs Ramsay's death is recalled by James as he sails to the lighthouse – a passage which had not appeared in the manuscript, was set in proof, but subsequently cancelled.[6]

Woolf's holograph drafts, exciting as they are as a record of the 'primal scene' of creation, thus only tell part of the story of her process of composition. It was often at a later stage of revision, that of the missing typescripts, that Woolf's formalist principles most evidently came into play. At this stage, she was less excited than she had been at the outset, and her diary and letters are consequently less informative about what she was planning and thinking. Any knowledge of these changes therefore depends on identifying differences – additions, omissions, and even the empty spaces that divide one unnumbered section from another – not quite the evidence of asterisks, nor that of the aposiopesis that Woolf was so fond of, yet scarcely more substantial. She nowhere described her practice as a reviser any more than she described her practice as a hand-printer, though both were clearly careful and methodical and took up considerable amounts of her time. Her work as a reviser can be partly reconstructed from the surviving evidence of different versions and from the occasional comments in her diary, letters, and elsewhere, but there is more to discover. While Woolf's revisions open up in several directions, some of them personal and political in the widest sense, my focus in what follows is upon the structuring of her novels, their division into numbered sections, and what those numbers may signify, as a development and extension of the previous essay. Thus it is all the more disappointing that the occasional sums written in the margins or on the verso pages of Woolf's notebooks so often refer merely to the numbers of words she had written.

Woolf's first two novels, though far from conventional, were written according to a contemporary formula – that of the novel of thirty-two chapters, referred to in her polemical essay on 'Modern Novels' (later, 'Modern Fiction'), where she complained that such novels were constructed 'after a design which more and more ceases to resemble the vision in our minds' (*Essays* iii, 33). *The Voyage Out* has twenty-seven chapters and *Night and Day* has thirty-four, but between them and her third novel, *Jacob's Room*, Woolf came to terms with modernism, as that novel graphically reveals. It reached her largely through the formalist theories of Roger Fry, but also through the modernist practice of Katherine Mansfield in *Prelude* (published by the Hogarth Press in July 1918), T. S. Eliot's *Poems* (in May 1919) and Hope Mirrlees's *Paris* (in May 1920), all of which Virginia typeset by hand for the Hogarth Press, which from April 1917 had stood on the Woolfs' dining-table at Hogarth House, Richmond.

The setting of *Paris*, in particular, familiarised Woolf with the use of space on the page as a form of punctuation, a way of indicating a pause in the movement of the text – which is how she used it in *Jacob's Room*, as my fifth essay has shown. This was a method visibly different from the asterisks used in Joyce's *Portrait of the Artist as a Young Man* (1916), for example – a printer's division, as contrasted to a writer's, perhaps. *Jacob's Room* is also the first of Woolf's novels to employ significant chapter numbers, though the process by which Woolf arrived at these can only be guessed from a comparison of the surviving (but incomplete) manuscript with the published text. Woolf made a number of major changes after completing the holograph draft; she added or omitted sequences, and altered the numbering of the chapters. The final scene of the manuscript, as in the published text, takes place in Jacob's room between his friend Bonamy and his mother, Betty Flanders, as she holds out his empty shoes. This scene is numbered 'XXX' in the manuscript, and thus is not so far from the thirty-two chapter total referred to in 'Modern Novels'. But the previous numbered chapter was 'XVIII' (it corresponds to chapter XI in the published text) and there are no chapters with numbers in the twenties, so perhaps 'XXX' was simply a slip for 'XX'.[7] In the published text, the last chapter has become 'XIV', making the penultimate one 'XIII'. The long and brilliant thirteenth chapter, which does not appear at all in the manuscript, takes place in London on the afternoon and evening of 4 August 1914, the day England declared war on Germany. The traditional ill-luck associated with thirteen is usually connected with the number of those present at the Last Supper, an allusion appropriate enough for a chapter whose outcome will be the betrayal, torture and death, not of an individual young man, but of an entire generation. The book as a whole points silently towards an ending signified as (MCM)XIV, a formula familiar from war memorials.

Woolf solved some of what she felt to be disruptions in the text of *Jacob's Room* by confining the action of her next novel, *Mrs Dalloway*, to a single day and providing a number of shared public sights and sounds that serve to unify the states of consciousness of individual characters. Above all, they share the novel's time continuum, signified as the regulating (and even patriarchal?) chimes of Big Ben (to which the feminine bells of St Margaret's refuse to conform). And in accordance with this unifying impulse, there are no longer any numbered chapter divisions. Instead, the blocks of text are broken up at irregular intervals by an extra line space. Counting these reveals a clear and appropriate twelve-part structure, reflecting the twelve hours of the day. The book had originally been entitled 'The Hours',[8] though individual sections do not correspond precisely to hours in the day, since (as Rosalind observes in *As You Like It*) 'Time travels in divers paces with divers persons' (Act III, sc. 2, 302–3). Noon forms the novel's natural break or *caesura* (as it would again in *The Waves*), constituting a turning point in the text between the eighth and ninth sections. The ninth (significantly longer than the others) begins

> It was precisely twelve o'clock: twelve by Big Ben; whose stroke was wafted over the northern part of London . . . twelve o'clock struck as Clarissa Dalloway laid her green dress on her bed, and the Warren Smiths walked down Harley Street. Twelve was the hour of their appointment . . . (The leaden circles dissolved in the air.) (MD, 103)

Big Ben strikes near the opening of the novel, and again at 11.30 a.m. (between the third and fourth sections), and finally at the end of the eleventh section. The sentence 'The leaden circles dissolved in the air' is repeated on each occasion (David Bradshaw has pointed out that from 1924 the chimes of Big Ben were regularly being broadcast on the radio[9]). Several sections are introduced by particular street noises overheard by different characters, thus linking their individual thoughts to one another. A car back-firing begins section two, an old woman singing section eight, and the ambulance bell begins section ten, on its way to fetch Septimus's body. A visual device creates an equivalent link in section two as various individuals look up at an aeroplane sky-writing, while section three begins with Clarissa wondering ' "What are they looking at?" ' (MD, 14, 88–90, 165, 30–1).[10] Through such moments of shared awareness, Woolf sought to smooth out what she had felt to be 'jumps and jerks' in *Jacob's Room*, the too arbitrary transitions from one consciousness to another.

Initially, the different sections seem to alternate between the consciousness of women and then of men, so that the first section opens with Clarissa (MD, 3), the second with the explosion and Septimus (though Clarissa and others will figure later) (MD, 14), the third reverts to Clarissa again (MD, 31), the fourth begins with Peter Walsh repeating Clarissa's words 'Remember my party, remember my party' (MD, 52), and the comparatively short fifth section is a visionary sequence that is not 'thought' by any individual character, but represents the mind in sleep or vision, a shared unconscious that anticipates the 'Time Passes' sequence in *To the Lighthouse* (MD, 62). Thereafter the alternations grow less clear. Section nine, which begins at twelve o'clock and is by far the longest, effectively starts a new movement within the novel (MD, 103). This takes place within the consciousness of Septimus and Rezia, Richard Dalloway, Clarissa, Miss Kilman, Elizabeth, and then Rezia and Septimus again, ending with Septimus's suicide. The ambulance bell at the beginning of section ten takes us back to Peter Walsh, whose consciousness had been absent from the preceding sequence, and redirects the action towards Clarissa's party (MD, 165).

Looked at as a time sequence, the first eight sections take place in the morning, before noon. The extended section nine includes all the events of the afternoon, and sections ten to twelve are devoted to Clarissa's evening party, so that a further three-part structure can be identified and set out as a ratio of 8 (morning): 1 (afternoon): 3 (evening). Woolf's next novel, *To the Lighthouse*, would employ a three-part time structure, this time beginning with an afternoon and evening ('The Window'), followed by a night ('Time Passes'), and a morning ('The Lighthouse'). The afternoon corresponds to the middle-age of Mr and Mrs Ramsay, while the morning corresponds to the ages of their children James and Cam. The complex interweaving of hours, times and seasons with human lives is further developed in the interplay between the interludes and the lives of the six characters in *The Waves*.

The manuscript of *Mrs Dalloway*, originally entitled 'The Hours', is not consistently divided into sections, although the rewrite of the first chapter is firmly identified as 'Chapter One' (but this is partly because it was redrafted, and does not appear until the second notebook – the original draft has not apparently survived). Sections are identified as 'III' and 'IV', though they correspond to the fourth and sixth published sections.[11] At the point where Clarissa is lying on her sofa in the middle of the afternoon (and in the middle of what will become the ninth section), Woolf reminds herself on a verso page '4 or 5 scenes more', and then lists them as 'Kilman & Elizabeth./ The Warren Smiths./ Peter./ London./ The party.'[12] Although the first two of these would later be absorbed into the long ninth section, Woolf already felt the rhythm of the rest of her book.

The passage of time is central to Woolf's next novel, *To the Lighthouse*, which has to traverse a ten-year gap, but Woolf dealt with this not by passing over it in silence, but by making it the central feature, the brush stroke through the middle of her novel (perhaps recalling Shakespeare's strategy in *The Winter's Tale* where the passage of time is conspicuously announced by Time himself). And the novel that followed, *Orlando*, makes fun both of 'Time Passes' and also of more conventional treatments of time in the novel (O, 67–8; see also 184). Its heroine arrives at the age of thirty-six (the age of Vita Sackville-West when the novel was published) more than 300 (and as many as 360?) years after we first meet him, years during which he changes sex and becomes a woman (a 180-degree turn?). A chapter is given to each of the five centuries that Orlando lives through (or across), plus an extra (third) chapter tucked between the seventeenth and eighteenth centuries for Orlando's transformation in Constantinople, on the edge of time and western civilisation (see essay 10). Thus the novel has six chapters in all, ending with 'the present moment', 11 October 1928, the day on which the novel was actually published (and a year since Woolf had begun it). This six-chapter model (numbered in roman figures) would also be used in the non-fictional *A Room of One's Own* (1929), whose structure parallels that of *Orlando*, with Judith Shakespeare introduced at the point corresponding to Orlando's sex-change, and again in *Flush* (1933).

As Woolf grew older and the events of European history became more disturbing, the significance of dates came to play a larger role in her fiction, though *The Waves*, with its extended comparison between human lives and the rhythms of nature, to some extent sidesteps historical particularity. Instead, it draws parallels and contrasts between its characters' lives (depicted in terms of nine, rather than seven ages) and the procession of days and seasons in the natural world. Like *To the Lighthouse*, it has a complex time scheme, focused upon inner time. By contrast, the fourth page of *The Years* has Colonel Pargiter picking up and throwing down a newspaper with a picture of Cologne Cathedral (Y, 5). In 1880 the Cathedral had been rededicated, an occasion employed by the Emperor Wilhelm I to celebrate the resurgent German nation (as David

Bradshaw has noted[13]). The arbitrary dates of political events measure a different kind of time.

*The Years* relates the history of a family over fifty years from 1880 to the present, a period roughly corresponding to Woolf's own lifetime (she was born in 1882) and one that had made enormous changes in middle-class family life and expectations. The opening episode, '1880', fascinated Woolf so much that it grew disproportionately long and, though she later cut away the 'essay' portions from what had begun as an 'essay-novel', what remained was still too long and required to be balanced out by an equally weighty 'present day' chapter. The '1910' chapter, which explores Woolf's sense that this was a key point of change, also grew out of hand as she became increasingly exhilarated by the feminist arguments that Elvira (later, Sally) and Maggie propose to their cousin Rose Pargiter. Later, she would cut these out as well, considering them too static and didactic. They were reworked as polemic in *Three Guineas*, the title of which first occurs in the manuscript draft of the '1910' chapter: here, in the course of a discussion on the need for contraception, Rose points out that the poor women of Battersea could not afford the standard three-guinea fee required for a medical consultation.[14]

From the beginning of *The Years*, Woolf's 'wide angle lens' approach to social history created technical problems for her: evidently the different episodes could not be depicted in comparable detail. It is not clear at what point the structure finally emerged, but *The Years* was planned to have twelve parts, like *Mrs Dalloway* (whose earlier title of 'The Hours', its own title recalls). The parts were identified as individual years (1880, 1891, 1907, 1908, etc.), but the whole system was to be flexible, so that individual parts could be as short or as long as seemed appropriate. Like *Mrs Dalloway* and *The Waves*, it would have a significant break or *caesura* about two-thirds of the way through, this time not after the eighth section (where 'twelve o'clock' had fallen in *Mrs Dalloway*), but during it, for the eighth section is '1914' and in Woolf's original scheme this chapter was split in half, with a sequence in May and another in September of that year. The May section ends with Kitty's train journey to the north, a passage that fulfils some of the functions of 'Time Passes' (Y, 198–9). As my next essay indicates, it represents the human sense of the passage of time, comparing our helplessness in the face of it with our helplessness in the face of historical determinism, here signified by the coming of the War.

The second, September half of '1914' was one of the 'two enormous chunks' that Woolf cut before publication on Leonard's advice, for the novel was unacceptably long, judged by the publishing norms of its day. It records a London full of young men in uniform and people anxiously reading newspapers. Kitty's train journey is echoed by Eleanor's travels on the underground and the bus as she goes to town and back to visit the theatre. At this stage, 'Everything seemed much as usual' (Y, 368)[15] and the War still seems somehow unreal. The West End is brightly illuminated – '[t]he streets were glaring with light' (Y, 366) – in contrast to the London of '1917', blacked out because of air raids. The second of the 'two enormous chunks', the '1921' episode, was cut in its entirety. Its inclusion would not only bring the number of chapters from eleven to twelve, but also rebalance the last third of the novel, both in terms of length and of content. Eleanor's rapturous pleasure in her new life in London described in the September section of '1914' is undermined by a dismal evening spent in a cheap restaurant in Oxford Street. She resents an outsize cinema poster of a couple kissing, is edged off the pavement by drunken louts, and feels a sudden premonition that civilisation is coming to an end (Y, 394–401).

Woolf's last novel, *Between the Acts*, explores the nightmare of history, taking in a huge sweep from the Jurassic age and prehistoric man, through a comic replay of English history, right up to 'the present moment' (a concept also employed in *Orlando* and *The Years*). Yet, formally speaking, its action is concentrated within a twelve-hour period and within an equally circumscribed physical space, never straying beyond the terrace, barn and greenhouse of Pointz Hall. Woolf herself had sacrificed the twelve-part structure of *The Years* when she cut out the 'two enormous chunks', but she did not live to see her last novel through the press, and that task was left to Leonard who conscientiously prefaced it by pointing this out: 'She would not, I believe, have made any large or material alterations in it, though she would probably have made a good many small corrections or revisions before passing the final proofs' (BA, 3). As published, *Between the Acts* is written as a sequence of unnumbered sections on the model of *Mrs Dalloway*. There appear to be thirty-seven of these, indicated by breaks of two white lines (Leonard had marked them in for the printers on the final typescript). Mitchell Leaska, who edited and transcribed two of the three typescripts, claimed that although 'the Earlier, Later and Final Typescripts differ in length and content, the number of scenes remains constant; that is, all three extant versions of the novel have thirty-seven scenes.'[16] This would be consistent with Woolf's earlier writing practice: when she was writing confidently and swiftly, as in *To the Lighthouse* or *Orlando*, for example, she made numerous small adjustments from her initial draft, but few major ones.

Leaska claimed that the thirty-seven scenes had been there from the beginning, and certainly thirty-seven sections can be identified in those typescripts, but they are nowhere numbered – the numbering of sections does not extend past '12' in the second of the two typescripts. Did Woolf consciously intend to have thirty-seven sections from the outset and, if so, what significance, if any, did that number hold for her? The pageant poses a number of problems: some of its sequences seem exceptionally long, and the dialogue, on and offstage, must all begin on new lines, so it is just possible that further sequence breaks in this area of the text have not been identified, particularly if they fall at the end of a page. But is it possible that two such divisions have fallen out? In other words, if Woolf had carried out the final revision, would *Between the Acts* have had thirty-nine sections, rather than thirty-seven, by analogy with the XIV chapters of *Jacob's Room*? The novel itself is conscious of this number: as Isa looks round the library for something to soothe the 'raging tooth' of love, the text pointedly wonders 'What remedy was there for her at her age – the age of the century, thirty-nine – in books?' (BA, 14). And later, as the pageant begins, 'At this very moment, half-past three on a June day in 1939 [the villagers] greeted each other' (BA, 47).

If Woolf had intended to have thirty-nine sections, the last section would become (19)39, and this is the section in which Giles and Isa finally speak to one another, fight, make love and perhaps beget an unknown future while at the same time being identified with 'savages', the cave dwellers who will open Miss La Trobe's next play. And it may be worth noting that the tenth section ('on or about December 1910 human character changed') is devoted to the unexpected (and indeed, uninvited) arrival of Mrs Manresa and William Dodge, the two outsiders who, in their different ways, invite a reassessment of traditional family values – Mrs Manresa through her freer and more open sexuality ('where she went others followed') while William Dodge introduces same-sex love, despised by Giles but warmly welcomed by Isa and Mrs Swithin. And section 14 is characterised by Giles's angry 'vision of Europe, bristling with guns, poised with planes. At any moment guns would rake that land into furrows; planes splinter Bolney Minster into smithereens and blast the Folly' (BA, 34).

What casts doubt not only on Leaska's assertion that there were always thirty-seven sections but also on my guess that Woolf might have planned thirty-nine is the absence of any numbers on the typescripts themselves: the second typescript numbers its early sections as far as twelve, but then gives up. Did Woolf actually know how many sections she had written, or remember which one was which? It seems unlikely. Stuart Clarke reminds me that Woolf counted on her fingers all her life, yet from *Jacob's Room* onwards, the different divisions in her novels were numbered, whether those numbers appeared as in *Jacob's Room*, or remained invisible as in *Mrs Dalloway*. And these numbers seem to carry significance. Twelve, the number of sections of *Mrs Dalloway/ The Hours*, and originally of *The Years*, is the traditional number of hours in the day and the number of months in the year. It is part of the process by which the natural cycles of the sun and moon are translated into the familiar units of time that we share and live by, the 'life of Monday or Tuesday'. A different kind of time, the dates of determining political events, is registered in the XIV chapters of *Jacob's Room*, where the final chapter in his now empty room records Jacob's death and the chapter number silently indicates how he died. The possibility remains that Woolf might have written a silent thirty-nine into the structure of *Between the Acts* had she carried out the final revision, for it was often at a late stage that her vision became explicit in terms of structure. And finally there are the personal numbers – the forty-two sections of *To the Lighthouse*, recalling the thirty-two years from Julia Stephen's death in 1895 to 1927, plus the ten years of 'Time Passes', or the thirty-six years and six chapters of Orlando that point to Vita Sackville-West as its source of inspiration.

Woolf deployed the numbers of time as part of her struggle to master contingency and happenstance, and embed them in a vision and a design. For although the father of modernism, Stéphane Mallarmé, had warned in his last poem that *Un coup de dés jamais n'abolira le hasard* ('a throw of the dice will never abolish chance'), modernism was beginning to recognise that the order of numbers might be as central to art as it had now become to the sciences.

## Notes

1. See George Bornstein's Introduction to *Representing Modernist Texts: Editing as Interpretation* (Ann Arbor: University of Michigan Press, 1991), pp. 2–3, and articles by Richard J. Finneran and Vicki Mahaffey in that volume.
2. T. S. Eliot, *The Waste Land: A Facsimile and Transcript*, ed. Valerie Eliot (London: Faber and Faber, 1971).
3. Christopher Butler discusses the work of Yeats and Joyce in *Number Symbolism* (London: Routledge and Kegan Paul, 1970), pp. 162–5; see also his essay on 'Numerological Thought' in *Silent Poetry: Essays in numerological analysis*, ed. Alastair Fowler (London: Routledge and Kegan Paul, 1970).
4. Frederic Spotts, ed., *Letters of Leonard Woolf* (London: Bloomsbury, 1990), pp. 259–60.
5. See James M. Haule, ' "Le temps passe" and the Original Typescript: An Early Version of the "Time Passes" Section of *To the Lighthouse*', *Twentieth Century Literature*, vol. 29, no. 3 (Fall, 1983), pp. 267–311.
6. *To the Lighthouse*, ed. Susan Dick (Oxford: Blackwell, Shakespeare Head, 1992), pp. 207–8. The status of this passage is discussed by Hans Walter Gabler in 'A Tale of Two Texts: Or, How One Might Edit Virginia Woolf's

*To The Lighthouse*', *Woolf Studies Annual* 10, ed. Mark Hussey (New York: Pace University Press, 2004), pp. 11–13, 17.

7. *Jacob's Room: The Holograph Draft*, ed. Edward L. Bishop, p. 274. There are comparable problems with the numbering of sections within chapters in the manuscript of *Orlando* – see *Orlando: The Original Holograph Draft*, ed. Stuart N. Clarke (London: S. N. Clarke, 1993), p. 18.
8. Though at one stage, Woolf seems to have envisaged a sixteen-hour day – see *'The Hours': The British Museum Manuscript of Mrs Dalloway*, ed. Helen M. Wussow (New York: Pace University Press, 1996), Appendix 2, p. 416. The novel's action seems to run to fourteen hours or more, if it begins at 10.00 a.m. and goes on till after midnight.
9. Virginia Woolf, *Mrs Dalloway*, ed. David Bradshaw (Oxford: Oxford University Press, 2000), pp. xxxiii–iv. Bradshaw also explores the novel's anomalies of time and travel noted by John Sutherland and Diderik Roll-Hansen, p. xiv.
10. Allen McLaurin explores these links, associating them with Unanimist writings, in his article 'Consciousness and Group Consciousness in Virginia Woolf', *Virginia Woolf: A Centenary Perspective*, ed. Eric Warner (New York: St Martin's Press, 1984), pp. 28–40.
11. *'The Hours'* – 'Chapter One' on p. 252, sections III, V, on pp. 8, 31.
12. Ibid., p. 193.
13. He spoke of the Cathedral as 'a symbol of German unity' and 'a sign of the strength of the armed forces' – David Bradshaw, ' "History in the Raw": Searchlights and Anglo-German rivalry in *The Years*', *Critical Survey*, vol. 10, no. 3 (September 1998), pp. 13–14.
14. 'But I don't see that woman down there going to Harley Street? With three guineas?' Rose's question, partly deleted, appears in the fourth MS Notebook of *The Years* on p. 27; the eight notebooks are held in the Henry W. and Albert A. Berg Collection of the New York Public Library.
15. The 'two enormous chunks' excised by Woolf are reprinted in the Appendix to Jeri Johnson's edition of *The Years* (London: Penguin, 1998), but here, as elsewhere, the September 1914 section is misidentified as '1917', a mistake corrected by Karen Levenback in 'Placing the First "Enormous Chunk" Deleted from *The Years*', *Virginia Woolf Miscellany* 42 (Spring 1994), pp. 8–9.
16. Virginia Woolf, *Pointz Hall: The Earlier and Later Typescripts of Between the Acts*, ed. Mitchell A. Leaska (New York: University Publications, 1983), p. 17.

Essay 8

# 'This Moment I Stand On': Virginia Woolf and the Spaces in Time

> Time . . . though it makes animals and vegetables bloom and fade with amazing punctuality, has no such simple effect upon the mind of man. The mind of man, moreover, works with equal strangeness upon the body of time. An hour, once it lodges in the queer element of the human spirit, may be stretched to fifty or a hundred times its clock length; on the other hand, an hour may be accurately represented on the time-piece of the mind by one second. This extraordinary discrepancy between time on the clock and time on the mind is less known than it should be and deserves fuller investigation. (O, 68)

Woolf did not require Einstein's theories to legitimate her sense of the relativity of time, the rapid or crawling passage of the hour. As a novelist centrally concerned with how to represent consciousness and subjectivity, she was intensely aware of time, both as an impersonal force and as a personal experience, as shared time and individual time, as the regulated and measurable time of clocks, public and private, and of seasons and stars. She was aware of time's asymmetrical relation to space, and of time in memory and thought, and also within the life of the body, moving from moment to moment towards that final obliteration of consciousness which is death. She was aware of time passed with family, friends or partners, of time as loss, and of time as history, whether personal, familial, cultural, social or political. Even the titles of her books suggest her sense of its passage – *Night and Day*, *Monday or Tuesday*, *The Hours*, *The Waves*, *The Years*, *Between the Acts*.

Towards the end of her life, Virginia Woolf agreed, as a labour of love, to write the biography of her friend, the artist and art historian, Roger Fry. It was her first serious biography, and she soon found herself struggling with the limits imposed not only by his sisters but also by the conservatism of her readers – there was so much that Roger had discussed uninhibitedly within Bloomsbury which could not be included in this public account of his life.[1] By way of compensation, she began to set down some of the details of her own life, some of the experiences that she felt a biographer might either fail to discover, or not feel able to publish. The resulting unfinished memoir, 'A Sketch of the Past', was included in Schulkind's collection of her autobiographical writings, *Moments of Being*. During the course of it, she criticised her father, the Victorian philosopher and man of letters, Leslie Stephen, for his displays of rage: 'There was something blind, animal, savage in them. Roger Fry said that civilisation means awareness. [Father] was uncivilised in his extreme unawareness' (MB, 149). Yet she also exonerated him on the grounds that

> Two different ages confronted each other in the drawing room at Hyde Park Gate. The Victorian age and the Edwardian age. We were not his children; we were his grandchildren. There should have been a generation between us to cushion the contact . . . Father himself was a typical Victorian . . . We were living say in 1910; they were living in 1860. (MB, 149–50)

She was exaggerating, of course. By 1910, Leslie Stephen had been dead for six years and his children had long since left Hyde Park Gate behind them, but the year 1910 still held a special significance for her as one of those turning points in time, a point where the continuity of past and present broke down, when the past came to a halt and the present – or perhaps *a* present – began. For Woolf, personal as well as political history consisted of such disjunctive moments, moments that change the way we think or feel. Often they were private, and some were linked specifically with sexual discovery, sometimes unpleasantly as when Gerald put his hand under her clothes and touched her private parts (MB, 82); enlighteningly, as when Jack Hills 'opened [her] eyes . . . to the part played by sex in the life of the ordinary man' (MB, 112); and disinhibitingly, as when Lytton Strachey pointed to a stain on Vanessa's white dress and enquired 'Semen?' (MB, 56).

Woolf celebrated what she termed 'moments of being' (experiences that gave their name to Jeanne Schulkind's collection), moments whose intensity she felt in their full presentness as meaningful, even ecstatic, moments that rose like mountain peaks out of daily life. Against these might be set moments of unmaking, moments when a particular way of seeing or thinking came to an end, when a set of meanings was loosed or unhinged, dissolved or dashed itself to pieces. For Woolf, such moments were linked with change, even with enlightenment, but they also brought sudden shocks, creating ruptures, gulfs or chasms that severed the past from the present. She examined her childhood shocks and her 'shock-receiving capacity' in 'A Sketch of the Past' (MB, 85).

It is scarcely surprising that Woolf pictured time as subject to such cracks and fissures since, both as an individual and as a member of a family, her own life had been subject to a series of violent disruptions. In 1895, when she was thirteen and on the brink of those major bodily changes that constitute puberty, the cheerful round of family life was broken by the unexpected death of her mother and was never fully restored. Two years later, her half-sister Stella died, and seven years after that, her father, and in 1906 her favourite brother Thoby, only a year and a half older than herself. Thoby's death was closely followed by the marriage of her sister Vanessa, so that the contented quartet of Stephens, who had lived for the previous two years at 46 Gordon Square, was dissolved, leaving her to construct a new life for herself and her more difficult younger brother Adrian. She sought refuge in beginning her first novel. Both *The Voyage Out* (1915) and its successor, *Night and Day* (1919) reflect her awareness of generational conflict, yet the moments of unmaking first appear explicitly not in her fiction but in her criticism where they are offered as an explanation of recent literary history, the history of her own generation of writers whom she felt to be as cut off from their predecessors as she had been from the Victorian father who might almost have been her grandfather.

Woolf's sense of a literary generation gap first appears in a letter to her friend and teacher Janet Case, written in May 1922 when she was finishing *Jacob's Room*. She and Leonard had been having 'a terrific argument' about the status of Bernard Shaw. Leonard claimed that Shaw had influenced the sexual behaviour of young people. She had disagreed – only poets could touch the human heart. She classified Shaw with the socially conscious Edwardians who had failed her generation through their lack of imagination (*Letters* ii, 529). In 'A Sketch of the Past' Woolf would define the difference between herself and her father as the difference between the Victorians and the Edwardians, but in writing to Janet Case in 1922 she applied the term 'Edwardian' to the generation of writers from 1895 to 1914:

> Don't you agree with me that the Edwardians . . . made a pretty poor show. By the Edwardians, I mean Shaw, Wells, Galsworthy, the Webbs, Arnold Bennett. We Georgians have our work cut out for us, you see. There's not a single living writer (English) I respect: . . . Orphans is what I say we are – we Georgians – (*Letters* ii, 529)

In an essay 'On Re-reading Novels' written for the *Times Literary Supplement* a couple of months later, she took her argument a step further, denouncing 'The failure of the Edwardians [as] comparative yet disastrous – . . . The Georgians, it seems, are in the odd predicament of turning for solace and guidance not to their parents who are alive, but to their grandparents who are dead' (*Essays* iii, 336). Though the terms are different, this essay shares with 'A Sketch of the Past' the sense of having lost an intervening generation, reflecting the way that personal experience coloured her reading of literary history. Her situation was further complicated by the fact that her own father, a Victorian by any definition, had influenced her early essays and reviews – though never, crucially, her fiction.

In a long letter to Gerald Brenan written on Christmas Day 1922, Woolf drew on her sense of belonging to an orphaned generation and the problems that brought. Brenan, a close friend of Dora Carrington, was himself an aspiring writer and had moved to Spain, where the Woolfs would visit him in the following spring. In his mountain fastness, he felt himself overcome with difficulties. Embarrassed by his generous (or possibly envious) praise of her work, Virginia tried to reassure him that he was not alone, that her writing, too, had come out of despair and a sense of inadequacy, while agreeing with him that the time was out of joint. For them, there had been more than the usual break between young writers and their predecessors, more than

> the usual smash and splinters . . .The human soul, it seems to me, orientates itself afresh every now and then. It is doing so now. No one can see it whole, therefore. The best of us catch a glimpse of a nose, a shoulder, something turning away, always in movement. (*Letters* ii, 598)

If writing is to be any easier for the next generation, her own must first 'break its neck'. She goes on to refer to those private orientations that take place every ten years and which 'match the vast one which is, to my mind, general now in the race' (*Letters* ii, 598).

According to this narrative, literary history had been interrupted, and the fragmented nature of modernist writing (though she does not use that term) was the result. The writer could only see in glimpses, see glimpses rather than the wholeness that the high Victorians had reached for, both in words and painting. She was approaching her famous declaration, comic in its arbitrariness, yet also demanding to be taken seriously – 'on or about December 1910 human character changed' (*Essays*, iii, 421), an assertion made in her 1924 essay 'Mr Bennett and Mrs Brown'.[2] This essay provides a critique of the realist novel in general and Arnold Bennett in particular. It was provoked by his sneer at *Jacob's Room*, that while he had seldom read a cleverer novel, its 'characters do not vitally survive in the mind'.[3]

Once again, 1910 was the date she selected to distinguish Bennett's generation, the Edwardians, from her own. Their generation had betrayed hers through an insistent materialism, a preoccupation with social conscience. Ignoring aesthetic criteria, they had made their readers feel that they must join a society or write a cheque. Woolf's rejection of their aims was, paradoxically, more forceful because they were aims she recognised and even shared. She too felt that fiction necessarily included social criticism, but she knew that their confidence in some absolute, external reality was misplaced; there were only individuals and what they saw.

What, then, was the significance of 1910? It was, most obviously, the year when the 'genial and phallic' King Edward VII died on 6 May, to be succeeded by his more respectable and commonplace son, George V. The specificity of December 1910 is usually explained in terms of Roger Fry's astonishing exhibition, 'Manet and the Post-Impressionists', which opened at the Grafton Galleries on 8 November. Nineteen-ten was also the year that Woolf first met Fry, an encounter she recalled in her biography of him: 'He talked that spring day in a room looking out over the trees of a London square, in a deep voice like a harmonious growl' (RF, 119).[4] His way of thinking about art and representation was to have a crucial influence upon her, underpinning her critique of Arnold Bennett as a realist, as well as the artistic aims she evolved for herself.

In *Vision and Design* ('probably the most important art criticism of our time', according to Virginia[5]), Fry pictured the emergence of the Post-Impressionists as a paradigm shift, and this is how some young artists experienced it. Mark Gertler, for example, compared their effect on him to that of the new quantum physics: 'The entry of Cézanne, Gauguin, Matisse etc., upon my horizon was equivalent to the impact of the scientists of this age upon a simple student of Sir Isaac Newton'.[6] According to Roger Fry's account, artists from the thirteenth century onwards had increasingly focused on representing 'the totality of appearance'.[7] The significance of Post-Impressionist painting was that it reinstated form as the central artistic value, and in so doing enabled a reassessment of much that had previously been dismissed as 'primitive' art, including African sculpture, children's paintings, the art of native Australians or native American Indians, art which valued form at the expense of realism.

In 'Art and Life', the opening essay of *Vision and Design*, Fry enquired 'whether the life of the past fifty years [had] shown any such violent reorientation as we have found in the history of modern art'. He concluded that he could not find an equivalent change in direction, though he did find 'something analogous in the new orientation of scientific and human endeavour. Science has turned its instruments in on human nature and begun to investigate its fundamental needs, and art has also turned its vision inwards'. He ended by speculating as to '[w]hether the differences between the nineteenth and the twentieth centuries will in retrospect seem as great in life as they already do in art', while noticing 'how much more conscious we are of the change in art than we are of the general change in thought and feeling.'[8]

'Mr Bennett and Mrs Brown' provides, among other things, an answer to Fry's question, assuring him that changes of a comparable magnitude had indeed taken place in society. For Woolf, a major shift in artistic taste such as separated her own generation of writers from Bennett and his contemporaries, or the Post-Impressionists from the Impressionists, could only flow from a deeper and more fundamental alteration in the nature of society. As a novelist and an observer of human behaviour, she was, perhaps, more alert to changing *mores* than Fry was. Nowhere had they changed faster than in Bloomsbury, and Fry himself had been implicated in some of those changes.

They were reflected in literature, too – her essay instances the books of Samuel Butler and the plays of Bernard Shaw (Leonard, it seems, had eventually won her round to his view of Shaw), but the deepest changes had affected society as a whole, altering the structure of 'All human relations . . . those between masters and servants, husbands and wives, parents and children. And when human relations change there is at the same time a change in religion, conduct, politics and literature' (*Essays* iii, 422). Woolf's essay located these changes in 1910, rather than identifying the 1914–18 War as the great and obvious agent of change. In her view, they were somehow peculiar to English society and had occurred earlier and independently of external or international forces. According to her time scheme, they were well under way before the War arrived.

She was not alone in that conviction: twenty-five years later, the historian George Dangerfield, introducing his account of *The Strange Death of Liberal England*, would identify the year 1910 as far more than a convenient starting point:

> It is actually a landmark in English history . . . For it was in 1910 that fires long smouldering in the English spirit suddenly flared up . . . That extravagant behaviour of the post-war decade, which most of us thought to be the effect of war, had really begun before the War. The War hastened everything – in politics, in economics, in behaviour – but it started nothing.[9]

Contemporaries agreed:

> The Post-Impressionists are in the company of the Great Rebels of the World. In politics the only movements worth considering are Woman Suffrage and Socialism. They are both Post-Impressionist in their desire to scrap old decaying forms and find for themselves a new working ideal

wrote Christina Walsh in the *Daily Herald*.[10] Woolf was sympathetic to both these causes. For her, 1910 had begun with a new year's resolution to contribute more actively to the Women's Movement. She joined the moderate Society for Adult Suffrage, but soon found herself bored: 'I spend hours writing names like Cowgill on envelopes', while the office was 'just like a Wells novel' (*Letters* i, 422), providing material for *Night and Day* (ND, 63, 137, 214).

For much of 1910, the Women's Social and Political Union maintained a truce in the hope that the Government would pass the 'Conciliation Bill' which would have granted the vote to a million propertied women. As Parliament was about to reconvene, efforts were stepped up; Woolf herself attended meetings at the Albert Hall in mid-November.[11] By the eighteenth, it was evident that the Prime Minister had no intention of promoting the Bill, and that afternoon a procession of women marched to Parliament Square to present a petition. There they were confronted with new and far more sexually aggressive forms of police brutality. After six hours of fighting, many women had been badly hurt. Black Friday, as it was called, opened a more militant phase in the history of the Movement.[12]

As Home Secretary, Winston Churchill was accounted responsible, as he was for the similarly violent interventions by the army and London policemen in the Rhondda Valley where 30,000 Welsh miners were currently on strike. A year of industrial disputes, strikes and lock-outs culminated in rioting, and on 21 November a pitched battle took place in the town of Tonypandy, put down with a violence that Churchill was never allowed to forget.[13] In addition to these eruptions of civil violence, a longer-term political crisis was brewing: the December election left the Liberal party locked in a constitutional crisis with the House of Lords and dependent on the support of Labour and Irish Members of Parliament which committed them to putting through Irish Home Rule (events that surface briefly in the later chapters of *Jacob's Room*[14]). According to some, 'England, on the eve of war, was in a state approaching revolution'.[15] Woolf's selection of December 1910, far from being arbitrary, was a reflection of her political astuteness.

As fascinating as the choice of December 1910 is the way that what began as cultural theory would, in her next novel, be transposed into artistic structure, becoming an aspect of that form which, for Fry, was the artist's highest goal. For the moment of rupture next appears as the 'Time Passes' section of *To the Lighthouse*, that central crossbar that supports and holds apart the novel's two narrative sequences. In 'Time Passes', the concept of cultural break is reworked as a quasi-musical, or even cinematic interlude. In accord with Fry's principle that the highest art transcends representation, Woolf largely abandons individual speakers or narrators, creating a fantasia of imagery that was 'the most difficult abstract piece of writing . . . all eyeless & featureless with nothing to cling to' (*Diary* iii, 76).

Unlike her essays (but like *Jacob's Room* and *Mrs Dalloway*), *To the Lighthouse* identifies the War with the moment of rupture, though its ten-year duration loosens its specificity a little. A ten-year gap also opens up in Woolf's essay on 'The Cinema' (1926), written during the composition of *To the Lighthouse*. Here it seems that an audience is watching a ten-year-old newsreel of 'a world which has gone beneath the waves':

> Brides are emerging from the Abbey; ushers are ardent; mothers are tearful; guests are joyful; and it is all over and done with. The war opened its chasm at the feet of all this innocence and ignorance. But it was thus that we danced and pirouetted, thus that the sun shone and the clouds scudded, up to the very end. (*Essays* iv, 349)

While this flashback finds in the cinema a mechanical analogy to memory, its time scheme is a little hazy, since 'ten years ago' only reaches back as far as 1916 – not quite far enough.

'One by one the lamps were all extinguished' (TTL, 137). The familiar domestic ritual that opens 'Time Passes' also serves to evoke the advent of war by echoing Lord Edward Grey's famous remark as he looked down from the Foreign Office into the dusk of 4 August 1914: 'The lamps are going out all over Europe; we shall not see them lit again in our lifetime'.[16] Woolf had made a similar allusion in *Jacob's Room* as 'Now one after another lights were extinguished. Now great towns – Paris – Constantinople – London – were black as strewn rocks' (J's R, 140). That novel, too, had made the War the moment of rupture, though its occurrence remains inferred rather than stated.[17] It was in *Jacob's Room* that Woolf first made full and deliberate use of that distinctive technique by which she exploited her readers' knowledge of recent events without necessarily referring to them, using them as a mode of irony.

Woolf's presentation of the break in 'Time Passes' brings with it the whole range of her concerns with time – as public and private, personal and historical. Indeed the abandonment of regulated clock time in favour of sequences of natural (diurnal or seasonal) change is also reflected in the quasi-Shakespearean 'double time scheme', according to which, the ten-year passage is simultaneously that of a single night: the Ramsay family and Lily Briscoe go to sleep at the beginning of it and wake up, as if it were next day, at the end of it. The events of the night are thus figured as their dreams, played out in the decaying house as if in a brain, drifting ever further from consciousness and the waking life of the body. While consciousness registers our existence in time, sleep, like death, eliminates time and, perhaps, individuality. The world of houses slowly delapidating, gardens overgrown, of walking, or rather floating, along the shore, and of seas stirred to storms and floods are the common language of our dreams of change and loss (experiences that most vividly mark out the passage of time). And though the deaths of Mrs Ramsay, of Andrew and Prue are isolated within parentheses, 'Time Passes' also registers their loss symbolically, just as it registers the War in nights 'full of wind and destruction' (TTL, 140) and in the ghastly appearance of the ashen-coloured ship, the *Dreadnought,* 'come, gone; there was a purplish stain upon the bland surface of the sea, as if something had boiled and bled, invisibly, beneath' (TTL, 146).

The troubled seas are part of a meditation on the human perception of nature, a perception of relationship which the War brought to an end, in another variant on the theme of history revising culture: 'That dream, then, of sharing, completing, finding in solitude on the beach an answer' – the dream of the romantic poets and, after them, of the Victorians – 'was but a reflection in a mirror . . . contemplation was unendurable; the mirror was broken' (TTL, 146). It was succeeded by a sense of nature's imperviousness in the face of human suffering, a sadly familiar theme in twentieth-century literature. 'Time Passes' is Woolf's most sustained meditation on time as artistic form; it portrays a world beyond the personal, a world 'on the mystical side of this solitude . . . not oneself but something in the universe' (*Diary* iii, 113).

In her next novel, *Orlando*, the passage of time and its disjunctions are more than ever present in a narrative that begins with its hero slicing at an African head (a scene that would be unacceptable today) (O, 11). Orlando will lose his masculinity and become female within a historical process that is marked by rupture at every turn. His radical physical change is heralded by a palace coup at Constantinople, as well as by a dislocation of the text in the form of a Jonsonian masque (O, 94–8). Later, the age of enlightenment is obliterated beneath storm clouds (O, 156) and a further storm interrupts Orlando's wedding ceremony, conveniently drowning out her promise to obey (O, 181). Her life is interrupted once again when she receives ten strokes on the head: 'it was ten o'clock in the morning. It was the eleventh of October. It was 1928. It was the present moment' (O, 206) – in fact, the day that *Orlando* was published and given to Vita Sackville-West, rather than the day on which Woolf wrote those words.

In *Orlando*, 'the present moment' is characterised (as the modernist movement so often is) by its fragmentation, its arbitrariness, typified by Orlando's abortive visit to Messrs Marshall & Snelgrove to buy 'boys' boots, bath salts and sardines' (O, 207). She struggles to come to terms with the sixty or seventy different times which beat simultaneously in every normal human system so that when eleven strikes, all the rest chime in unison, and the present is neither a violent disruption nor completely forgotten in the past. . . .The true length of a person's life, whatever the *Dictionary of National Biography* may say, is always a matter of dispute. For it is a difficult business – this time-keeping; nothing more quickly disorders it than contact with any of the arts (O, 211).

The idea that time is experienced differently by different individuals, and that each of us has a series of different internal clocks measuring different times plays upon Einstein's *Special Theory of Relativity* (1905) which established that time was not absolute but flowed at different rates for different observers moving at different speeds relative to one another. On the following page, Woolf links her multiple internal clocks with the multiple selves that inhabit us. As Gillian Beer has observed, 'Woolf, like most educated people of the 1920s, was well aware of Einstein as an intellectual presence. And like many others, she found his theories both baffling and magical'.[18]

Although the sense of time as disrupted sequence may be said to shape *Orlando*, one episode in particular embodies quite literally that 'smash and splinters' that Woolf had earlier associated with generational break: Orlando's great love affair turns out to be the most disruptive experience of all, taking place in a virtually non-existent time and space that anticipates T. S. Eliot's impossible 'midwinter spring' in *Little Gidding* – the middle of the frozen Thames in the mythically cold winter of 1608. The ice becomes the stage for a drama of love as Orlando first catches sight of Sasha, the impossible and perfect love object, skating towards him. Her departure coincides with the flood that breaks up the ice, bringing the hugest smash Woolf ever described: 'All was riot and confusion. The river was strewn with icebergs. Some of these were as broad as a bowling green and as high as a house; others no bigger than a man's hat, but most fantastically twisted' (O, 44). The river in spate is a figure for time itself, carrying away a bizarre medley of human and non-human life: 'Among other strange sights was to be seen a cat suckling its young; a table laid sumptuously for a supper of twenty; a couple in bed; together with an extraordinary number of cooking utensils' (O, 45). The dissolution of what had once seemed solid provides an unforgettable image of past experience, intensely remembered yet leaving no trace on the everyday world. Love turns to loss and is sluiced away by time. The end of the fair – or the end of the affair – on the ice is at once the most imaginative and the most violent of Woolf's moments of rupture.

What Woolf termed 'The little platform of present time on which I stand' (MB, 96)[19] also offered perspectives in her last two novels: *The*

*Years* ends with a section entitled 'The Present Day', while Miss La Trobe's pageant in *Between the Acts* ends with 'The Present Time', in which the actors hold up mirrors to the audience, for the present time consists of 'ourselves' (BA, 105–10). These present moments, present days, present times cut themselves loose from a past already selected and distorted by the mind. The past is continually being mythologised which makes it difficult to decide what power such moments of rupture actually possess – both *Orlando* and *Between the Acts* speculate as to whether people change fundamentally, or merely their clothes (O, 131–2; BA, 103–4).

The strange yet transitory nature of the present moment is explored most fully in a central passage from *The Years*, a passage which involves a train journey and the consciousness of a woman traveller, thus recapitulating elements of Woolf's essay, 'Mr Bennett and Mrs Brown' (and, before that, the third chapter of *Jacob's Room*, and her seminal short story 'An Unwritten Novel'). Woolf's exploration of the train's movement through time and space also recalls Einstein's repeated use of the figure of the railway carriage and its relation to an external observer in his 'plain exposition' of relativity theory for the lay reader. Later accounts such as Bertrand Russell's *ABC of Relativity* (1926) adopted this analogy.[20]

In the first half of the 1914 section of the novel it is spring, and Kitty, Lady Lasswade, gives a party. As the evening draws on, she becomes intensely aware that '[t]ime was passing', glancing at the hands of the clock, hearing it chime eleven, 'a succession of petulant little strokes' (Y, 193), for she plans to catch the overnight train to her country house in the North, and is anxiously aware that she had 'Run it rather fine' (Y, 197). Swiftly, she changes her clothes, snatches up her bags and is driven to the station where 'The yellow station clock showed that they had five minutes to spare' (Y, 196). 'Only just in time', says the railway guard, as he hands her into the compartment, echoing her thoughts (Y, 197).[21] The tightly regulated clock time of London is contrasted with Kitty's inner sense of time and the different time of the train journey which, like 'Time Passes', will also be a journey into the unconscious for Kitty. It is contrasted with seasonal time with which Kitty feels more at home and which she recovers as she reaches the countryside where 'the spring was late . . . the trees were not fully out yet' (Y, 199).

The train's movement in space parallels movement in time as Kitty travels: 'She seemed to be passing from one world to another; this was the moment of transition'. Climbing into her bunk,

> she felt a faint vibration against her head . . . The years changed things; destroyed things; heaped things up . . . The train rushed her on . . . How could

> she sleep? How could she prevent herself from thinking? . . . *Now* where are we? she said to herself. Where is the train at this moment? *Now*, she murmured, shutting her eyes, we are passing the white house on the hill; *now* we are going through the tunnel; *now* we are crossing the bridge over the river . . . A blank intervened; her thoughts became spaced; they became muddled. Past and present became jumbled together. (Y, 198–9)[22]

At this point she falls asleep. Kitty's attempt to equate her 'now', the present moment, with a 'here', a particular spot on her journey, suggests another recent theory in contemporary physics, Heisenberg's Uncertainty Principle (1927), according to which two variables, such as position and momentum or energy and time, cannot both be measured, since as one becomes more precise the other becomes less so, according to an exact formula, though the rule applies only to the sub-atomic particles studied in quantum mechanics.[23]

In the everyday world, Kitty's thoughts draw attention to the non-equivalence of time and space since, when travel through space stops, travel through time goes on as before, just as it goes on even when Kitty's consciousness surrenders to sleep. When she wakes, it is next morning although her country estate with its slow, seasonal time is also linked with the past rather than the present (and not only with Kitty's past, but also with her author's as Kitty watches the rubber-shoed pony pulling the lawn-mower, one of Virginia's enduring memories of St Ives). London, by contrast, stands for the present moment.

The train suggests the passage of time, though its movement is not identical with it. So too does Kitty's experience of travelling, releasing a series of involuntary memories and questions about time passing: 'All their clothes are the same, she thought; all their lives are the same. And which is right? . . . Which is wrong?' (Y, 198). Meanwhile her body tosses restlessly on the ledge of her bunk, cramped as if already in her coffin, yet finally absorbed into sleep, itself a brief rehearsal for death, the body's terminus and final escape from time. 'This is sleep . . . thank goodness, she said to herself, shutting [her eyes] again, this is sleep. And she resigned herself to the charge of the train' (Y, 199). She gives herself up to its care like a tired child with a nanny. Yet 'charge' can also signify a headlong movement that cannot easily be interrupted, as in 'The Charge of the Light Brigade'.

The charge of time carrying Kitty into the dark, takes her, she feels, from one world to another, from London to the country. But it does so in a further sense than she realises, a sense available to the reader but not to her, since this episode is dated '1914'. Within three months, war would be declared and would change the lives of most of those who lived through it in ways that wars had hardly done before, being less universal, more local and contained. So Kitty also stands for Everywoman. She cannot choose but resign herself to the charge of time that is also the determinism of history. The section ends with a moment of consolation as, gazing at the sky and the landscape, Kitty recovers her sense of self and happiness. For a moment she felt that 'Time had ceased' (Y, 203).

'That a break must be made in every life when August 1914 is reached seems inevitable. But the fracture differs, according to what is broken' (RF, 160), Woolf had written in her biography of Roger Fry. As she described the charge of the train that was time and history, carrying Kitty with it, and later when she wrote of the War closing in on Roger Fry (RF, 162), Woolf was conscious that she herself was caught up again in the charge of time and history, as it threatened to interfere once more with individual freedoms: the lessons of 1914 had not been learned; hopes for better international relations and an effective League of Nations had been disappointed; Europe was once more on track for a conflagration.

The combination of time and train travel in *The Years* suggests relativity theory, yet viewed simply as an analogy the train represents a classically linear conception of time. Seen from this point of view, the moment of rupture might threaten to become an accident, were there any such accidents in Woolf's work (as there are in Forster's *The Longest Journey*, for example). Instead, she links railway journeys with change or transition, passages from one stage of life to another, as in the third chapter of *Jacob's Room* (23–4) or the sixth chapter of *Orlando* (190). But thinking of time as running along railway lines creates further problems: some of these are articulated in Rachel Bowlby's book, *Feminist Destinations*, which takes Woolf's use of railway journeys for its central metaphor. Bowlby resists defining Woolf's sense of time as linear, since in her view such end-directed movement is too often the product of patriarchal attitudes and institutions – linked with Big Ben, and the determinism of clock time or Mr Ramsay's teleological logic. Female time, she feels, should be circular.[24]

Modernist time, too, is commonly regarded as circular, from Bergson's 'durée' (time as a continuous process of 'becoming'), through Nietzsche's concept of eternal recurrence, Yeats's spiralling and modal gyres, James Joyce's Viconian cycles, and even T. S. Eliot's sense of time as awaiting Christian redemption:

> Time present and time past
> Are both perhaps present in time future
> And time future contained in time past.
> If all time is eternally present
> All time is unredeemable.

Eliot's meditation on time at the beginning of 'Burnt Norton' was composed a little over a year after Woolf wrote Kitty's railway journey.[25]

Woolf too imagined time as cyclical and that vision finds its most powerful expression in *The Waves* where those changing, changeless, impersonal forces, 'time & the sea' (*Diary* iii, 264), the hours and the seasons are counterpointed to human repetitiveness and human mortality in images of still life and empty rooms. Cyclical time as 'woman's time' is most vividly evoked in a passage that only occurs in an early manuscript, a kind of dirge or lament for women as procreators, doomed to be broken and lost:

> Many mothers, & before them many mothers, & again many mothers have groaned and fallen. Like one wave succeeding another. Wave after wave, endlessly sinking & falling as far as the eye can stretch. And all these waves have been the prostrate forms of mothers, in their nightgowns, with the tumbled sheets about them holding up, with a groan, as they sink back into the sea.[26]

Like *Orlando*, if very differently, *The Waves* pits continuity and repetition against disjunction and change. As she worked on it, Woolf wondered

> Now is life very solid, or very shifting? I am haunted by the two contradictions. This has gone on for ever: will last for ever; goes down to the bottom of the world – this moment I stand on. Also it is transitory, flying, diaphanous. I shall pass like a cloud on the waves. (*Diary* iii, 218)

But always when Woolf moved from 'Un-' to 'Dis-' (BA, 119), from humanity united to humanity dispersed, from the body of the people to the body of the individual, she showed herself conscious of the body as subject to linear growth, development, decay and death, those forces at once within us, and beyond us. And though memory runs backwards across breaks and ruptures, losses and changes, the ability to remember and relive past events cannot alter the fact that they belong to the past. Writing is one way of stemming a sense of human loss, a way of recovering the past, recapturing its moments of plenitude, restoring the decayed house and recalling the dead. Woolf formulates and re-formulates her various breaks and spaces in time because it is across time's chasms, its gaps and fissures, that she must cast her art.

## Notes

1. See Diane Gillespie's edition of *Roger Fry* (1940; Oxford: Blackwell, Shakespeare Head, 1995), pp. xxv–xxxiii. For example, Woolf reprinted Fry's own account of his horror at school floggings, but, after consultation, omitted the words 'by my having an erection' – see pp. xxxii, 28.

2. McNeillie entitles it 'Character in Fiction' in his edition of Woolf's *Essays*, since this was the title she gave it when she published it in the *Criterion* in July 1924, and it distinguishes it from an earlier and shorter version of the same essay, also entitled 'Mr Bennett and Mrs Brown' – for further publication details, see *Essays* iii, 436.
3. *Virginia Woolf: The Critical Heritage*, ed. Robin Majumdar and Allen McLaurin (London: Routledge and Kegan Paul, 1975), p. 113.
4. Their meeting probably took place at Ottoline Morrell's house in Bedford Square. A 1938 diary entry (*Diary* v, 155) puts it at 1909, but this seems to be a mistake.
5. In a review published 18 February 1921 in the *Woman's Leader*, and reprinted in *Roger Fry*, p. 381.
6. 'Mark Gertler: The Man and His Art', *The Studio*, September 1932, cited by Jane Hill, *The Art of Dora Carrington* (New York: Thames and Hudson, 1994), p. 19.
7. 'Art and Life', *Vision and Design* (1920; London: Chatto and Windus, 1928), p. 11.
8. Ibid., pp. 12, 14, 15.
9. George Dangerfield, *The Strange Death of Liberal England* (1935; London: Paladin, 1970), p. 14. I am indebted to Peter Stansky, *On or About December 1910: Early Bloomsbury and its Intimate World* (Cambridge, MA: Harvard University Press, 1996), p. 4, for the reference to Dangerfield, and to both books for the summary of the political events of November 1910 that follows.
10. Stansky, ibid., p. 7.
11. 'Twice in one week the great Albert Hall was filled to overflowing, and enthusiasm and hope ran high', wrote Ray Strachey in *The Cause: A Short History of the Women's Movement in Great Britain* (1928; London: Virago, 1978), p. 316. Virginia wrote to Violet Dickinson in mid-November 1910, 'My time has been wasted a good deal upon Suffrage. We went to two meetings, at which about a dozen people spoke, like the tollings of a bell. If they spoke faster all their words went into one. It was at the Albert Hall. The only amusement was that a baby cried incessantly, and this was taken by some as a bitter sarcasm against women having the vote' (*Letters* i, 438).
12. Dangerfield, pp. 148–50.
13. Stansky, pp. 164–7; Dangerfield, p. 221.
14. See references to 'Mr Asquith's Irish policy' (J's R, 91); ' "I say, will King George give way about the peers?" ' (113); 'nor was he altogether in favour of giving Home Rule to Ireland' (121).
15. Paul Johnson, preface to Dangerfield, p. 10.
16. Dangerfield, p. 372.
17. Allusions to the coming war occur on pp. 83, 136 and 150–4, and are embedded in Jacob's surname and his place of birth. Scarborough was the site of the first civilian casualties in Britain in December 1914, when it was shelled from the sea by German warships – see Martin Gilbert, *First World War* (London: HarperCollins, 1995), p. 110.
18. 'Physics, Sound and Substance: Later Woolf' in *Virginia Woolf: The Common Ground* (Edinburgh: Edinburgh University Press, 1996) p. 117. Beer examines Woolf's use of contemporary physics, here and in *Wave,*

*Atom, Dinosaur: Woolf's Science* (London: Virginia Woolf Society of Great Britain, 2000).

19. The Cambridge Apostles had apparently attempted to define 'the present' – in a letter to Lytton Strachey, Leonard Woolf refers to a discussion on the topic between G. E. Moore and Bertrand Russell, 13 July 1903, *The Letters of Leonard Woolf*, ed. Frederic Spotts (London: Bloomsbury, 1990), p. 32.
20. Einstein refers frequently to 'our old friend the railway carriage' in *Relativity: The Special and General Theory: A Popular Exposition*, trans. Robert W. Lawson (London: Methuen, 1920). Bertrand Russell's *ABC of Relativity* was reviewed in *The Nation and Athenaeum* (of which Leonard Woolf was literary editor) on 13 June 1925. See also Alan J. Friedman and Carol C. Donley, *Einstein as Myth and Muse* (Cambridge: Cambridge University Press, 1985), p. 14.
21. Avrom Fleishman, *Virginia Woolf: A Critical Reading* (Baltimore, MD: Johns Hopkins University Press, 1975) points out and discusses the recurring references to time 'built up with Proustian regularity' throughout the 1914 section, pp. 188–90.
22. The last ellipsis is Woolf's.
23. Friedman and Donley identify the influence of the Uncertainty Principle on *The Waves* (1931), p. 141. For them, 'Woolf, like many other modern writers, recognised the necessity to create literary form which could carry the concepts of relativity, uncertainty and complementarity', p. 146.
24. Bowlby, *Feminist Destinations* (Oxford: Basil Blackwell, 1988), esp. pp. 75–8, 89–91 (though there is extensive discussion of Woolf's treatment of time throughout).
25. This sequence was originally written for the Second Priest in *Murder in the Cathedral*, first performed in June 1935. Woolf had finished the 1914 episode by 17 December 1933 (*Diary* iv, 193).
26. *The Waves: The Two Holograph Drafts*, ed. J. W. Graham (Toronto and Buffalo: University of Toronto Press with University of Western Ontario, 1976), Draft 1, p. 7.

Essay 9

# 'Like a Shell on a Sandhill': Woolf's Images of Emptiness

> To show how very little control of our possessions we have – what an accidental affair this living is after all our civilisation – let me just count over a few of the things lost in our lifetime, beginning, for that seems always the most mysterious of losses – what cat would gnaw, what rat would nibble – three pale blue canisters of book-binding tools? Then there were the bird cages, the iron hoops, the steel skates, the Queen Anne coal-scuttle, the bagatelle board, the hand organ – all gone, and jewels too. Opals and emeralds, they lie about the roots of turnips. (CSF, 84)

As the narrator of 'The Mark on the Wall' implies, the unexpected disappearance of material objects can highlight their normal durability, and, for Woolf, things were too often harder and more enduring than human beings. Things frequently outlast us, becoming mementos of human brevity, of the ephemeral nature of our lives. The famous question she asked in her diary at the beginning of 1929, 'Now is life very solid, or very shifting?', suggests that, while life itself can feel one way or the other, ultimately it is 'things', 'solid objects', that survive us, while we remain trapped in the inevitable processes of time, change, decay, loss and death – 'one flying after another, so quick so quick' (*Diary* iii, 218).

Minta, in *To the Lighthouse*, loses her pearl brooch on the beach,[1] and Paul attempts to mark the place with his stick, determined to come back next morning at low tide and find it for her before the waves carry it away, to leave it lying among the roots of seaweed. Sand and stones are constant elements in this novel, and Mr Ramsay contrasts their duration with that of human life: 'The very stone one kicks with one's boot will outlast Shakespeare' (TTL, 41). His remark gains a special force in a novel where footwear is oddly recursive: Mrs Ramsay runs 'across the lawn in galoshes to snatch a child from mischief' (TTL, 35); Mr Bankes approves Lily's 'excellent' shoes which 'allowed the toes their natural expansion' (TTL, 22), while Lily praises Mr Ramsay's 'beautiful boots!' when she is at a loss as to what else to say to him (TTL, 167–8). Boots belong to the particular type of things with which this account is concerned – things as containers that silently, unconsciously, mourn the life they once held, that nurse an imprint of a former life; for objects are imprinted with human life, and it is this that gives them their particular significance for Woolf – not only in *To the Lighthouse*, but also in *Jacob's Room* and *The Waves*, all novels that are, in some sense, elegies (*Diary* iii, 34). This aspect of things is summed up in the last two lines of *Jacob's Room*: ' "What am I to do with these, Mr Bonamy?" She held out a pair of Jacob's old shoes' (J's R, 155).

*Jacob's Room* searches for its central figure through the various spaces, places, people and objects that once held him – his shoes, his rooms, his loves, and the life he left behind in them, evident even in his chair: 'One fibre in the wicker arm-chair creaks, though no one sits there' (J's R, 31; 155). Indeed, the novel itself is just such an empty container, recording the traces and imprints of Jacob's life, and the narrator's search for those traces, as he disappears, the representative of a whole generation of young men lost in the killing fields of Flanders, anticipated in his surname. But the novel also questions whether one can ever know another human being, whether it is even possible to record the facts about another person. This wider epistemological crisis is deftly and touchingly concealed behind the appearances of familiar places, people and things, even though these things themselves further underscore the impossibility of such knowledge.

*Jacob's Room* begins on a beach, where Betty Flanders is writing a letter, a scene that is replayed in *To the Lighthouse* as Lily's memory of Mrs Ramsay after her death. Lily remembers her sitting on the beach writing letters, while she and Charles Tansley skimmed flat stones across the surface of the water (TTL, 174–5). Their activity recalls another scene concerned with the elusive nature of things, in the short story 'Solid Objects'. Here, another Charles also skims stones while his friend John burrows his fingers deep into the sand, finding that 'the water oozes round your finger-tips; the hole then becomes a moat; a well; a spring; a secret channel to the sea'. In the sand he encounters 'something hard – a full drop of solid matter' which he gradually brings back to the surface. It turns out to be 'a lump of glass, so thick as to be almost opaque' (CSF, 103), a solid object that is almost fluid, an object shaped by nature to resemble a work of art, brought to the surface after burrowing deep into consciousness to the watery place beneath, for by now the recovery of this mysterious object has become an allegory of the creative process that Woolf elsewhere described in terms of diving or fishing.[2]

The scene of Mrs Flanders writing on the beach which begins *Jacob's Room* is the novel's primal scene of writing, but it is also a scene of mourning, for Betty Flanders is writing about her dead husband Seabrook, and weeping, her tears blurring her vision as she writes. Her husband Seabrook lies buried, 'enclosed in three shells' – that is, in three coffins (J's R, 3, 10). In her own way, Betty too is writing an elegy, rather like Lily Briscoe as she remembers, mourns for and celebrates Mrs Ramsay through her painting – or even like Woolf herself as she remembers her brother Thoby through Jacob Flanders, and her mother through Mrs Ramsay.

While Betty Flanders writes and weeps, little Jacob is running across the sands, feeling lost and abandoned, when he catches sight of 'a whole skull – perhaps a cow's skull, a skull, perhaps, with the teeth in it. Sobbing but absent-mindedly, he ran farther and farther away until he held the skull in his arms' (J's R, 5). His action is at once naturalistic and psychologically plausible, and yet at the same time emblematic – it is as if Jacob is reaching out for his own death. 'Throw it away, dear, do' (J's R, 6), says his mother as they walk home from the beach, but he can't let it go. Back at their lodgings, the children are put to bed and the wind begins to rise (as it does at the end of 'The Window' in *To the Lighthouse*). Betty Flanders, anticipating Mrs Ramsay with Cam, attempts to soothe the restless Archer: 'Think of the fairies . . . the lovely, lovely birds settling down on their nests . . .' (J's R, 7–8; TTL, 124–5).

Archer's restlessness prefigures that of the sleepers in 'Time Passes': he 'spread out, with one arm striking across the pillow'. As consciousness, the most familiar form of life, drains away, Woolf creates an early version of the nocturnal scene that will ultimately become 'Time Passes', but here she treats it as if she were an impressionist painter, recording the light as it falls upon the different surfaces in the children's room:

> The wind actually stirred the cloth on the chest of drawers, and let in a little light, so that the sharp edge of the chest of drawers was visible, running straight up, until a white shape bulged out; and a silver streak showed in the looking glass.
>
> In the other bed by the door Jacob lay asleep, fast asleep, profoundly unconscious. The sheep's jaw with the big yellow teeth in it lay at his feet. He had kicked it against the iron bed-rail. (J's R, 9)

Sleep is the brother of death. The book that begins with Jacob holding a sheep's skull in his arms, and ends with his empty shoes, traces the outline of a man who cannot in the end be captured or pinned down, a man who no longer inhabits his own skull. He is as elusive, as ephemeral as the light that traces the edges of the furniture, as if the external surface is all that we can know of another person. The movement of the light in this scene anticipates its action in the interludes of *The Waves*.

*Jacob's Room* is haunted by what Jacob will not survive to become, so that clichés about the lives of great men become a recurrent theme, exemplified in his Cambridge essay, 'Does History consist of the Biographies of Great Men?' (J's R, 31). Miss Julia Hedge, the feminist, sitting beneath the hollow dome of the British Museum Reading Room (itself a figure for a skull crowded with knowledge) reads the names written in gilt letters 'all round the dome – the names of great men which remind us – "Oh damn," said Julia Hedge, "Why didn't they leave room for an Eliot or a Brontë?" ' Woolf's wording here recalls a favourite Victorian schoolroom poem, Longfellow's 'Psalm of Life':

> Lives of great men all remind us
> We can make our own sublime,
> And, departing, leave behind us
> Footprints on the sands of time.

The novel begins with Jacob running across the sand, and ends with his empty shoes. Longfellow's 'sands of time' suggest a desert or a waste land, levelling out all human life – a setting like that in which Shelley's Ozymandias warned the traveller of his own oblivion: 'Round the decay/ Of that colossal wreck, boundless and bare/ The lone and level sands stretch far away.' Sands are the product of slow time and are themselves very ancient – in this respect, they resemble the 'little sandy beaches where no one had been since the beginning of time' (TTL, 76) and which will still be there when human life has come to an end. The tiny grains of sand – minute things in themselves, yet too small and too numerous to be treated individually – are themselves often used to stand for time and its passing, our lost and irretrievable minutes as they slip through the waist of an hourglass (formerly the standard way of measuring the passage of an hour). Figuring both the uncountable and the particular, sands are not only paradoxical but also liminal, for sandhills lie, quite literally, at the ends of the earth where 'The waves broke on the shore' (W, 228).

For Woolf, sand was an essential element in some of her earliest and happiest memories, memories of Cornwall, and of Talland House at St Ives where the Stephen family had stayed for several months each summer from 1882 (the year Virginia was born) until 1894 when she was twelve years old – the years of happiness and security before her mother's sudden death in May 1895. 'If life has a base that it stands upon', she wrote in her unfinished autobiography,

> if it is a bowl that one fills and fills and fills – then my bowl without a doubt stands upon this memory . . . of lying half asleep, half awake, in bed in the nursery at St Ives . . . of hearing the waves breaking . . . of hearing the blind draw its little acorn across the floor as the wind blew the blind out . . . of feeling the purest ecstasy I can conceive. (MB, 78–9)[3]

Both the acorn and the waves are traditional images of genesis, birth or rebirth.

Talland House and its garden with scented escallonia hedges, geraniums tumbling from stone urns and red hot pokers and, below the garden, the sandhills, rock pools and waves were for Woolf an archetype or figure of paradise, an idealised pastoral landscape. Yet, as in traditional pastoral, it already contained the threat of its own ending, implicit from the beginning, for 'et in Arcadia ego', I too am in Arcadia, says death. Talland House, so full of life, seemed doomed to be deserted, abandoned, to be

> left like a shell on a sandhill to fill with dry salt grains now that life had left it. The long night seemed to have set in; the trifling airs, nibbling, the clammy breaths, fumbling, seemed to have triumphed. The saucepan had rusted and the mat decayed . . . Idly, aimlessly, the swaying shawl swung to and fro. (TTL, 149–50)

Mrs Ramsay had used her green cashmere shawl to cloak or disguise the threat of death implicit in the boar's skull nailed to the nursery wall – an object which delights James and distresses Cam (who is also Virginia herself as a little girl). The skull, lying on the sand in the opening scene of *Jacob's Room* and hung up on the nursery wall in *To the Lighthouse*, is perhaps the most familiar of all *memento mori*. Mrs Ramsay's attempt to protect her children from the knowledge of death will prove vain, in the literal sense of empty. The empty shell on the sandhill stands for both the empty house and the empty skull – things or containers now emptied of the life they once held, *memento mori* set among the blowing sandhills of time. The vision of death occurring in the midst of life (a theme echoed from *Mrs. Dalloway*[4]) corresponds to the tripartite structure of *To the Lighthouse* as it progresses from the plenitude of life ('The Window') to the emptiness of death ('Time Passes'), returning to life once more in 'The Lighthouse'.

From the novel's opening page, things are heavy with the possibility of human loss or destruction, whether they are actual objects – furniture or clothes – mere representations like the pictures that James is cutting out from the Army and Navy Stores catalogue, or else creations of the imagination whose significance lies in the fact of their absence. The most unexpected example of this last category is the scrubbed deal table, 'grained and knotted' and upended in the fork of a tree, that Lily Briscoe associates with Mr Ramsay's studies (TTL, 28, 169–70). Philosophically speaking, this too is a figure signifying absence, since Andrew had explained his father's work by telling Lily to 'Think of a kitchen table . . . when you're not there' – an idea derived from Mr Ramsay's (and perhaps Leslie

Stephen's) study of the British empiricists, Locke, Hume and Berkeley. Berkeley had enquired whether a thing existed when there was no one to see it and his question occasions the opening of E. M. Forster's novel, *The Longest Journey* (1907), which begins with an undergraduate argument as to whether there can be a cow in the meadow, if there is no one there to see it: 'It was philosophy. They were discussing the existence of objects. Do they only exist when there is someone to look at them? or have they a real existence of their own?' More serious concerns as to the nature of reality underpin the rest of the novel.

Mr Ramsay is comparably concerned with 'Subject and object and the nature of reality' (TTL, 28), philosophical problems that fascinated Woolf herself as she struggled to envisage 'the thing that exists when we're not there', to imagine the world in the absence of a human eye to record it. Lily Briscoe aspires to a comparable vision when she reflects that 'distant views seem to outlast by a million years . . . the gazer and to be communing already with a sky which beholds an earth entirely at rest' (TTL, 25). And just such a vision of non-human peace – of an empty house, traversed by sunlight, moonlight and light winds, free of the perpetual frets of human joy or pain – will be created in the interludes of *The Waves*.

'Time Passes' was Woolf's first conscious attempt to describe 'an empty house, no people's characters, the passage of time, all eyeless & featureless' (*Diary* iii, 76), but *Jacob's* [empty] *Room* and *The Waves* all, in their different ways anticipate or enlarge upon her explorations. Thus Bernard's soliloquy in the ninth chapter of *The Waves* confronts 'the world seen without a self', a wordless place, emptied of meaning, where 'there is nothing. No fin breaks the waste of this immeasurable sea . . . No echo comes', a vision of the absence of colour, 'like the eclipse when the sun went out' which 'left the earth . . . withered, brittle, false', 'a waste of shadow', a 'dust dance' of lives (W, 218–19). Yet gradually, just as light returns to the world after the eclipse, life recovers and 'for a moment [Bernard] had sat on the turf somewhere high above the flow of the sea and the sound of the woods, had seen the house, the garden, and the waves breaking' (W, 221). Beyond the old labour of being a 'self', there lies a place of immunity from the burden of consciousness 'where no one had been since the beginning of time' (TTL, 76).

The antithesis of this cherished yet imaginary refuge is the world of things, with their unresponsive capacity to survive. The Ramsays' holiday home is furnished with the 'crazy ghosts of chairs and tables' (TTL, 32), cast-offs from the family's London life. The first things encountered in the novel are merely the objects illustrated in the catalogue that James is cutting out, yet they acquire a strange life of their own – a refrigerator, a rake, a mowing machine, and later 'the picture of a pocket knife with six blades which could only be cut out if James was very careful' (TTL, 21). This last recalls James's Oedipal desire for 'an axe . . . a poker, or any weapon' with which to gash 'a hole in his father's breast', while Mr Ramsay, in turn, is as 'lean as a knife, narrow as the blade of one' and quite as cutting (TTL, 8). James would always keep 'this old symbol of taking a knife and striking his father to the heart' (TTL, 199). Against this imagined violence, Mrs Ramsay fills the house up with herself and her family, both literally and metaphorically: soothing her difficult husband,

> she created drawing-room and kitchen, set them all aglow . . . (as a nurse carrying a light across a dark room assures a fractious child) . . . the house was full; the garden blowing. If he put implicit faith in her, nothing should hurt him. (TTL, 43–4)

Yet the vision she creates to reassure her husband is interrupted by a presentiment of danger that her very promises open up: 'So boasting of her capacity to surround and protect, there was scarcely a shell of herself left for her to know herself by; all was so lavished and spent' (TTL, 44). She empties herself to fill his needs. When Mr Ramsay departs, 'like a child who drops off satisfied', Mrs Ramsay collapses and 'the whole fabric fell in exhaustion upon itself' (TTL, 44) as physical tiredness is succeeded by a sense of unease at her husband's evident dependence on her. This is the first of the novel's images of the empty shell, yet, like the house that it suggests or stands in for, the shell can also symbolise plenitude and fullness: in the form of a cornucopia (literally, a horn of plenty), it stands at the centre of the Ramsays' dinner table, surrounded by lush fruit. Rose (a version of Virginia's sister Vanessa) has created a miniature work of art using a 'horny pink-lined shell', an image that brings together female fecundity and masculine desire. Rose's beautiful arrangement makes her mother think of 'a trophy fetched from the bottom of the sea', of Neptune's banquet or Bacchus' vine leaves (TTL, 105). And, as Mrs Ramsay gazes at it, 'she felt more and more serene' (TTL, 118).

The figure of the shell combines life and plenitude – the fruitfulness of Mrs Ramsay as the eternal mother, pink-lined, birth-giving – with fragility and, ultimately, emptiness. Alone, Mr Ramsay condescendingly thinks of his wife and son as 'children picking up shells, divinely innocent and occupied with little trifles at their feet and somehow entirely defenceless against a doom which he perceived' (TTL, 39), as if half remembering Newton's words,

> to myself I seem to have been only like a boy playing on the sea-shore and diverting myself in now and then finding a smoother pebble or a prettier

> shell than ordinary, whilst the great ocean of truth lay all undiscovered before me.[5]

Mr Ramsay's perception unconsciously anticipates his wife's barely suppressed sense of looming disaster. The empty shell that expresses her exhaustion in the face of her husband's demands also foretells her death. The shell is thus linked with the skull, the *memento mori* which (like Paul Rayley's watch that he keeps in its own wash-leather bag) is a symbol of time running out and so, once again, of death which must be covered or concealed as the ultimately 'fetishised' object. The word 'shell' (cognate with shale or scale) is derived from the Old Germanic 'skalj' or 'skal', something bowl-shaped, concave or hollow, and so is likely to be connected with the word 'skull' (whose origin, according to the *OED*, is obscure). Whether or not there is a philological connection, the shell and the skull are linked as containers of a former life. In a sudden outburst in her diary as she worked on *Jacob's Room*, Woolf wrote, 'Our generation is daily scourged by the bloody war. Even I scribble reviews instead of novels because of the thick skulls at Westminster & Berlin' (*Diary* ii, 51). Perhaps she was thinking of the battlefield as another Golgotha ('the place of the skull').

In the context of the battlefield, the word 'shell' had a very different meaning: unlike the skull which encased the brain matter, the shell encased material intended to destroy human flesh, and this is the sense that Mr Ramsay invokes, as he marches up and down the terrace, uttering 'a loud cry, as of a sleep-walker, half roused, something about "Stormed at with shot and shell" ' (TTL, 21). He is reciting from Tennyson's 'Charge of the Light Brigade'. 'The Window' section of *To the Lighthouse* is intermittently interrupted by loud, threatening sounds; the first, heard only by Mrs Ramsay, sounds

> like a ghostly roll of drums [that] remorselessly beat the measure of life, made one think of the destruction of the island and its engulfment in the sea, and warned her whose day had slipped past in one quick doing after another that it was all ephemeral as a rainbow – this sound . . . suddenly thundered hollow in her ears and made her look up with an impulse of terror. (TTL, 20)

Later, another silent explosion, this time of Lily's thoughts, is immediately followed by a gunshot as Jasper attacks a flock of starlings with his rifle, and Mr Ramsay 'boomed tragically at them, "Someone had blundered!" ' (TTL, 30). Sudden startling sounds, like the evening gun-salute on the Piraeus near the end of *Jacob's Room*, foretell the coming of the war, or recall it, as does the explosion heard by Mrs Dalloway in Bond Street (MD, 14) – just as the empty shells and the skull, even the

Shakespeare sonnet that Mrs Ramsay reads to herself ('From you have I been absent in the spring') anticipate her departure in death. Lily later pictures Mrs Ramsay raising a wreath of white flowers to her forehead, a bride walking beside a shadowy companion across the fields of death (TTL, 196–7).

'Time Passes' is the novel's place of absence and emptiness, beginning with the sleepers' absence of consciousness, and figured initially as a downpouring of darkness. Blowing winds and the encroaching sands of time attack the empty house. Objects within the house – 'the bare legs of tables, saucepans and china . . . a pair of shoes, a shooting cap . . . in the emptiness indicated how once they were filled and animated', while the looking glass 'had held a world hollowed out' (TTL, 141). The folds of her green shawl that Mrs Ramsay had used to conceal the skull, with all the slowness and vastness of an avalanche, work loose and swing in the air – death, after all, cannot be hidden or confined to parentheses. More ominous sounds like huge hammer-blows further loosen the shawl and crack the tea-cups. The thud of some nameless object falling presages the fall of the shell that will kill Andrew in France (TTL, 145).

Woolf adopts the imagery of wind and storm to suggest the coming of war, as Yeats had done in his poems on the Irish Civil War.[6] Yet even as she does so, she also analyses the cultural process involved in the creation of imaginary links between man and nature, and sees the experience of war as bringing such habits of thinking to an end. For with the Great War came the end of the romantic vision of nature as responding to the human world or working in subtle harmony with it, and in its wake, nature came to be regarded as an alien, incomprehensible force. Storms could no longer figure or prefigure human violence, since such habits of thought had been exposed as part of a larger process of self-deception. Mystics and visionaries, walking beside the sea, could no longer believe that the 'beauty outside mirrored beauty within': 'Did Nature supplement what man advanced? Did she complete what he began? With equal complacence she saw his misery, condoned his meanness and acquiesced in his torture' (TTL, 146). As in war poems such as Wilfred Owen's 'Exposure', nature was now revealed as indifferent, or worse. The romantic vision had collapsed – 'the mirror was broken', and the passage that follows demonstrates nature's chaos and violence – the mindless, meaningless tossing of winds and waves, 'battling and tumbling in brute confusion and wanton lust . . . eyeless and so terrible' (TTL, 147).

'The house was left; the house was deserted . . . left like a shell on a sandhill . . . the long night seemed to have set in . . .' (TTL, 149). 'Time Passes' brings together the transition from consciousness to unconsciousness, from life to death, from peace to war, and from the cultural values of the nineteenth to those of the twentieth century – a process that involves not only an emptying out of the numinous, a sense of man's changed relationship to his environment, a draining of things – of chairs and tables, houses and shells, and of the life that once inhabited them, but also an alteration and a darkening of their significance, so that familiar objects – Mrs Ramsay's grey cloak or her galoshes – become reminders of absence, loss and death. 'There were boots and shoes; and a brush and comb left on the dressing-table, for all the world as if she expected to come back to-morrow' (TTL, 148). 'The Lighthouse' section wakes to a world that is bare and empty, with a hole at the centre corresponding to the gap at the centre of Lily's painting. It can only be filled by the vision of Mrs Ramsay, her shadow cast over the step once more. As Mr Ramsay steps onto the solid rock beneath the enduring lighthouse, and Lily's moment of vision dissolves, the novel ends, as if anticipating Woolf's question of 1929 as to whether life is very solid or very shifting.

The shell thus acquires at least three different significances in *To the Lighthouse*: as cornucopia, it is female, fecund, life-giving – both Mrs Ramsay's fragile shell of self, and the pink shell at the centre of the dining-room table that pleases her so much. Thus linked with Mrs Ramsay, it is also associated with the first section of the novel, 'The Window'. Its second meaning is military, man-made and destructive – Mr Ramsay shouting 'Stormed at with shot and shell . . . ', and, as the survivor, Mr Ramsay is most closely linked with the third section, 'The Lighthouse' (though there he recites Cowper's self-pitying lines – 'But I beneath a rougher sea/ Was whelmed in deeper gulfs than he', rather than 'The Charge of the Light Brigade'). Its third meaning is that of a container emptied of life, a place of silence and absence – the world of 'Time Passes'; yet that world is potentially generative since its silence and emptiness acts as an invitation to the imagination.

In her final novel, *Between the Acts*, Woolf returned to these images and reworked them: now the dining room of Pointz Hall has become an empty shell, 'a shell, singing of what was before time was' (BA, 24), an alabaster urn singing of its own emptiness. It is contrasted with the fecund, muddy lily pond (BA, 28), the novel's place of creativity, but ultimately the two are one, for the emptiness of the shell is the necessary precondition to the fullness of the pond. In the preface to her first novel, *Madeleine*, Woolf's friend Hope Mirrlees had written, 'Art is like the dauntless, plastic force that builds up stubborn, amorphous substance cell by cell, into the frail geometry of a shell.'[7] Perhaps Woolf remembered that when she came, reluctantly, to describe the composition of *Mrs Dalloway* for her American publisher: 'the idea started as the oyster starts or the snail to secrete a house for itself. And this it did without any conscious direction' (*Essays* iv, 550).

## Notes

1. Woolf recorded losing her own 'little mother of pearl' brooch on 3 March 1926 as she was drafting this episode (*Diary* iii, 64) – see *To the Lighthouse: The Original Holograph* ed. Susan Dick (London: Hogarth Press, 1983) p. 126. She was to begin the following section on 5 March (p. 129).
2. See, for example, *Letters* iv, 223; 'Professions for Women', CE ii, 287.
3. As children, the Stephens compared 'Kensington Gardens with St Ives, always of course to the disadvantage of London. That was one of the pleasures of scrunching the shells with which now and then the Flower Walk was strewn. They had little ribs on them like the shells on the beach'. Behind the Flower Walk had been a swamp, where Nessa and Thoby had found the skeleton of a dog (MB, 88).
4. 'Oh! thought Clarissa, in the middle of my party, here's death, she thought' (MD, 201).
5. David Brewster, *Memoirs of Newton*, (1855) vol. 2, chapter 27.
6. For example in 'Meditations in Time of Civil War' (1923). Woolf read Yeats's *Autobiographies* at the end of 1926, and also knew his poetry (he had been awarded the Nobel prize in 1923).
7. *Madeleine, One of Love's Jansenists* (London: W. Collins, 1919), p. vii.

Essay 10

# Constantinople: At the Crossroads of the Imagination

In *A Room of One's Own*, Virginia Woolf describes the novel as 'leaving a shape on the mind's eye, built now in squares, now pagoda shaped, now throwing out wings and arcades, now solidly compact and domed like the Cathedral of Santa Sofia at Constantinople' (ROO, 64). She had learned from Roger Fry and her brother-in-law Clive Bell to think of her own art, as well as the plastic arts, in terms of 'significant form'. Indeed, in his account of the subject, Bell had posed the question,

> What quality is common to Sta. Sophia and the windows at Chartres, Mexican sculpture, a Persian bowl, Chinese carpets, Giotto's frescoes at Padua, and the masterpieces of Poussin, Piero della Francesca, and Cézanne? Only one answer seems possible – significant form.[1]

Was Woolf thinking, as she wrote these words, of *Orlando*, her most recent novel, in which the third chapter is actually set in Constantinople, or was it *To the Lighthouse* that seemed to her so 'solidly compact and domed'? Yet for Woolf, Santa Sofia was not merely 'very solid', it was also 'very shifting' (*Diary* iii, 218):

> like a treble globe of bubbles frozen solid, floating out to meet us. For it is fashioned in the shape of some fine substance, thin as glass, blown in plump curves; save that it is also as substantial as a pyramid . . . beautiful & evanescent & enduring . . .[2]

That was how the great mosque (or cathedral) had appeared to her when she first visited it with Vanessa and Violet Dickinson in October 1906. And as Lyndall Gordon has shown, it became for her a metaphor for 'delicacy of treatment with strength of form'.[3] That paradox of weight and weightlessness, of granite and rainbow, dominates Woolf's sense of *To the Lighthouse*, just as it dominates Lily Briscoe's artistic aims, so that her portrait of Mrs Ramsay parallels the novel itself. Lily too envisages her painting in terms of a paradox, 'the colour burning on a framework of steel; the light of a butterfly's wing lying upon the arches of a cathedral' (TTL, 54, and see 186).

Historically speaking, Santa Sofia is itself a series of paradoxes: formerly a great Christian cathedral built by Justinian at the height of the Byzantine Empire, inheriting the mantle of Rome after its fall, it stands at the crossroads of East and West, not simply geographically but spiritually too, since after 1453 it became the greatest mosque in Constantinople. The city itself became the seat of the Caliph, spiritual leader of the Moslems, just as it had been the seat of the Patriarch of the Greek Orthodox Church. It stood not only on an East–West axis (where Asia met Europe met Russia; where Moslem met Christian Orthodox met Roman Catholic), but also on a North–South axis: high in the gallery of Santa Sofia is a runic inscription, dating from the tenth century, which records that the Vikings too reached Constantinople. The city, renamed Istanbul in 1930, thus stands at the crossroads – and not merely of the imagination.

Of course, Woolf thought of the structure of *To the Lighthouse* in various ways as she began writing, yet looking back from the late 1930s she recalled its composition in terms of '[b]lowing bubbles out of a pipe' (MB, 92), and her early memories of Constantinople also surface within the novel itself. In her 1906 journal, the young Virginia Stephen had recorded that

> the most splendid thing in Constantinople . . . is the prospect of the roofs of the town, seen from the high ground of Pera. For in the morning a mist lies like a veil that muffles treasures across all the houses & all the mosques; then as the sun rises, you catch hints of the heaped mass within; then a pinnacle of gold pierces the soft mesh, & you see shapes of precious stuff lumped together. And slowly the mist withdraws, & all the wealth of gleaming houses & rounded mosques lies clear on the solid earth, & the broad waters run bright as daylight through their midst.[4]

This classic view of the city reappears on the second page of Woolf's first novel, *The Voyage Out*, now transposed to London, where '[s]ometimes the flats and churches and hotels of Westminster are like the outlines of Constantinople in a mist' (VO, 4).

In *To the Lighthouse*, as Nancy walks with Minta Doyle 'along the road to the cliff' and down to the beach, she repeatedly catches Nancy's hand; each time she does so, Nancy wonders 'What was it she wanted?' For a moment, Nancy shares her author's vision of 'the whole world spread out beneath her, as if it were Constantinople seen through a mist'. It seems that she must ask ' "Is that Santa Sofia?" "Is that the Golden Horn?" ', as unidentified forms emerge – 'a pinnacle, a dome; prominent things, without names'. But when Minta drops Nancy's hand to run down the hillside, 'whatever it was that had protruded through the mist, sank down into it and disappeared' (TTL, 81). But what is it that emerges from the mist as Minta clasps Nancy's hand? Is it Minta's hopes for the future, her excitement at her impending engagement, which she communicates through touch, or is it some unspoken sexual charge that briefly unites the two young women on the threshold of life? In the third section of the book, Nancy's younger sister Cam again links Constantinople with form or design emerging from chaos, as drops of joy illuminate 'the dark, the slumberous shapes in her mind; shapes of a world not realised but turning in their darkness, catching here and there, a spark of light; Greece, Rome, Constantinople' (TTL, 205) – moments of high civilisation, briefly redeemed from the nightmare of history.

Constantinople had figured glancingly in *Mrs Dalloway* as a site of sexual crisis, the place where Clarissa, 'through some contraction of this cold spirit . . . had failed' her husband Richard (MD, 34, 129). It may be that both here and in *To the Lighthouse* we should read the city as standing for love between women, as David Roessel has argued,[5] (402), though it may equally signify the return of the repressed, the visible rising of desire from the mists of the unconscious. But in *Orlando*, Woolf's next novel, Constantinople is quite explicitly linked with women, and women who love women, from the moment of its inception. Before she had even decided what that book was to be about, or that it would portray her beloved Vita Sackville-West, Woolf wrote a preliminary sketch for it in a diary entry for March 1927, only weeks before the publication of *To the Lighthouse*. It was to be called 'The Jessamy Brides' and would focus on lesbian love: 'Two women, poor, solitary, at the top of a house . . . the ladies of Llangollen . . . Sapphism is to be suggested . . . The Ladies are to have Constantinople in view. Dreams of golden domes' (*Diary* iii, 131). Were those golden domes the voluptuous curves of the female body? In the event, most of this scheme was abandoned as self-censorship transmuted homosexual into heterosexual love. Almost the only element to survive was Constantinople itself: with its 'Dreams of golden domes', it became both the literal and, arguably, the psychic centre of *Orlando*, a place of transit from one state of being to another, from manhood to womanhood – it was a natural setting for transition, both geographical and spiritual.

Sent as ambassador to Constantinople, Orlando enjoys exactly the same view of the city that Virginia had described in 1906, and Nancy had glimpsed as she held Minta's hand. He gazes down from his house,

> entranced. At this hour the mist would lie so thick that the domes of Santa Sofia and the rest would seem to be afloat; gradually the mist would uncover them; the bubbles would be seen to be firmly fixed; there would be the river; there the Galata bridge. (O, 84)

Vita's ancestors, the Sackvilles (whose history Orlando incorporates), had often acted as ambassadors abroad, but it was actually her future husband, Harold Nicolson, who was attached to the British Embassy in Constantinople when he first proposed to her in January 1912.[6] He was in the diplomatic service and it was his second posting. The couple began married life in Constantinople in October 1913, living in a 'wooden Turkish house, with a little garden . . . and such a view over the Golden Horn, and the sea, and Santa Sophia!'[7] – exactly the view that had so delighted Virginia (and would later entrance Orlando). The city, which Vita had expected to find 'beastly', turned out to be 'lovely':

> She has an early morning of her own,
> A blending of mist and sea and sun
> Into an indistinguishable one,
> When Saint Sophia, from her lordly throne
>
> Rises above that opalescent,
> A shadowy dome and soaring minaret,
> Visible though the base be hidden yet
> Beneath the veiling wreaths of milky shroud.[8]

Vita and Harold came back to England for the birth of their son Ben in August 1914. With the outbreak of war, they could not return but both of them remembered the city with affection – Vita wrote eight poems on *Constantinople* (1915, privately printed), and Harold wrote a romantic thriller about the old Ottoman empire, *Sweet Waters* (1921), which included portraits of himself and Vita. During his posting there, Harold had learned something of the extraordinarily complex rivalries between Greece, Turkey, Russia and the West in that part of the world, and thereafter his expertise would be called upon when plans for its future were discussed – as at the Paris Peace Conference of 1919, at San Remo in 1920 and Lausanne in 1922.

In *Orlando*, the hero reaches the summit of his success as a man in Constantinople, scaling the heights of that world of male honours that Woolf alternately giggled at and despised. Like various historical Sackvilles and indeed like her own father, Leslie Stephen, Orlando is dubbed Knight Commander of the Order of the Bath (KCB) and at the same time acquires the grandest of British aristocratic titles, being crowned duke (as some of the Sackvilles had been). Orlando celebrates the occasion publicly, with a grand reception and a display of fireworks. But privately, he consummates a clandestine marriage to the gypsy Rosina Pepita (in reality, Vita's grandmother) who apparently bears him several children (though the book's time scheme scarcely allows for this). Yet at the climax of his achievements as a man, both professionally and personally,

Orlando once more falls into a deep coma during which a revolution takes place not only around him, but also within him: 'The Turks rose against the Sultan . . . set fire to the town, and put every foreigner they could find, either to the sword or the bastinado' (O, 95). In this, there may be distant echoes of Shelley's *Revolt of Islam*, of Vita's (then unpublished) novel *Challenge* (which Woolf had read in June 1927), as well as of the actual political crisis of Chanak in September 1922.

Orlando, meanwhile, awakes to find himself a woman. This startling transformation is heralded by a change of genre – from fiction or mock-biography to a form expressly designed to present transformation: the Jacobean, or more precisely, the Jonsonian masque. Woolf's sense of the appropriateness of the court masque as a form within her fantasia had already been evident from the first draft which included two references to masques, though these were subsequently changed or deleted. During the fair on the ice in the opening chapter, there is a performance before King James of 'a masque by one of the popular Elizabethan poets – Jonson, Shakespeare or another'.[9] In the published text, this is replaced by a performance of *Othello*. With its allusion to the eclipse that Vita and Virginia had watched together, *Othello* underlines both Orlando's jealousy of Sasha and the jealousy that Vita aroused in Virginia.

The second masque to appear in Woolf's manuscript, performed as part of the celebrations for Orlando's new honours, is Milton's *Comus*, though again this was cut from the published text.[10] Milton's masque includes Jonsonian elements (among them, the figure of Comus himself, derived from Jonson's *Pleasure Reconcil'd with Virtue*), but it was not structured on such simple lines as Jonson's masques were, and it seems to have been the Jonsonian masque that provided Woolf with the format she used to mask Orlando's mysterious change of sex. Jonson invented the 'antimasque' in which a group of undesirables (such as witches in *The Masque of Queens*) appear and identify themselves, only to be dismissed by the forces of virtue. It is this structure that Woolf employs for the 'Masque of Truth' in *Orlando*, but with the added twist that her vices or antimasquers are figures traditionally considered virtues. It is Chastity, Purity and Modesty who are bid 'Avaunt! Begone . . . !' (O, 96). At times during this episode, Woolf's continuous prose threatens to slither into Jonsonian rhymed couplets:

> Hide deeper, fearful Truth.
> For you flaunt in the brutal gaze of the sun
> things that were better unknown and undone;
>
> those who prohibit; those who deny;
> those who reverence without knowing why. (O, 96, 97; my re-alignment)

While Woolf clearly grasped the structure (and even the tone of the stage directions) of the Jonsonian masque, it is difficult to decide where she first encountered the form. Nearly ten years previously, Lytton's mother, Lady Strachey, had read to her from Jonson's masques: 'They are short & in between she broke off to talk a little . . . I enjoyed it', she observed (*Diary* i, 106). Had she remembered them ever since? Though she briefly discusses Jonson's comedies in her essay 'The Elizabethan Lumber Room' (*Essays* iv, 58), she does not there refer to his masques. A great deal has been written, and more might be said on the subject of Orlando's sex change, but instead I shall follow Woolf's example in appropriating a dismissive manoeuvre from Austen's *Mansfield Park*: 'let other pens treat of sex and sexuality; we quit such odious subjects as soon as we can' (O, 98).

Leaving Constantinople, Lady Orlando goes to live among the gypsies in Bursa (or Broussa), the old capital of the Ottoman empire, visited by Virginia Stephen in April 1911 when she travelled out to help Vanessa who had had a miscarriage while on holiday there with her husband Clive and lover Roger Fry. Out in the wilderness, the gypsies offer an alternative society; untroubled by social hierarchy, authority or law, a way of life that constitutes a utopian vision in the novel as a whole, since the great determinants of class and gender are here temporarily in abeyance. Class does not exist among the gypsies and gender is less conspicuous as everyone wears Turkish trousers, so that 'the gipsy women, except in one or two important particulars, differ very little from the gipsy men' (O, 108). For a while, Orlando can disappear among them, yet their divergence of outlook remains a source of tension. Her urge to write, her worship of nature and her very dissimilar cultural experiences set up anxieties on both sides. The issue of religious difference, avoided in the Constantinople scenes, now arises: and though Orlando tries to sort it out through open discussion,

> much bad blood was bred between them. Indeed, such differences of opinion are enough to cause bloodshed and revolution. Towns have been sacked for less, and a million martyrs have suffered at the stake rather than yield an inch upon any of the points here debated. No passion is stronger in the breast of man than the desire to make others believe as he believes. Nothing so cuts at the root of his happiness and fills him with rage as the sense that another rates low what he prizes high (O, 105).

A hundred years ago, the themes of religious conflict, intolerance and violence were as closely associated with Constantinople as they are with Jerusalem today. *Orlando*, Woolf's most optimistic fiction, lightens these themes, presenting them amusingly; but when she had first turned to the question of faith in her 1906 journal, she observed that 'it was not ten years ago that the Turks and Armenians massacred each other in the streets'.[11] Massacres had indeed taken place in 1894 and 1896. Leonard Woolf recalled one of his earliest teachers being highly exercised over them:

> The terrible stories and Mrs Cole's passionate indignation had a great effect upon me: for the first time I had, I think, a vague feeling or dim understanding of the difference between civilisation and barbarism. I could almost see the helpless Armenians being bayoneted by the Turkish soldiers and the women and children fleeing and floundering through the snowdrifts. And I had a shadowy feeling . . . that each of these victims was a person, like me an 'I'.[12]

It was Clarissa Dalloway who

> cared much more for her roses than the Armenians. Hunted out of existence, maimed frozen, the victims of cruelty and injustice (she had heard Richard say so over and over again) – no, she could feel nothing for the Albanians, or was it the Armenians? (MD, 132)

'Who remembers the Armenians today?' Hitler had cynically asked;[13] evidently not Clarissa. No excuse is offered either for Clarissa's failure of sympathy or for her ignorance. Although both Albania and Armenia had been ravaged by armies of occupation during the First World War, their problems were substantially different. The Armenians became the victims of Turkish genocide once again in 1915, in the wake of a massive defeat inflicted on the Turks by the Russians. In retaliation, the Turks drove the Armenians from Eastern Anatolia, continuing attacks on them until 1919 when their numbers were further decimated by famine. In a moment of Clarissa-like coldness, Woolf wondered how her friend Janet Case could get so exercised over 'the quantities of Armenians. How can one mind whether they number 4,000 or 4,000,000? The feat is beyond me' (*Diary* i, 271).

Despite her apparent lack of sympathy, Woolf was merely being honest about the sincerity of responses towards sufferings that we cannot alleviate. She put the question more directly to herself two years later, while thinking about the War Reparations Committee and the civil war in Ireland, where

> People go on being shot & hanged . . . The worst of it is the screen between our eyes and their gallows so thick. So easily one forgets it – or I do . . . Is it a proof of civilisation, to envisage suffering at a distance? (*Diary* ii, 100)

Constantinople endured a series of political crises in the years following the First World War, and in the debates over its future Vita's husband, Harold Nicolson, played a small but significant part. Given his expertise in that area, it was inevitable that he should be at the great European Peace Conference (as he described in his book, *Peacemaking*, 1919). There, he worked closely with the Greek Prime Minister Eleutherios Venizelos as the delegates tried to determine the fate of the old Ottoman empire: the Turks had allied themselves with Germany in 1915 and had subsequently shared in its defeat. In April 1919, Venizelos, buoyed up by British and French encouragement, sailed into the Turkish port of Smyrna, intending to invade the Turkish mainland. Turkey and Greece had had a long history of religious and territorial rivalry. In the panic that ensued, the British gave the task of restoring order in the interior to a young, blue-eyed and highly charismatic Turkish officer who had already distinguished himself at the Dardanelles and was currently in Constantinople – one Kemal Mustafa Ataturk. He left immediately for the mainland, where he set about co-ordinating a nationalist movement.[14]

Meanwhile, back in Paris, Lloyd George and Georges Clemenceau pored over Harold Nicolson's maps, trying to construct a workable future for Thrace, Constantinople and Anatolia. In March 1920, British troops entered Constantinople where they arrested leading nationalists, but Ataturk, now established at Ankara, responded by arresting any Allied officers he could find. A conference held at San Remo granted Smyrna and Thrace to Greece, but Ataturk had different plans. He renegotiated the border between Turkey and the new Russian Soviet, but rejected all proposals for peace with Greece until all Greek troops had withdrawn from the Turkish mainland.[15] In August 1922, Ataturk marched his nationalist army to Smyrna where the Greek quarter was burnt to the ground – 'a disagreeable incident', was his comment.[16] The collapse of Greek forces in Turkey left British and French troops in Constantinople exposed, and the French marched their men out of Chanak on the Asian side of the straits. As endless lines of Greek refugees began to pour out of Turkey and Thrace, a peace conference was held at Lausanne, attended by Lord Curzon with Harold Nicolson in tow.

Ataturk did not attend the conference in person, but he was now negotiating from a position of strength, having gained control of mainland Turkey. The conference was obliged to grant Turkish-speaking territories, from Eastern Thrace as far as Syria, to Turkey, and it set up a compulsory transfer of populations: Muslims were returned to Turkey in exchange for the Greeks who were fleeing for their lives. Ataturk would transform the old Ottoman empire into a new secular state, based on the Turkish language rather than on a shared religion. By 1923, the last foreign troops had left Constantinople. The Sultan was in exile and the Caliph would soon follow him. Ataturk ruled from Ankara, the capital of the new Turkey he was creating – a man who gave birth to a nation or the first of the new dictators, depending on your point of view.

Harold Nicolson's book of memoirs, *Some People*, presents the Lausanne conference in terms of domestic farce by focusing on 'Arketall',

Curzon's hastily acquired valet. Silent and permanently drunk, he was in charge of the Marquis's foot-rest and wardrobe. Nicolson's account begins at Victoria Station where 'on the linoleum of the gangway Lord Curzon's armorial dressing-case lay cheek by jowl with the fibre of Miss Petticue's portmanteau'.[17] At the Conference, Lord Curzon had to cope not only with the intransigent Turks but with the rapid decline of his valet who eventually left under a cloud, having hidden or mislaid all his master's trousers. Curzon's death, three years after the conference, gave Nicolson the freedom to write the kind of gossipy, affectionate account that he would have hated. In September 1927, Virginia Woolf wrote a review of *Some People* for the *New York Herald Tribune*. Her account, 'The New Biography', contrasts the truth of fact ('of granite-like solidity') with the truth of fiction ('of rainbow-like intangibility'), arguing that the two are fundamentally incompatible. So far, no biographer had been subtle or bold enough

> to present that queer amalgamation of dream and reality, that perpetual marriage of granite and rainbow . . . But Mr Nicolson with his mixture of biography and autobiography, of fact and fiction, of Lord Curzon's trousers and Miss Plimsoll's nose, waves his hand airily in a possible direction. (CE iv, 229, 235)

As her diary reveals, Nicolson's approach in *Some People* stimulated Woolf to wonder whether she might not sketch, 'like a grand historical picture, the outlines of all my friends. I was thinking of this in bed last night'. His example opened a door for her, suggesting

> a way of writing the memoirs of one's own times during people's lifetimes. It might be a most amusing book. The question is how to do it. Vita should be Orlando, a young nobleman . . . & it should be truthful; but fantastic. (*Diary* iii, 156–8)

This is the first time Orlando is mentioned by name. The rest is literary history. Behind Woolf's fiction, as always, lay an extraordinary range of reading, a weight of serious thought and knowledge, worn so lightly that we are scarcely aware of it: the butterfly wing of fiction, fantasy and imagination are, after all, always underpinned by the stone arches of history and politics, and clamped together with the iron bolts of fact.

## Notes

1. Clive Bell, *Art* (1914; London: Chatto and Windus, 1923), p. 8. He returns to Santa Sofia as an example in the second half of the book, pp. 128, 129.
2. Virginia Woolf, *A Passionate Apprentice: The Early Journals, 1897–1909*, ed. Mitchell A. Leaska (London: Hogarth Press, 1990), pp. 347–8. The

description of the first view of Constantinople from the sea, with the dome of Santa Sofia rising from the mist, is almost 'a literary genre with its own rules', as Umberto Eco points out in his foreword to Edmondo de Amicis, *Constantinople* (1877; London: Hesperus, 2005), p. vii, and see also p. 13.

3. Lyndall Gordon, *Virginia Woolf: A Writer's Life* (Oxford: Oxford University Press, 1984), pp. 111–12.
4. *A Passionate Apprentice*, p. 351.
5. David Roessel, 'The Significance of Constantinople in *Orlando*', *Papers on Language & Literature*, vol. 28, no. 4 (Fall 1992), p. 402; Krystyna Colburn analyses the scene between Minta and Nancy in similar terms in 'Spires of London: Domes of Istanbul', *Virginia Woolf: Texts and Contexts, Selected Papers from the Fifth Annual Conference*, ed. Beth Rigel Daugherty and Eileen Barrett (New York: Pace University Press, 1996), p. 252.
6. Victoria Glendinning, *Vita: A Biography of Vita Sackville-West* (New York: Alfred Knopf, 1983), p. 69.
7. Ibid., p. 69.
8. 'Morning in Constantinople', Vita Sackville-West, *Collected Poems* (Garden City, NY: Doubleday, 1934), p. 201, quoted by Roessel in his article, p. 403.
9. Virginia Woolf, *Orlando: The Original Holograph Draft*, ed. Stuart N. Clarke (London: S. N. Clarke, 1993), p. 38. This masque is particularly linked with Ben Jonson since, as Orlando listens, 'Something was already being said about the Chariot of love' (*Holograph*, 40), words that recall Jonson's 'Celebration of Charis', which opens 'See the Chariot at hand here of Love'. Woolf could have found this poem in her favourite anthology, A. T. Quiller-Couch's *Oxford Book of English Verse* (Oxford: Clarendon Press, 1908), p. 217, although it is not in fact part of a masque but a poem describing a triumphal procession.
10. Holograph, p. 102. Woolf was as familiar with Milton's poetry as with Shakespeare's. She had quoted the invocation, 'Sabrina fair, Listen where thou art sitting . . . ' from *Comus* in her first novel, *The Voyage Out*, where its underwater imagery had contributed to Rachel's growing delirium (VO, 309).
11. *A Passionate Apprentice*, p. 357.
12. Leonard Woolf, *An Autobiography, vol. 2: 1911–1969* (London: Oxford University Press, 1980), p. 388.
13. Margaret MacMillan, *Paris 1919: Six Months that Changed the World* (New York: Random House, 2002), p. 377.
14. Ibid., pp. 369–72; 433–4.
15. Ibid., p. 449.
16. Ibid., p. 451.
17. Harold Nicolson, *Some People* (1927; London: Constable, 1931), p. 187. Compare 'a piece of a policeman's trousers lying cheek by jowl with Queen Alexandra's wedding veil' (O, 55).

Essay 11

# The Conversation behind the Conversation: Speaking the Unspeakable

> Shall I ever 'write' again? And what is writing? The perpetual converse I keep up. (*Diary* iv, 57)

Any discussion of what lies behind the conversation in Woolf's novels must take into account the several modes of literary anteriority. There is the anteriority of earlier versions: if we picture writing as a chronological sequence, these will normally take the form of the various manuscripts or typescripts that precede the final text. There is also the quite different but equally significant anteriority of social or cultural context, which exerts its own pressure on what and how a writer writes. And then, behind speech, in yet another sense are 'the things people don't say'. In Woolf's first novel, *The Voyage Out*, Terence Hewet voiced an ambition to write 'a novel about Silence . . . the things people don't say. But the difficulty is immense' (VO, 204). His (or his author's) concern with the as-yet-unsaid, or even the not-to-be-said remained a feature of Woolf's fiction from first to last – one might even see it as constituting her project, a project in which anteriority would be intimately linked to interiority (construed as a prior, and to-be-privileged mode of being). Such interiority, 'that stream which people call, so oddly, consciousness' ('Middlebrow', *CE* ii, 202) provided the basis for Woolf's first liberated writing for the Hogarth Press in 1917, her short story 'The Mark on the Wall'.

In this experiment, Woolf gives us the interiority of a woman's thoughts as she sits silently by the fire – they flow richly and creatively around the unidentified 'mark' until, in the story's final lines, they are interrupted (or disrupted) by an intrusive male voice, talking about the War. The speaker collapses the woman's extended meditation around an absent centre by reductively identifying the mark (itself a figure for writing) as neither more nor less than a snail (CSF, 89). Interiority of an essential yet perhaps of an indefinable kind also stamps *The Waves*, begun ten years later, which could be regarded as the summit of Woolf's achievement in this line, the ultimate outcome of that project.

Other forms of the unsaid or the unspeakable, words and thoughts that cannot be spoken in polite society, also exert their pressure on what does get said: some of these are connected with the needs or urges of the body, and reflect public regulation or repression of bodily desires or actions. And there is a further, indeed a comprehensive aspect of the unsaid which itself constitutes the condition on which acts of communication seem to depend: that essential space or gap within which the reader's imagination operates, which Woolf referred to when she wrote that Jane Austen 'stimulates us to supply what is not there' ('Jane Austen', *Essays* iv, 149) – precisely the quotation which Wolfgang Iser used to introduce his own discussion of the 'blank' or 'gap' in the text that makes literary communication possible at all.[1] It also serves to link these several other unspeakables – or at the very least, it comprehends them.

Later in the same essay, Woolf suggests that, had Jane Austen lived longer, she 'would have devised a method, clear and composed as ever, but deeper and more suggestive, for conveying not only what people say, but what they leave unsaid' (*Essays* iv, 155) – an observation that defines Austen as potentially Woolf's ancestor, mother or grandmother, within the tradition of women's writing. This essay will focus upon two particular examples of the unspoken within or behind conversations, with the intention of illustrating the continuous conflict or creative tension between Woolf's impulse to say 'the things people don't say' and her recognition of the limits on what could be said – limits that she chafed against at times, and saw as one of the undesirable effects of patriarchy, not to be cured 'until men have become so civilised that they are not shocked when a woman speaks the truth about her body' (P, xl). But while Woolf experienced convention and censorship as constraining, she also found a certain exhilaration in exploring the limits of the permissible, or (to change the metaphor), patrolling the delicate border between the acceptable and the forbidden – between the allowed and acknowledged and the unspoken and unspeakable. To find a language at once precise and suggestive in which to address and even expose cultural taboos is an extraordinary challenge, one that Woolf often rose to, and nowhere with greater energy or more positive delight than in *Orlando*.

Woolf's profound ambivalence over the whole question of the speakable, the 'decent', is everywhere in evidence in her writings: she resented the limits placed on free expression, associating them with the physical constraints that had been imposed on her as a young woman – constraints that had prevented her from going out alone, walking through London's West End unaccompanied, riding in a hansom cab without both the flaps down, etc. (P, 37). Yet at the same time she criticised Joyce for his 'indecency' ('Character in Fiction', *Essays* iii, 434; 'Modern Fiction', *Essays* iv, 161–2) and sneered at D. H. Lawrence's single-minded harping on sexuality, as she saw it, though usually without identifying him by name (P, xxxix; O, 187; ROO, 90). She displayed a Janus-like ability to look back contemptuously at the hypocrisy of the Victorians (in the approved fashion of Bloomsbury – and Lytton Strachey in particular), while at the same time understanding their values from within. Indeed, these two central and alternating views might be seen as constituting the motor that drives *To the Lighthouse*.

The great Victorians had, in their turn, found how to convert contemporary limitations on what might 'decently' be said to their own advantage (as Woolf herself would): it has often been observed that George Eliot does not need to take her reader into her heroines' bedroom in order to show us the nature of their marriages at an intimate level: Casaubon's failure is evident from Dorothea's tears in the Via Sistina; Grandcourt's brutality when he kicks his little spaniel. And the Victorian tradition of using the signifying power of language to do what language does best – that is, to suggest, rather than limitingly to state – finds its 'most rich inheritor' (to borrow Yeats's phrase) in Henry James.

Woolf was among the earliest critics to draw attention to this aspect of James's style, in the course of reviewing an anthology of his ghost stories for Bruce Richmond and the *Times Literary Supplement* late in 1921. Writing of James's story, 'The Friends of the Friends', in which the hero's secret encounters with a dead woman prevent him from marrying a living one, Woolf described the story's effect as 'tranquil, beautiful, like the closing of chords in harmony; and yet, somehow [lewd]' ('Henry James's Ghost Stories', *Essays* iii, 322). Almost immediately, the editor, Bruce Richmond, was on the telephone:

> 'Mrs Woolf? I want to ask you one or two questions about your Henry James article . . . now you use the word "lewd". Of course, I dont wish you to change it, but surely that is rather a strong expression to apply to anything by Henry James. I haven't read the story lately of course – but still my impression is . . .
>
> But you know the usual meaning of the word? It is – ah – *dirty* – Now poor dear old Henry James – At anyrate, think it over, & ring me up in 20 minutes.' (*Diary* ii, 151)

'So', Woolf's diary entry continues ruefully, 'I thought it over & came to the required conclusion in twelve minutes & a half. But', she wonders, in a characteristic afterthought, 'what is one to do about it?' (*Diary* ii, 152). On that particular occasion, she submitted to the pressure to comply, yet her compliance itself annoyed her, fuelling a determination to speak out that was increasingly in evidence during the early 1920s. A year earlier she had written a letter to the Editor of the *New Statesman* complaining that their reviewer, 'Affable Hawk' (the pseudonym of her old friend Desmond MacCarthy), had endorsed the contemptuous account of women's achievements advanced by Arnold Bennett ('The Intellectual Status of Women', *Diary* ii, 339–42).

Woolf altered 'lewd' to 'obscene', in response to Richmond's complaint (made, she suspected, not so much for the sake of 'poor old Henry' as to preserve the reputation of the *TLS* – *Diary* ii, 152). But her line of investigation had not confined itself to a single word: in the final paragraph of her review, she had considered *The Turn of the Screw*, and in particular James's evocation of the moment when the governess first catches sight of Peter Quint, standing on the tower in the twilight – the moment when '"The rooks stopped cawing in the golden sky, and the friendly evening hour lost for the unspeakable minute all its voice"' ('Henry James's Ghost Stories', *Essays* iii, 325). Woolf picks up James's use of the adjective 'unspeakable' in order to expose '[s]ome unutterable obscenity [that] has come to the surface'. Her careful retrieval of the word 'unspeakable' brings together both the sexual horror evoked but never stated, and the notorious dependence of this particular story upon gaps and silences, on what cannot be spoken – or even written. James's combination of great precision and silence, she recognised, is played off against what his society cannot speak about, and is indeed deeply reluctant to contemplate – namely, sexual relations between children and adults. In writing thus, Woolf observes, James makes us 'afraid of something, unnamed, of something, perhaps, in ourselves' (*Essays* iii, 325).

*The Turn of the Screw* deliberately took as its ground what, culturally speaking, cannot be said, exploring how far words can carry the reader across that forbidden territory. Woolf, too, from her first novel, had followed James in exploring the forbidden, and had also concerned herself with what could not be said – the life of outcast London (VO, 6), prostitution (VO, 72, 202), a haunting vision of old women slaughtering chickens to feed the hotel guests (VO, 238–9), the 'ruined' women who die 'with bugs crawling across their faces' (VO, 284). But it was above all the First World War that came to stand for the unspeakable, the unspoken, exerting its silent pressure on the texts of *Jacob's Room*, *Mrs Dalloway* and even *To the Lighthouse*. As late as the 'Present Day' section of *The Years*, Peggy sneers at the statue of Edith Cavell, saying that it always reminds her of an advertisement for sanitary towels, while Eleanor recognises that the actual source of her bitterness has been displaced: it is not sanitary towels but the War and her brother's early death that constitute the real obscenity (Y, 246). *Orlando* could be seen as interrupting this sequence since it ignores the War altogether, substituting for it an utterly different discourse of the unspeakable – that of homosexuality, 'the love that dare not speak its name'. Arguably, lesbian love is the 'unspoken' of that novel in much the same way as the War had been in Woolf's earlier novels, exerting its silent pressure on our reading of it.

Woolf was to introduce the theme of male homosexuality more explicitly into her novels of the 1930s, and in particular, through the characters of Neville in *The Waves*, Nicholas Pomjalovsky in *The Years* and William Dodge in *Between the Acts*.[2] Sometimes, her treatment of these figures includes a plea for tolerance, usually indirect, but sometimes direct, though Sara, who is devoted to Nicholas, perversely announces that he 'ought to be in prison . . . Because he loves . . . the other sex' – by which, a little oddly, she means 'the same sex' (Y, 217). In *Between the Acts*, William Dodge becomes the focus of Giles Oliver's silent anger during the course of a lunchtime conversation in which words 'rose, became menacing and shook their fists at you' (BA, 38):

> [Dodge's] expression . . . gave Giles another peg on which to hang his rage . . . A toady; a lickspittle; not a downright plain man of his senses; but a teaser and twitcher; a fingerer of sensations; picking and choosing; dillying and dallying; not a man to have straightforward love for a woman – his head was close to Isa's head – but simply a – At this word, which he could not speak in public, he pursed his lips; and the signet-ring on his little finger looked redder, for the flesh next it whitened as he gripped the arm of his chair. (BA, 38)

Isa, his wife, responds equally silently:

> Isabella guessed the word that Giles had not spoken. Well, was it wrong if he was that word? Why judge each other? Do we know each other? Not here, not now. But somewhere, this cloud, this crust, this doubt, this dust – she waited for a rhyme, it failed her; but somewhere surely one sun would shine and all, without a doubt, would be clear. (BA, 39)

Giles and Isa never exchange a word in the whole book, but like many married couples they are intensely engaged in a ceaseless if hostile dialogue which operates at some deeper level. The passage as a whole (intervening conversations have been omitted) makes a continuous and highly suggestive play with hand movements and gestures, from William catching the coffee cup that Isa had half purposely knocked over, through Mrs Manresa's comic (and provocative) demonstration that she does not know how to hold a pen, to William's 'very delicately' setting the cup back on its saucer. His catching and replacing of the cup frame the whole passage, and the allusions to china may themselves include sexual suggestion (as they do, for example, in William Wycherley's comedy, *The Country Wife*, Act 4, sc. 3).

The word that Giles 'could not speak in public' ('aloud', in an earlier version[3]) creates an explicit gap in the text, though its pressure is nevertheless exposed by his pursed lips and white knuckles as he grips the arm of his chair. Isa recognises that Giles is looking for an object on which to focus his anger, and she identifies the word he hasn't said, countering his silent accusation with an equally silent plea for tolerance. While this is deftly and concisely handled in the published text, it is interesting to look back at how Woolf arrived at that wording. Three pages of manuscript of this section of *Between the Acts* (or *Pointz Hall*, as it was originally called) have survived – unusually, since the earlier drafts exist almost entirely in the form of typescript.

In this early formulation, dated 'Sept. 16th' [1938], as Woolf was drafting the first version of her novel, Isa guessed 'the very word' that Giles had not spoken, and wondered whether it was 'true that William Dodge was that thing?'[4] Almost immediately, Woolf changed 'thing' to 'word' – probably that very afternoon, since the passage in the earlier typescript where this passage first appears is also dated 'Sept. 16th' and is likely to have been typed out by Woolf herself later that day.[5] With that change, it becomes a matter of what Dodge 'is called', rather than what he actually 'is'. In the middle of any Woolf novel, let alone a novel as intensely word-conscious as *Between the Acts*, we can scarcely fail to respond to the power of language: but the status of Giles's silent accusation is reduced to that of 'a word', and one that expresses vulgar prejudice rather than objective truth.

In comparison with the surviving manuscript, the published text sheers away from the argument much more rapidly, burying itself in that strange and private language that mingles nonsense and poetry that Isa continually talks to herself. Her language accords with a development also apparent in the writing of *The Years*, which reflects Bernard's yearning (as set out in his final soliloquy in *The Waves*) for 'some little language', for stories that don't 'come down beautifully with all their feet on the ground' (W, 183) – for an admission that the chaos and flux of nature find their counterparts in the chaos and flux of human thought and conversation. Such a recognition constantly undermines, and sometimes dismantles the direct statements and developed arguments evident in the earlier drafts of *The Years* and to a lesser extent those of *Pointz Hall / Between the Acts*. Finally, in both the manuscript and typescript versions, Isa asks 'Why do we all hate each other?', thus posing too early and too explicitly the question that links the narrative of Giles and Isa's relationship (a narrative of significant silences) to that of the coming war in Europe.

Bernard's acknowledgement that human experience, like the alien and contingent world of nature, is not story-shaped, and that the artist must confront the tenuous and precarious character not only of language but also of its meanings, should encourage us to re-examine the ways in which we think about Woolf's practice of revision; and in particular the ways in which direct political statements are reworked, qualified, modified or even cut out altogether to the detriment – as it has sometimes seemed to her critics – of her forcefulness as a feminist reformer. Such changes, often regarded as part of a process of self-censorship imposed on Woolf by contemporary attitudes, may have other and more complex causes. Woolf herself enjoyed that 'indirection' that 'finds direction out', as all her work attests; and her ambivalent, and sometimes contradictory feelings, often over issues of great importance to her (such as England and Englishness, for example, as discussed in essay 13) are a source of richness and complexity within her work. To illustrate this point, let us return to *Orlando*, a case example of a novel whose central topic was unspeakable from the very beginning: this paradox may itself have given rise to the novel's proliferating fantasy, what could not be said requiring the invention of what could.

Even before Woolf knew that her next novel was to focus on Vita Sackville-West, she had designated it, in a diary entry for March 1927, 'The Jessamy Brides' – a title that redeploys the eighteenth-century slang term 'Jessamy' (often in the form 'Jemmy Jessamy') for a gay man ('jessamy' was an old-fashioned name for jasmine, so perhaps the use of this flower name corresponds to 'pansy'). Woolf coined the term 'Jessamy Brides' for their female equivalent – for lesbians. The rest of Woolf's diary entry makes her intention explicit: the projected book was to be about 'two women, poor, solitary at the top of a house . . . [it was to be] on the ladies of Llangollen . . . Sapphism is to be suggested . . .The Ladies are to have Constantinople in view . . . And it is to end with 3 dots . . . so' (*Diary* iii, 131; only the last three dots are Woolf's – the rest indicate omissions from her text). *Orlando* will indeed end thus, and the novel does provide a vision of Constantinople, but very little of the rest of her plan was – or even could have been – fulfilled. Only a month after *Orlando*'s publication in October 1928, Radclyffe Hall's novel *The Well of Loneliness* was prosecuted for obscenity, and found guilty.

*Orlando* is a novel full of feelings that could not be mentioned and events that could not be described under existing conventions – events such as love-making, pregnancy, giving birth, and even a sex-change – but all of them occasion lavish and conspicuous displays of concealment. Indeed, Woolf goes so far as to invent a Jonsonian masque in which the antagonists of the antimasque – identified as Purity, Chastity and Modesty – are dismissed by the trumpet of Truth (O, 95–7). In the fourth chapter, Orlando, now a woman, but still dressing from time to time as a man, encounters a woman called Nell in Leicester Square, and is introduced to her circle. Nell's friends provide a female and underworld counterpart to the clubs and coffee houses that were such a feature of male social life in the eighteenth century when men proclaimed their supposed 'rationality' by identifying women as their irrational 'other'. In the passage that follows, Woolf brought together two unspeakable discourses – that of women's intimacy and same-sex love, and that of prostitution, which for Woolf always implied a critique of patriarchy. Out of these two discourses, she created a double subversion, though subtly and indirectly. Nell's unidentified gentleman visitor refuses to believe that women can hold any interest for one another, or even that women have individual desires as opposed to affectations. Tidied up a little, the passage runs thus in the manuscript draft:

> So they would draw round the punch bowl which Orlando made it her business to keep furnished; & many were the fine tales they told of the other sex, & how to practise on their weaknesses. For it cannot be denied that when women get together – but hist! They are always careful to see that the doors are shut, & that not a word of it gets into print & the gentlemen have the field all to themselves in the matter of deriding the other sex. All they desire is – but hist again! – is not that the voice of the manly __ upon the stairs? Women have no desires he said, only affectations. Without desires, & only affectations to take their place, their conversation cannot be of the slightest interest to anyone.[6]

In the published text, however, the last two sentences read 'women have no desires, says this gentleman, coming into Nell's parlour; only affectations. Without desires (she has served him and he is gone) their conversation cannot be of the slightest interest to anyone' (O, 152). It may be that in the earlier version, too, we were intended to understand that the gentleman heard climbing the stairs was also Nell's client or customer, but the new parenthesis lies like an unexploded bomb in the text, a reminder of the (male) assumptions that make prostitution possible. By suggesting (without stating) the physical aspect of Nell's self-effacing sexual 'service', the text now dramatises male indifference to female feeling in a peculiarly disturbing way. Not only have we been denied the tales that Nell and her friends tell among themselves (tales which Orlando found more amusing than the conversation of Pope and Dryden), because men do not consider them interesting enough, but women's desires (which may be very different from what men suppose) are also censored on the same grounds. Thus Woolf exploits male conventions and assumptions as a way of avoiding writing about female intimacy, whether as shared narrative or even as relationship, while at the same time drawing our attention to the existence, even to the strength, of that intimacy. Women's meetings, taking place behind closed doors, may be even more sexually and politically subversive than those of the coffee houses but, by dismissing them as of no interest, men have incidentally guaranteed that their secrets will remain secret.

This added parenthesis is a good example of a process that is easily overlooked, yet often occurs in the course of Woolf's revisions: while the transition from draft to published text usually tones down Woolf's social critique or voices it less directly, it could, on occasion, tune it up, announcing it more emphatically. In this passage, words are used both precisely and suggestively to convey an act that cannot decently be shown. The words chosen are at once clear yet indirect: in the context of a prostitute and a male visitor, we know exactly what 'she has served him' means, although in a different context it might become a wholly innocent remark.

*Orlando* makes delighted and self-mocking play with the various forms of the unspeakable or the unspoken proposed at the beginning of this essay – opening up the gap between writer and reader, drawing our attention to the culturally unspeakable, and representing interiority. This novel simultaneously celebrates 'High battlements of thought' (O, 124) while ironically scolding Orlando for her thoughtlessness in sitting down to write, and thus depriving her biographer of the action necessary for any account of her activities:

> If only subjects . . . had more consideration for their biographers! What is more irritating than to see one's subject, on whom one has lavished so much time and trouble, slipping out of one's grasp . . . to see all this dumb show of emotion and excitement gone through before our very eyes when we know that what causes it – thought and imagination – are of no importance whatsoever?

With these words Woolf's text comically denounces the very act that brought it into being.

## Notes

1. Wolfgang Iser, *The Act of Reading: A Theory of Aesthetic Response* (Baltimore, MD, and London: Johns Hopkins University Press, 1978), p. 168.

2. See Stuart N. Clarke, '"Out": Homosexual Men in Virginia Woolf's Fiction', *Virginia Woolf Bulletin*, no. 10 (May 2002), pp. 10–21.
3. Virginia Woolf, *Pointz Hall: The Earlier and Later Typescripts of 'Between the Acts'*, ed. Mitchell A. Leaska (New York: University Publications, 1983), p. 472.
4. Ibid., p. 473.
5. Ibid., p. 81.
6. Virginia Woolf, *Orlando: The Holograph Draft*, ed. Stuart N. Clarke (London: S. N. Clarke, 1993), pp. 176–7.

Essay 12

# 'Sudden Intensities': Frame and Focus in Woolf's Later Short Stories

'I w[oul]d like to write a dream story about the top of a mountain. Now why? About lying in the snow; about rings of colour; silence . . . & the solitude' wrote Woolf in June 1937 as she laboured over the arguments of *Three Guineas*:

> I cant though. But shant I, one of these days, indulge myself in some short releases into that world? Short now for ever. No more long grinds: only sudden intensities . . . And its useless to repeat my old experiments: they must be new to be experiments. (*Diary* v, 95–6)

For Woolf, as for other novelists such as Dickens or Henry James, the short story was a playground or exercise yard, or else a sketchbook in which she renewed her search for 'the essential thing', developing through fiction her thoughts on the connections between experience, perception and imagination, and their expression in words or paintings. Because she used her stories to carry her thinking forward, their publication was comparatively unimportant to her: she published eight of them in *Monday or Tuesday* (1921), while others – for example, 'The Evening Party' or 'Sympathy', by no means her slightest – remained uncollected and unpublished during her lifetime. 'Lappin and Lapinova', dating from around 1918 as those did, was published in the United States in 1939 when she felt short of money. Stories often clustered significantly around a novel. *Mrs Dalloway* began and ended in short stories: growing out of 'Mrs Dalloway in Bond Street' and 'The Prime Minister', it was followed by a series of further episodes from Clarissa's party as viewed by different individuals. These stories are tinged with social satire such as Woolf had used in her first two novels, and in 'A Society' and 'The Evening Party'.

This essay examines three groups of short stories, from the last twelve years of Woolf's life: the first three, a kind of tuning-up for *The Waves*, provide self-reflexive commentary on the nature and outcome of the creative process. Two of the three stories written after *The Waves* are uncharacteristically melodramatic, creating a surprisingly violent satire on the English establishment – their distance from Woolf's usual inwardness suggesting a parody that never becomes explicit. The last two stories from the end of Woolf's life revert to questions of art and imagination, now seen in relation to the workings of memory, or the 'shock-receiving capacity' behind the impulse to write that Woolf was exploring in her 'Sketch of the Past' (MB, 85).

Late in May 1929, Woolf interrogated herself about the book that became *The Waves*:

> How am I to begin it? And what is it to be? I feel no great impulse; no fever; only a great pressure of difficulty. Why write it then? Why write at all? Every morning I write a little sketch to amuse myself. (*Diary* iii, 229)

One of these sketches was 'The Lady in the Looking-Glass', a fantasia woven around a vision of Woolf's friend, the painter Ethel Sands, coming in from her garden and not reading her letters. One of its typescripts is dated 28 May 1929, the date of this diary entry, while that of 'The Fascination of the Pool' is dated the following day (CSF, 306). 'Three Pictures', written that June, according to Leonard Woolf's note,[1] followed them closely. Bracing herself to begin her 'very serious, mystical, poetical work' (*Diary* iii, 131), Woolf used these three stories to explore a series of conceptual problems that she often returned to: the relation of experience to imagination, and the crystallisation of meaning, both in the mind and in a work of art. The complex vision of 'The Lady in the Looking-Glass' gives place to the simpler and more individual voices of 'The Fascination of the Pool'. 'Three Pictures' is the most conventional, its setting and ironic twists recalling Thomas Hardy, yet it too explores the way apparently static pictures suggest narratives.

'The Lady in the Looking-Glass', with its punning subtitle, 'A Reflection', plays with the cliché of art as a mirror of life, bringing out both the mastery and the loss involved in the act of recording. The mirror's frame, with its sharp exclusions (it cuts and slices off), holds a static world, a world already fixed and finished. It also suggests the way in which paintings differ from writing. Like 'Kew Gardens', this story sets up a series of binary oppositions: life and art; room and garden; inside and outside (the frame); words and pictures; imagination and reality; change and stillness; light and shadow; convolvulus and aster; perception ('one's eyes') and truth. The still world of the mirror is opposed to the constant motion of living thoughts as they flush and darken in rhythm with the fluctuating feelings within the room. In a reversal of normal expectation, it is the inside of the house (the imagination) that is full of forms of life, fantastic creatures pirouetting or stepping delicately while 'in the looking glass things had ceased to breathe and lay still in the trance of immortality' (CSF, 222).

Like a changeless work of art, the looking glass exaggerates what is lost between conception and expression. Woolf had pictured 'the greatest book in the world' as one 'made entirely solely & with integrity of one's thoughts. Suppose one could catch them before they became "works of art"? Catch them hot & sudden as they rise in the mind – ' (*Diary* iii, 102). Lily Briscoe echoes that insight and frustration: 'Beautiful pictures. Beautiful phrases. But what she wished to get hold of was that very jar on the nerves, the thing itself before it has been made anything' (TTL, 209).

With a backward glance at *Jacob's Room*, the Lady's room, 'very narrow and long and fashionable' like her shoes (CSF, 224), contains her imagined presence. As in earlier short stories, Woolf celebrates the potential of imagination at the expense of achieved art: the figure of the Lady is mysterious, suggesting secrets within secrets, hidden like her letters tied with bows of ribbon or shut within the little drawers of her cabinets. The arrival of further letters, delivered by a 'large black form', a harbinger of change or death from the temporal world beyond, is at once interrupting and confusing. At first the messages seem part of the mirrored world, a 'packet of marble tablets'. Then they briefly share in the changing life of the room, and are 'all dripping with light and colour'. Restored once more to the mirror's world, they become 'tablets graven with eternal truth', their pages 'cut deep and scored thick with meaning' (CSF, 223). When the Lady returns from the garden, the fantasies that have accumulated in her absence suddenly collapse, as such fantasies had done in earlier stories like 'The Mark on the Wall' or 'An Unwritten Novel'. Interrupted, the rich world of the imagination falls in on itself. Finally, 'Everything dropped from her'. The looking glass exposes the Lady entirely drained of meaning, 'naked in that pitiless light. And there was nothing. Isabella was perfectly empty . . . no thoughts . . . no friends . . . nobody. As for her letters, they were all bills' (CSF, 225).

'The Fascination of the Pool' extends and transforms the contrast between the reflective surface and 'the brooding, the ruminating of a mind' (CSF, 226) at the heart of 'The Lady in the Looking-Glass'. Whereas the looking glass had evoked the stillness of the plastic arts in contrast with the flux of words, this story begins with a scene recalling the various paintings of the pool at Charleston by Vanessa Bell, Duncan Grant and Roger Fry, and their play of light across the water.[2] Again, there is a contrast between depth and surface appearance – in this case, the water's rippling reflection of a poster advertising a sale, a figure for the 'here and now', the immediate material focus of consciousness ('farm horses, agricultural implements and young heifers'). But if the surface is visual, the depths are figured as so many half-heard voices from the past, like those of 'The Haunted House'. The disembodied voices of 1851, 1662, 1805 – voices of pleasure, love, sorrow – rise from a shared unconscious. Behind them lies some ultimate voice which might lift the others 'as a spoon lifts all the things in a bowl of water', yet this too is another illusion, for 'There was always another face, another voice' (CSF, 227). As the mind floats upward, the pool becomes a painter's image once again, its surface a reflection of the poster pinned to a tree-stump.

'Three Pictures' juxtaposes pictures and voices, the painter and the writer, in a third formulation. This time, the picture-forming habit is explicitly defined as an illusion, but an unavoidable one: 'We cannot possibly break out of the frame of the picture by speaking actual words'. The narrator, apparently the village blacksmith (Rodmell's Mr Dean? see *Diary* v, 247), (mis)interprets the 'you' in a car (Woolf herself?) as 'a picture of old luxurious aristocratical England' (CSF, 228). 'The Lady in the Looking-Glass' had contrasted those Post-Impressionist flushes of colour in the room with the unchanging reflections in the mirror (photography? traditional painting?). 'The Fascination of the Pool' contrasts the Impressionist reflections on the surface of the water with the voices from the depths. 'Three Pictures' evokes Victorian 'genre' painting: the first picture represents 'The Sailor's Homecoming', complete with neighbours, 'a cottage garden ablaze with flowers', and a young wife expecting a baby – a picture heavy with ideological content, designed to makes life 'sweeter' or 'more enviable'. The second picture is not so much seen as heard – a cry in the night followed by 'dead silence', creating fear and apprehension in the hearer (CSF, 229). In the third picture (or pictures), the peace and stability of the summer (which have become 'a little unreal') are disrupted, torn apart by the cry in the night. The narrator creates for herself further scenes of the sailor's homecoming, 'so that one picture after another of happiness and satisfaction might be laid over that unrest, that hideous cry, until it was crushed and silenced'. But as she descends into the village (Rodmell) and the churchyard (at the back of Monk's House), she sees a grave being dug, and the gravedigger's family picnicking beside it: ' "Here, Tommy, you're all covered with earth!" ' (CSF, 230). The grave is for the sailor; the cry was that of his bereaved wife.

Now the three pictures form a new and tragic sequence, constructing a narrative meaning different from each taken individually. The story illustrates how we continually rewrite the tales we tell ourselves about what is going on around us, commenting self-reflexively on the making of private fictions, as 'Sympathy' and 'An Unwritten Novel' had done previously.

And as in those two stories, Woolf uses the short story's traditional 'twist in the tail', in this case to bind the three pictures into a different plot. The workings of the imagination, its delight in its own richness, and its ability to fill up the emptiness of the material world anticipate *The Waves*, as does the linking of art and loss, and the blend of individual voice with a shared consciousness. The Lady's room, emptied of the creatures of the imagination, anticipates the deserted room, house, garden and landscape of the interludes.

The stories that precede *The Waves* participate in its abstraction, its exploration of inner consciousness. Those that follow it focus, as if in compensation, on the fabric of the material and social world: on dials and telescopes, dead pheasants 'with soft warm bodies, with limp claws, and still lustrous eyes' (CSF, 255), on fake pearls. At the end of 1931, exhausted from finishing *The Waves*, Woolf lapsed into a pensiveness, rich with possibilities: 'Books come gently surging round me, like icebergs. I could write a book of caricatures' (*Diary* iv, 57). In January and February 1932, she wrote three 'caricatures', but then abandoned the project. Six years later, she published two of these – 'The Shooting Party' and 'The Duchess and the Jeweller' – in *Harper's Bazaar*. A third, 'Scenes from the Life of a British Naval Officer', or 'Life on a Battleship', remained unpublished. But she had not exhausted her impulse to satire, and in 1937, with *The Years* finally dispatched, she began a sequence of short 'Portraits' for a book she planned to write with Vanessa, to be called 'Faces & Voices'. Eight of these have survived, and the last four (along with 'Uncle Vanya', dating from the same period) are written as self-justifying soliloquies, miniature versions of Alan Bennett's 'Talking Heads' (CSF, 244–6, 247).[3] The contemporary popularity of satire as practised by Huxley, Orwell, Waugh, Wyndham Lewis and others may have encouraged her to experiment with it.

Woolf's 'Caricatures' or 'Scenes from English Life' portray stereotypes satirising aspects of the British establishment – in particular, its militarism, capitalism, patriarchy and decaying aristocracy. Woolf's response to 'the inherited glory of the rich' was ambivalent: while Vita Sackville-West and her ancestral home at Knole are celebrated in *Orlando*, and various society hostesses such as Ottoline Morrell, Sibyl Colefax and Christabel Aberconway appealed to Woolf's sense of tradition, she disliked their often imperialist or conservative politics, and suspected them of being Philistines. Like Martin Pargiter in *The Years*, she could sneer at their lack of taste while enjoying their hospitality (Y, 191–3). On questions of patriarchy and militarism, however, Woolf's views are clear: she would analyse their pernicious nature in *Three Guineas*.

The sketchiest of these, 'Life on a Battleship', is also the one most closely connected with the stories about pictures through its focus on 'seeing', and in particular a mode of seeing that occludes imagination and perception, and so prevents sympathy for, or even relations with others. One point of origin for this piece was the comic yet sinister 'Dreadnought Hoax' of 1910 in which the young Virginia Stephen and her brother Adrian, bearded and blacked up, had posed as the retinue of Abyssinian royalty – part of an elaborate practical joke played on the British navy by Adrian's friend Horace Cole. In its day, the *Dreadnought* battleship represented the height of technology, the pride of the Admiralty. Absurdly disguised, Virginia, Adrian, Duncan Grant, Cole himself and two others were given an official reception and a tour of the ship by members of the Royal Navy, including Virginia's first cousin Willy (later, Sir William) Fisher who never forgave her (*Diary* v, 100). Towards the end of her life, Woolf turned this story into a comic history to amuse the Rodmell Women's Institute (*Diary* v, 303), yet it left her with a profound horror of battleships, evident from the fifth chapter of *The Voyage Out* (VO, 60) and *To the Lighthouse* (TTL, 146). More relevant, in its concern with military precision, is the episode in *Jacob's Room* where 'The battleships ray out over the North Sea, keeping their stations accurately apart. At a given signal all the guns are trained on a target which (the master gunner counts the seconds, watch in hand – at the sixth he looks up) flames into splinters' (J's R, 136).

In 'Scenes from the Life of a British Naval Officer', Captain Brace is discovered seated in his cabin, with a map in front of him and a wall of dials behind him, drawing figures with extreme exactness on squared paper. When the ship's gong is struck, he proceeds with measured tread onto the deck, salutes his crew, and marches to the dining room, his officers falling into step behind him. Here he leaves them, preferring to dine alone, rejecting the muddle of human relationships (CSF, 232–3). The final paragraph explores the nature of his viewpoint, at once rigid and piercing. As he places a telescope to his eye, as if emphasising his alien view of the world, it becomes 'a horn casing that had formed itself to enclose the penetration of his sight. When he moved the telescope up and down it seemed as if his own long horn-covered eye were moving' (CSF, 234), transforming the Captain from a creature of flesh and blood into some kind of armoured monster – a snail, whose eye on its long stalk, far from demonstrating a Keatsian 'snailhorn sensibility',[4] is rigid and hard, like the bony extrusion of a dinosaur. Analogies between extinct dinosaurs and over-armoured military regimes were not yet commonplace, but Woolf exposes how military attitudes deny the wincing tenderness of the human body, figuring its servants as invincibly armoured machines. *Three Guineas* with its critique of militarism, its processions marching in mindless conformity towards destruction, is never far off.

Very little happens in this story, and its meaning partly depends on the significance of 'seeing', of perception and viewpoint in Woolf's work. In the two remaining 'Caricatures', almost too much happens and events carry more of the meaning than usual. Both stories satirise wealthy Edwardian life with its lavish weekend shooting parties, its extravagance and its 'upstairs, downstairs' mentality. 'The Great Jeweller', later 'The Duchess and the Jeweller', is in some ways the more disturbing. Like 'The Shooting Party', it comprehends social extremes only to acknowledge their distance.

'[T]he richest jeweller in England' is a social climber, a Jew living in a fashionable flat looking out onto Green Park and Piccadilly – and thus very far from the 'filthy little alley' in the East End where he grew up. In fact, the distance is less than he supposes, since the Jew(eller) is haunted by memories of his own origins that disrupt his consciousness. He is constantly admonished by the voice of his mother whose picture hangs on the wall in front of him (CSF, 248–9). At his shop off Bond Street, the Duchess of Lambourne persuades him to pay her twenty thousand pounds in return for ten pearls and an invitation to her weekend house party, knowing that he is infatuated with her daughter Diana. Though his mother's voice warns him against it, he allows himself to be deceived. On closer inspection, the pearls turn out to be fakes but he has supposedly saved the Duchess's honour. The Jew pays to maintain the aristocratic society he is in love with, while recognising its dishonesty: like the fake pearls, it is '[r]otten at the centre – rotten at the core!' (CSF, 253).

Both the Duchess and the Jeweller are crudely drawn – the Duchess is 'very large, very fat, tightly girt in pink taffeta, and past her prime' (CSF, 251). The Jew combines two equally disturbing (though more often antithetical) racial stereotypes: that of the poor refugee, growing up in the overcrowded East End slums – he had begun his career by selling stolen dogs in Whitechapel (with an echo of the fourth chapter of *Flush*), but he also belongs to that imaginary international conspiracy of bankers who master-mind world finance, familiar from Eliot's 'Bleistein', Pound's 'Usura' and the caricatures of Nazi propaganda. Both his racial identity, and his character are evident from his physical appearance:

> [H]is nose, which was long and flexible, like an elephant's trunk, seemed to say by its curious quiver at the nostrils (but it seemed as if the whole nose quivered, not only the nostrils) that he was not satisfied yet; still smelt something under the ground a little further off. Imagine a giant hog in a pasture rich with truffles; after unearthing this truffle and that, still it smells a bigger, blacker truffle under the ground further off. (CSF, 249)

The Jeweller's nose is only the most obvious of a series of traits and gestures that betray his origins. A traditional source of racist jokes, the phallic connotations of the nose reflect social anxieties about sexual contamination. Woolf's description develops that theme by comparing the Jeweller to a truffle-hunting pig, not only implying his greed but also referring to the pig's uncleanness and the Jewish taboo against eating pork (itself another mark of racial difference). Originally Theorodoric or Isidore Oliver, Woolf renamed the Jeweller Oliver Bacon. And though it is the well-born English duchess who sells him her fake pearls, an early draft of the story refers to the 'crowds of Jewesses' remembered from his youth,'beautiful women, with their false pearls, with their false hair' (CSF, 309).[5]

Woolf was apparently unconscious of her anti-Semitism. In 1937, the year she revised this story, she published *The Years* which includes a quite different but equally disturbing episode in which the crippled Sara complains to her nephew North of sharing her bath with a Jew, a Mr Abrahamson, who leaves a grease mark and hairs behind him. Here the Jew is more explicitly associated with contamination. Its defenders maintain that the scene offers a critique rather than an endorsement of anti-Semitic myth, but Sara's singsong repetition, 'all because of a Jew in my bath, all because of a Jew', and North's 'Pah!' evoke a mood of disgust that the narrative makes no attempt to extenuate (Y, 248–50).[6]

Revising her story in August 1937, Woolf felt 'a moment of the old rapture – think of it! – over copying The Duchess & the Jeweller . . . there was the old excitement, even in that little extravagant flash' (*Diary* v, 107). She had been working at *Three Guineas* since the beginning of that year, struggling with its arguments and documentation, so that a brief escape into 'the space & irresponsibility of fiction' (*Diary* v, 109) delighted her. But *Three Guineas* displays an utterly different attitude to Jews, comparing their persecution as outsiders to the oppression of women. Readers are warned that under fascism they risk suffering as their mothers had done,

> because you are Jews, because you are democrats, because of race, because of religion. . . . The whole iniquity of dictatorship, whether in Oxford or Cambridge, in Whitehall or Downing Street, against Jews or against women, in England, or in Germany, in Italy or in Spain is now apparent to you. (TG, 228)

Though Woolf herself apparently failed to notice the prejudice on display in 'The Duchess and the Jeweller', it was evident enough to the New York agent Jacques Chambrun who had commissioned it. After accepting her synopsis, he backed down, explaining that a 'psychological study of a Jew' would be unacceptable to his client – at this point Chambrun himself attracted a racist slur as 'that maroon coloured sharper, as we suspect him' (*Diary* v, 107, 112–13).[7] It was Leonard who intervened to effect a compromise, persuading Virginia to remove the more explicit references to the Jeweller's Jewishness, and Chambrun to accept her changes.

Ironically and unknowingly, Leonard himself was partly responsible for Woolf's crude stereotype. At Cambridge he had absorbed the anti-Semitism of his upper-middle-class English friends, and it is reflected in his early fiction. It was Leonard's description of the Jewish nose in his short story 'Three Jews' and, Leonard's assertion of Jewish energy in his novel *The Wise Virgins* that Virginia had echoed, feeling (if she thought about it at all) that if Leonard wrote thus about his own race, there could be 'no offence, no offence in the world' in following his example.[8] Despite, or perhaps because of, her love for Leonard, Virginia found her mother-in-law and relatives by marriage at best tedious and at worst distasteful, as successive diary entries reveal. It may or may not be an accident that the name of the Jew in the bath in the awkward episode in *The Years* is Abrahamson: obviously a generic name for the sons of Abraham, it was also the name of Leonard's cousin, Sir Martin Abrahamson (*Diary* v, 117). The Jew in 'The Duchess and the Jeweller', like Abrahamson in *The Years* episode, may articulate suppressed irritation with her in-laws who no doubt represented all that she found most alien in Leonard (as in-laws often do).[9] If that was the case, there may be an analogy to be drawn with the figure of the Duchess of Lambourne who recalls another 'mother-in-law' figure, in this case, Vita's mother, Lady Sackville-West. For Woolf's story also reworks elements of a scene of four years earlier when Lady Sackville-West had accused her daughter of having changed twelve of her pearls for fakes.

Woolf consistently linked Vita with pearls, picturing her as 'pink glowing, grape clustered, pearl hung' (*Diary* iii, 52). When she sat on the floor beside her at Tavistock Square, Virginia would knot 'her pearls into heaps of great lustrous eggs' (*Diary* iii, 117). The ten pearls in the story, taken from a wash-leather pouch that 'looked like a lean yellow ferret', resemble 'the eggs of some heavenly bird' as they roll out of 'the slit in the ferret's belly' (CSF, 252).[10] On 18 April 1928, while Vita was visiting the family solicitor, her mother turned up and began to scream abuse at her: 'Give me your pearls, . . . twelve of them belong to me, and I wish to see how many you have changed, you thief' (as Suzanne Raitt has shown, she was obsessed with the idea that her jewellery was fake[11]). Lady Sackville-West marched back to her Rolls, sending her chauffeur to order Vita to go to the jeweller and have twelve pearls cut from her necklace. Vita went straight out to her mother's car and there and then cut up the pearl necklace in front of her, handing over the twelve largest pearls in the middle of the street. Later that afternoon, Vita visited Virginia who reported the episode in her diary, commenting, 'The woman is said to be mad' (*Diary* iii, 180).[12]

If Lady Sackville-West was indeed a model for the Duchess, Woolf's position in loving her daughter (Diana/Vita) becomes analogous to that of the Jew. A further verbal echo suggests that she may have shared the Jeweller's subversive desire to blow up the existing social order. Gloating over his jewels, he sees them as

> 'Tears!' said Oliver, looking at the pearls.
> 'Heart's blood!' he said, looking at the rubies.
> 'Gunpowder!' he continued, rattling the diamonds so that they flashed and blazed.
> 'Gunpowder enough to blow up Mayfair – sky high, high, high!' (CSF, 250)

Woolf's diary for February 1932, the month she drafted 'The Great Jeweller', refers to the feminist sequel to *A Room of One's Own* she was planning,'for which I have collected enough powder to blow up St. Paul's' (*Diary* iv, 77). The Jeweller also resembles Woolf in being haunted by the voice of his dead mother, as she was before she exorcised it by writing *To the Lighthouse* (MB, 92). And Phyllis Lassner has noticed that the Jeweller's original name – Isidore Oliver – is transformed into that of Isa Oliver, the very English heroine of *Between the Acts* (and the victim of gender rather than of racial oppression).[13]

Preparing 'The Duchess and the Jeweller' and 'The Shooting Party' for Jacques Chambrun, Woolf may have thought that an American audience would be more sympathetic to her satires on the English class system. In the event, the stories appeared simultaneously in the London and the New York editions of *Harper's Bazaar* in the spring of 1938. If one source for 'The Duchess and the Jeweller' lies in Vita's biography, that of 'The Shooting Party' is recorded in a diary entry for 29 December 1931: 'Christabel's story of the Hall Caines suggested a caricature of Country house life, with the red-brown pheasants' (*Diary* iv, 57). Christabel (the Hon. Mrs Henry McLaren, soon to be Lady Aberconway) was a friend, a society hostess who had visited Virginia earlier that month. Thomas Hall Caine was the author of popular novels and had lived on the Isle of Man until his recent death. But what exactly was the story that Christabel told Woolf?[14] The Hall Caines had lived at Greeba Castle, which was not an ancestral home (as in Woolf's story), but merely a crenellated house that Hall Caine had bought and done up. The single link between Hall Caine and Woolf's story was a scandal concerning an illegitimate son, supposed to have been born to one of his domestic staff, though this hardly explains the centrality of 'the red-brown pheasants' in both diary entry and story.

'The Shooting Party' (or 'Scenes from Country Life') is surely Woolf's most untypical fiction in terms of setting, characters and its violent denouement, yet it finds a curious echo in *Three Guineas* (written five years later). Observing that before 1919 marriage 'was the only profession open' to women, Woolf added, '[t]he influence of the pheasant upon love alone deserves a chapter to itself' (TG, 160). An endnote explains that a mother's concern to marry off her daughters was potentially in conflict with a father's requirement that a shooting party guest should be a 'decent shot' (TG, 288). While the heaps of dead pheasants remain the story's central image, it has nothing to say about love. Instead, it links the degeneracy of the upper classes with what Woolf saw as the wanton – and essentially masculine – destructiveness of hunting. As *Three Guineas* would point out, 'Scarcely a human being in the course of history has fallen to a woman's rifle; the vast majority of birds and beasts have been killed by you [i.e. men], not by us [women]' (TG, 120). Within Woolf's immediate circle it was another in-law – her brother-in-law Clive Bell – who went in for shooting. In 1908, Vanessa reported to her sister that Clive had 'killed three rabbits. Oh Billy! poor little furry beasts. It surpasses my imagination entirely, this wish to kill – does it yours?'[15] The cruelty of pheasant shooting also occurs in fiction, most memorably in Hardy's *Tess of the D'Urbervilles* where it is used to make a similar point about the carelessness of the British upper classes.[16]

'The Shooting Party' represents the killing of large numbers of pheasants as an example of wanton brutality, an indulgence in mass-destruction that ultimately recoils upon those who practise it – in this case, the (suggestively named) Rashleighs, an old English family, whose last members live on in their decaying stately home on the family estate. Their way of life dramatises the danger of separate spheres that Woolf would expose in *Three Guineas*: the men are preoccupied with war, womanising, or hunting and shooting, while their womenfolk sit by the fire and sew, complacently, even complicitly, gloating over those male sexual exploits. The younger generation has died violently on the battle or the hunting field, and now only the squire and his two aging sisters survive, and though powerless to resist his violence they are also evidently proud of him. Confined to the house, the two old sisters are clawed and feathered like the pheasants he shoots, and like them, helpless victims, as stupid as they are doomed.

When the squire returns from the shoot, his three huge gun-dogs set upon his sisters' spaniel. As the squire curses and lays about him with a whip in an effort to regain control of his dogs, he knocks his elder sister into the fireplace where the family shield falls on top of her and kills her. The emblems on the shield – grapes, mermaids, spears – reflect the family weaknesses for drinking, womanising and war-making. Upper-class English life is here characterised by a passion for imperial conquest and pillage, reflected in miniature in the enthusiasm for blood sports. The fall of more than the house of Rashleigh seems foretold by the final sentence: '[t]he wind lashed the panes of glass; shots volleyed in the Park and a tree fell. And then King Edward in the silver frame slid, toppled and fell too' (CSF, 270).

The original holograph and the earlier typescript of 'The Shooting Party' are both dated 19 January 1932 (CSF, 309), the day after the Woolfs drove to Ham Spray to visit the dying Lytton Strachey. That version begins with Miss Antonia embroidering as she listens to the firing of the shooting party growing ever closer to home. It introduces Wing, the keeper, and Milly Masters, the handsome housekeeper with a long scar along her jaw – the squire's mistress and the mother of his illegitimate son. It ends with the words quoted above. Rereading the story in July 1937, before sending it to Chambrun, Woolf added some framing paragraphs at the beginning and the end, resorting to a familiar figure from earlier work – the middle-aged woman sitting in the corner of a railway carriage who appears in 'An Unwritten Novel' (1920), in the third chapter of *Jacob's Room* (1922), and most famously in her essay 'Mr Bennett and Mrs Brown' (1924).

The published text thus begins with a woman 'telling over the story now, lying back in her corner' (CSF, 254). The initials on her suitcase, 'M.M.', the long scar on her jaw and the brace of pheasants identify her as Milly Masters, the Rashleighs' housekeeper. '[L]ike somebody imitating the noise that someone else makes, she made a little click at the back of her throat: "Chk. Chk." ' – precisely the noise Miss Antonia made while embroidering, and itself an echo of the whirring cries of the doomed pheasants. '[W]hy should not the eyes there, gleaming, moving, be the ghost of a family, of an age, of a civilization dancing over the grave?' (CSF, 260). Milly Masters, in the corner of the railway carriage, seems to contemplate the fall of the family with a certain grim satisfaction.

Revising 'The Shooting Party', Woolf suddenly

> saw the form of a new novel. Its to be first the statement of the theme: then the restatement: & so on: repeating the same story: singling out this and then that: until the central idea is stated . . .. What happened was this: when I finished the S[hooting]. P[arty]. I thought, now that the woman [Milly Masters] has called a taxi; I will go on to meet, say, Christabel [Aberconway, who had originally told her the story], at T[avistock]. Square who tells the

> story again: or I will expatiate upon my own idea in telling the story; or I will find some other person at the S[hooting]. P[arty]. whose life I will tell: but all the scenes must be controlled, & radiate to a centre . . . c[oul]d. be a concentrated small book: c[oul]d. contain many varieties of mood . . . I must keep the idea at the back of my mind for a year or two, while I do Roger [Fry] &c. (*Diary* v, 114–15)

The search for a frame that would enhance the significance of her story suggests that Woolf was uncertain whether she had communicated everything she had in mind, even after the addition of the scene on the train (her phrase, 'the woman has called a taxi', picks up more or less where the published short story leaves off). This concern to provide a clarifying frame recalls Woolf's 'novel-essay', *The Pargiters*, the initial draft of the '1880' section of *The Years*, in which fictional episodes alternate with a framing commentary on their social significance (an experiment abandoned a few months later).[17] If 'The Shooting Party' also required further exposition, Woolf had in mind for it a subtler method of framing and interrogating her narrative, and one which would allow for further reflections on her art, the theme at the heart of so many of her short stories. This scheme is further connected with *The Years* through the image of a circle with spokes that radiate from a centre, a motif that recurs in the novel (indeed, Ruth Miller considers it the novel's organising principle[18]). But Woolf never found an opportunity to try out this new form.

Other late short stories create frames or draw on images of focusing to show how the casual accidents of life can be endowed with the force and pressure of a work of art. The most satisfying of these is 'The Searchlight', 'the old Henry Taylor telescope story that's been humming in my mind these 10 years', Woolf called it at the end of January 1939, turning to it from her biography of Roger Fry (*Diary* v, 204). The telescope, employed in 'Life on a Battleship' and elsewhere, focuses on a distant object, isolating, enlarging and enclosing it in a circular frame, but as Woolf worked on successive drafts of this story,[19] she combined the telescope with the image of the searchlight, a more up-to-date version of the lighthouse beam, which also focuses upon and illuminates its object, rather as the process of fiction-making does. Holly Henry, in contextualising this story, points out that both the telescope and the searchlight had been developed for military purposes, and that Woolf particularly associated the searchlight with war.[20] As its 'rods of light wheeled across the sky', we learn that '[i]t was peace then; the air force was practising; searching for enemy aircraft in the sky' (CSF, 269).

Setting the action of 'The Searchlight' between the wars is one of several links with Woolf's final novel *Between the Acts* which also takes place as war approaches. It, too, begins on a summer's night and is similarly steeped in dramatic imagery. 'The Searchlight' adopts a deliberately theatrical style and setting: it is played out on the balcony of one of London's Pall Mall clubs, against the backdrop of Green Park and the play of the searchlight / spotlight. And as in *Between the Acts*, the narrative itself is merely an overture or 'curtain-raiser' to another play that will take place offstage. Mrs Ivimey (almost the only character named) promises her listeners a story. 'If they liked, she would try to tell it. There was still time before the play' (CSF, 269). It tails off in mystery – ' "The light . . . only falls here and there." The searchlight had passed on . . . And it was time they went on to the play' (CSF, 272). Within the time allowed, Mrs Ivimey performs her story with a strong sense of drama, though at one point she is interrupted by a fragment from a different play, when 'a voice behind them said:

"Right you are. Friday."

They all turned, shifted, felt dropped down on to the balcony again' (CSF, 271).

'The Searchlight' plays upon time and space, their complex correspondences and sudden foreshortenings, not merely through acts of memory but through more mechanical means of expansion or illumination. As the searchlight strikes the balcony, highlighting a single 'bright disc', Mrs Ivimey 'sees' the bright disc of her great-grandfather's telescope, thus prompting her to relate the story (CSF, 268).[21] Her listeners are transported to a ruined tower looking out onto the 'green and blue' distance of the Yorkshire moors, and the Ivimeys' party is replaced by a lonely boy, a hundred years earlier, for the telescope's action of making far-off things seem close also operates through time as well as space, and what is framed and focused in its circular field acquires the intensity, stillness and permanence of a work of art.

'So much depends then, thought Lily Briscoe . . . upon distance: whether people are near us or far from us' (TTL, 207). The romantic vision of a decaying tower and a lonely boy recreate a distant, timeless world that corresponds to 'that great Cathedral space which was childhood' (MB, 93). Gazing up at the stars ('very permanent, very unchanging'), the boy wonders about their origins, and his own: ' "What are they? Why are they? And who am I?" ' Then he turns the telescope onto the earth, and 'focussed it', growing ever lower and closer to the unknown object of his search (CSF, 270–1). What he ultimately sees, with all the intimacy that the telescope can confer, is a man and a woman kissing – metaphorically, a primal scene – his own point of origin, as it is more explicitly Mrs Ivimey's – ' "if there hadn't been a telescope . . . I shouldn't be sitting here now!" ' (CSF, 270). And just as his excitement carries the boy across the moors to the girl, so

Mrs Ivimey then becomes the girl that awaits him, her own great-grandmother, encountering the boy in the theatrically lit circle of the searchlight:

> [a] shaft of light fell upon Mrs Ivimey as if someone had focussed the lens of a telescope upon her . . . She had risen. She had something blue on her head. She had raised her hand, as if she stood in a doorway, amazed. (CSF, 272)

Between them, searchlight and telescope have fulfilled the purposes of art, crossing and overcoming the cold distances of time and space, focusing upon and illuminating origins.

*Between the Acts* ends with the approach of war and the possibilities of new life. When it was virtually finished, Woolf turned to a short story she had had in mind for three years or more: 'I shall brew some moments of high pressure. I think of taking my mountain top – that persistent vision – as a starting point' (*Diary* v, 341). The outcome of that impulse, 'The Symbol', is more provisional and less finished than 'The Searchlight' but, as in the earlier story, distant events are brought into close-up, this time through the use of field glasses. More explicitly than in 'The Searchlight', 'The Symbol' takes place on a balcony that overlooks 'the main street of the Alpine summer resort, like a box at a theatre'. As in the sitting room of 'The Lady in the Looking-Glass', there is 'something fantastic' about the street entertainment played out below, something 'airy, inconclusive'. Beyond the street stands the mountain, immutable and inescapable. ' "The mountain," ' the lady writes from her hotel balcony, ' "is a symbol . . ." She paused. She could see the topmost height through her [field] glasses. She focussed the lens, as if to see what the symbol was' (CSF, 288).

As in 'The Searchlight', 'so much depends . . . upon distance'. The mountain changes its appearance, from white to blood red; sometimes appearing close, at other times distant as a cloud, yet it never disappears. Its looming presence is at once oppressive, yet longed for – in the letter she is writing, the lady links the summit of the mountain with her own yearning for freedom as her mother lay dying, her sense that 'when I reach that point – I have never told anyone for it seemed so heartless; I shall be at the top' (CSF, 289). Both the lady's letter and Woolf's several revisions of the story repeatedly try to pin down the meaning of the mountain: it was 'a cliché . . . The symbol of effort', yet it was also 'not at all a cliché: in fact it was something that far from running into ink spontaneously, remained almost unspeakable even to herself' (CSF, 312, nn. 2, 3). Whether that 'something . . . almost unspeakable' refers to the lady's long-suppressed yearning for freedom or to the mountain's phallic appearance or to its nature as a source of sudden death remains obscure. According to a further revision, the lady would 'be happy to die . . . in the crater', would 'find the answer' there. And she goes on to wonder why we want 'to climb to the top of the mountain. Why . . . have we the desire? Who gave it us?' (CSF, 313, n. 4).

'The Symbol' is a story about a woman writing and Woolf adds to this metafictional dimension a specific connection with the process of writing itself. In 'The Lady in the Looking-Glass', letters had acted as messages from a temporal world beyond, but here the lady's struggle against cliché as she writes reflects the writer's sustained commitment '[t]o purify the dialect of the tribe'.[22] And her letter registers the author's imaginative intimacy with violence and death, echoing Woolf's sense that 'the shock-receiving capacity is what makes me a writer' (MB, 85). The sudden disappearance of the climbers from the lady's field of vision finds its equivalence on the written page:

' "They are now crossing a crevasse . . ."

The pen fell from her hand, and the drop of ink straggled in a zig zag line down the page. The young men had disappeared' (CSF, 290).

Here, the printed marks across the page, imitating the ink marks of the lady's letter, reproduce the disaster visually – the climbers are like the dots of the aposiopesis, momentarily strung out across the page. When they fall, they form a zigzag repeated by the movement of her pen.

'The Symbol' (originally entitled 'Inconclusions') explores the obscure connections between desire, death, and language, as the pen and print marks themselves directly record the climbers' fall. In this, probably her last short story, Woolf reached through a series of different frames – theatrical, epistolary – to focus upon the permanent mystery of our environment, and the continual shock of death. Returning to her interrupted letter, the lady writes 'They died in an attempt to discover . . .', but she does not know how to end either the sentence or her letter. 'There seemed no fitting conclusion'. The date on the typescript is 1 March 1941.

## Notes

1. Virginia Woolf, *The Death of the Moth and Other Essays* (London: Hogarth Press, 1942), p. 14.
2. Vanessa Bell, *Charleston Pond*, 1916 (Charleston Trust), Duncan Grant, *Landscape, Sussex*, 1920 (Tate Britain) and *The Barn by the Pond*, 1925 (Aberdeen Art Gallery), and Roger Fry, *Farm Pond, Charleston*, 1918 (Wakefield Art Gallery), all reproduced in *Bloomsbury: The Artists, Authors and Designers by Themselves*, ed. Gillian Naylor (London: Pyramid Books, 1990), pp. 247, 246, 215, 214.
3. See Maggie Humm's recent account, 'Visual Modernism: Virginia Woolf's "Portraits" and Photography', *Woolf Studies Annual*, vol. 8 (New York: Pace University Press, 2002), pp. 93–106.

4. 'To . . . select from [Roger Fry's writings on art history] so as to show his snailhorn sensibility trembling this way and that would require the skill of a trained hand', Woolf wrote of Fry (RF, 96), recalling Keats's phrase, 'that trembling delicate and snail-horn perception of Beauty' (from his letter to Benjamin Haydon, 8 April 1818).
5. It was customary among East-End Polish Jews for the women to shave their heads on marrying, thereafter wearing wigs – another marker of visible difference.
6. David Bradshaw defends *The Years* in 'Hyams Place: *The Years*, the Jews and the British Union of Fascists', in *Women Writers of the1930s: Gender, Politics and History*, ed. Maroula Joannou (Edinburgh: Edinburgh University Press, 1999), pp. 179–89.
7. See also Hermione Lee, *Virginia Woolf* (London: Chatto and Windus, 1996), p. 679.
8. Compare the description of the cemetery-keeper's nose in 'Three Jews' (London: Hogarth Press, 1917), p. 11 (reprinted in *Virginia Woolf Bulletin*, no. 5 (September 2000), p. 7): 'a nose, by Jove, Sir, one of the best, one of those noses, white and shiny . . . immensely broad, curving down, like a broad high-road from between the bushy eye-brows down over the lips. And side face, it was colossal; it stood out like an elephant's trunk with its florid curves and scrolls'. See also the end of chapter 3 of *The Wise Virgins* (1914; London: Persephone Books, 2003), p. 59.
9. See Lee, pp. 314–15.
10. In 'A Sketch of the Past', Woolf recalled Mr Gibbs giving 'Vanessa and myself two ermine skins, with slits down the middle out of which poured endless wealth – streams of silver' (MB, 86).
11. Suzanne Raitt, 'Fakes and femininity: Vita Sackville-West and her mother' in *New Feminist Discourses*, ed. Isobel Armstrong (London: Routledge, 1992), pp. 113–18, esp. 116.
12. Victoria Glendinning, *Vita: A Biography of Vita Sackville-West* (New York: Alfred A. Knopf, 1983), pp. 192–3.
13. Phyllis Lassner, ' "The Milk of Our Mother's Kindness Has Ceased to Flow": Virginia Woolf, Stevie Smith and the Representation of the Jew', in Bryan Cheyette, ed., *Between 'Race' and Culture: Representations of 'the Jew' in English and American Literature*, (Stanford, CA: Stanford University Press, 1996), pp. 138–9.
14. Christabel Aberconway's friendship with Virginia Woolf is described and Woolf's letters to her are transcribed in Stephen Barkway, ' "What tiara did you wear?": Lady Aberconway and Mrs Woolf', *Virginia Woolf Bulletin*, no. 15 (January 2004), pp. 4–68, but unfortunately they throw no further light on the story behind 'The Shooting Party'.
15. To Virginia, 21 August 1908, *Selected Letters of Vanessa Bell*, ed. Regina Marler (London: Bloomsbury, 1993), p. 69.
16. *Tess of the D'Urbervilles* (1891), §5, the end of chapter xli; see also Hardy's 'Triolet','The Puzzled Game-Birds', *Collected Poems of Thomas Hardy* (London: Macmillan, 1970), p. 135.
17. *The Pargiters: The Novel-Essay Portion of The Years*, ed. Mitchell A. Leaska (London: Hogarth Press, 1978).

18. C. Ruth Miller, *Virginia Woolf: The Frames of Art and Life* (London: Macmillan, 1988), p. 33.
19. John W. Graham, 'The Drafts of Virginia Woolf's "The Searchlight", *Twentieth Century Literature*, 22:4 (December 1976), pp. 379–93. Stuart N. Clarke transcribed a version entitled 'A Scene from the Past', *Virginia Woolf Bulletin*, no. 1 (January 1999), pp. 6–11. Clarke dates this draft to January 1941 and observes that other versions also belong to the last months of Woolf's life.
20. Holly Henry, *Virginia Woolf and the Discourse of Science: The Aesthetics of Astronomy* (Cambridge: Cambridge University Press, 2003), p. 65; see also her account of Henry Taylor, pp. 51–2, and ch. 2 more generally, pp. 51–70.
21. Woolf discusses 'seeing' – 'by wh[ich]. I mean the sudden state when something moves one' – in a diary entry for 1 November 1937 *(Diary* v, 118).
22. T. S. Eliot, *Little Gidding*, §2, line 127, translating Stéphane Mallarmé's 'Donner un sens plus pur aux mots de la tribu', 'Le Tombeau d'Edgar Poe', line 6 (and one aim of modernism).

Essay 13

# 'Almost Ashamed of England Being so English': Woolf and Ideas of Englishness

In the sixty years since her death, Virginia Woolf's England has vanished. Many English country houses and homes, both large and small – Knole and Sissinghurst, Charleston Farmhouse and Monk's House – have been adopted by societies committed to preserving them for the heritage industry, and they have been redesigned for the enjoyment of visitors, a process of democratisation that has altered their identity for ever. The fabric of English society has also radically changed. We aspire to be a multi-racial, multi-cultural society, for whom the concept of 'Englishness' is at best an empty myth, the invention of an imaginary past; at worst an occasion for prejudice and political reaction. It has become a potential embarrassment, almost a dirty word. As Raphael Samuel observed, 'British history makes "Englishness" problematical and invites us to see it as one among a number of competing ethnicities.' As for English literature, its teaching is now 'associated with the missionary position in sexuality, parochialism in high politics and tea-shop gentility in the world of letters.'[1] This outworn concept of Englishness, tied to lost ideals of continuity and community, evolved partly as a reaction to the speed of change, resisting the process even as it responded to it. Yet the conflict that has accumulated around the various meanings of Englishness had begun well before Woolf's death. Her responses to it were themselves conflicted, but also subtle, amusing and acute.

The concept of Englishness has its own history. It is usually thought to have come into being in the last quarter of the nineteenth century – like Woolf herself, born in 1882.[2] It grew out of changing economic and social conditions: as British industry lost ground to Germany and the United States in world markets, and wealth began to migrate from north to south, an ideal of the past was generated that bypassed factories and cities to dwell upon the countryside and, in particular, the 'South country' – a country of downland and manor house, thatched cottage, church spire and village green. As an ideal, it depended upon assumptions of a social harmony that had never existed.[3] Class and gender warfare, increasingly visible on contemporary city streets, were normally excluded from the picture, and foreign commerce was considered as a potential threat. Alongside more formal expressions of national pride such as the *New English Dictionary* (1884–1928) and the *Dictionary of National Biography* (1885–1900 – Woolf's father, Leslie Stephen, was its first editor), myths of a distinctive national identity came into being, although these were to change substantially under the impact of two world wars.[4] As the countryside was increasingly invaded by tarmac roads and suburban estates, the preservation of 'the sweet especial rural scene' became an urgent issue. E. M. Forster's fiction is always preoccupied with what it might mean to be English, whether at home or in Italy or even India. In his novel *Howard's End* (1910), representatives of different social groups struggle for possession of the Surrey farmhouse whose significance lies in its continuity with the past, both communal and personal, as well as its symbolic links with 'the whole island . . . lying as a jewel in a silver sea', with a conscious echo of John of Gaunt's speech from *Richard II* – a *locus classicus* for patriotic sentiment in which England becomes 'This precious stone set in a silver sea', at once loved and at risk.[5]

Both Forster and Woolf celebrated those aspects of Englishness that brought back a sense of the past, while deploring the more sinister aspects of nationalism. In *To the Lighthouse*, Woolf would evoke English seaside holidays, family games of cricket in the garden, walks on the sands, and the long summer twilight. In *Mrs Dalloway*, Clarissa and her friends look back at life in the archetypal English country house at Bourton, with its terraces, park, lake, kitchen garden. On a far grander scale, *Orlando* recreates for her friend Vita Sackville-West the long and literary history of her ancestral home, Knole, with its ancient hall, hundreds of bedchambers, whispering galleries, wide grounds and aged oak trees – the home that Vita was debarred from inheriting because she was a woman. In *The Waves*, a lady writes at a table between two long windows at Elvedon while gardeners sweep the lawn. Pointz Hall in *Between the Acts* is another English country house. The view from the terrace takes in the 'spire of Bolney Minster, Rough Norton woods and on an eminence rather to the left, Hogben's folly' (BA, 34). It has survived unchanged for a hundred years and Mrs Swithin is saddened at the thought that the view will still be there when they are all dead, but her nephew Giles burns with the knowledge that war is coming and bombers could destroy the view in a few moments. In their various ways, each of these landscapes is either already lost in the past, or else under threat.

For Woolf, the English landscape was inextricably bound up with English literature. In April 1926, Virginia and Leonard spent five days at Iwerne Minster, a village in Dorset close to Cranborne Chase. 'We stole off and were divinely happy', she told Raymond Mortimer, 'in a country, at a moment, which really made one almost ashamed of England being so English; and carpeting the woods, and putting cuckoos on trees, and doing exactly what Shakespeare says'.[6] The woods had been there so long that Shakespeare had described them in the spring song at the end of *Love's Labour's Lost*. In an old country, poetry, like landscape, can bring back the imagined past. But Woolf's pleasure in coming upon an enchanted landscape recorded in a much-loved literary tradition was countered by a sense of embarrassment that the carpeted woods and the cuckoo's song had become clichés, and during the war such obvious 'Englishness' had been exploited for patriotic propaganda.

Literature and the discussion of literature were a constant source of pleasure and passion for Woolf, and perhaps not coincidentally, it was during her lifetime that the teaching of English language and literature came to be established as an independent discipline, taught and researched in schools and universities.[7] In general, she had little time for academe, and indeed disliked institutional approaches to the subject she loved; yet through her reviewing for the *Times Literary Supplement* and the two volumes of *The Common Reader*, she built up her own less conventional canon of English literature, linking its idiosyncrasies to those of the climate: 'It's atmosphere that makes English literature unlike any other – clouds, sunsets, fogs, exhalations, miasmas' (*Essays* iii, 181). Fifteen years after her death, Nikolaus Pevsner, in his Reith lectures on *The Englishness of English Art* (1956) would consider the damp climate and the monosyllabic language as possible influences on the character of English art – changeable features, yet constant in their changeability.[8] Woolf herself delighted in the English language: 'those of English birth', she observed, were 'brought up from childhood . . . to disport themselves now in the Saxon plainness, now in the Latin splendour of the tongue . . . stored with memories . . . of old poets exuberating in an infinity of vocables' (ND, 258). The early drafts of *The Years* paid tribute to Joseph Wright, author of *The English Dialect Dictionary*, not only for his academic achievements, but also for the determining role that his own life, and that of his working-class mother had played in those achievements.[9] The '1911' section of the finished novel celebrates many traditional features of English country life – the village fête (with its mingling of small folk and gentry), the country house, the owl glimpsed from the terrace in the summer twilight, and again the beauty of the English language as

Eleanor listens to her sister-in-law Celia talking about a possible water shortage:

> 'Oh, but there's quite enough for everybody at present' . . . And for some reason [Eleanor] held the sentence suspended without a meaning in her mind's ear, '. . . quite enough for everybody at present,' she repeated . . . What a lovely language, she thought, saying over to herself again the commonplace words, spoken by Celia quite simply but with some indescribable burr in the 'r's, for the Chinnerys had lived in Dorsetshire since the beginning of time. (Y, 151–2)

Language and family are thus linked through their roots in a common past. Woolf's pleasure in language here is that of 'the most rich inheritor'. For a moment, she allows herself to enjoy 'the advantages of being Virginia Stephen',[10] the privileged daughter of Sir Leslie; for a moment, she is an insider revelling in traditions whose exclusions can be temporarily ignored; for a moment (and unusually), she catches up the modernist concern with a lost past, more familiar from the work of the Americans, T. S. Eliot[11] and Ezra Pound, or the Irishman, W. B. Yeats.

One seminal text for an understanding of Woolf's ideal of Englishness is her 1919 essay, 'Reading', set in a country house in a summer garden with views to the sea. Here she basks in the carved and panelled library, 'lined with little burnished books, folios, and stout blocks of divinity' (*Essays* iii, 141) that house the long canon of English classics from Chaucer to Wordsworth and beyond. As she sits reading beside an open window, the book and the world beyond it become indistinguishable:

> [I]t seemed as if what I read was laid upon the landscape not printed, bound, or sewn up, but somehow the product of trees and fields and the hot summer sky, like the air which swam, on fine mornings, round the outlines of things. These were circumstances, perhaps, to turn one's mind to the past. (*Essays* iii, 142)[12]

A sunlit avenue seems to stretch all the way back to Queen Elizabeth's day, reminding her of an early favourite, Thomas Hakluyt's *Traffics and Discoveries*.[13] His travel volumes had been loved by the late Victorians for their foretaste of imperial trade and exploration, and by Virginia herself as a young girl for their outlandish adventures. Her childhood is also written into her essay on 'Reading', for the garden it describes is that of Talland House at St Ives, where the young Stephens had spent their childhood holidays. The escallonia hedges and the beds of fuchsia and geranium, like the gardener mowing the lawn with his rubber-shoed pony, are remembered from summer holidays in Cornwall (MB, 134), as is the vivid account of a moth hunt by night in the second half of the essay (later reworked in *Jacob's Room*) (*Essays* iii, 150–2; MB, 113; J's R, 25).

'There is no difficulty in finding poetry in England', she announces. 'Every English home is full of it'. It is 'sunk very deep', yet it is both as familiar and as 'strangely persistent' as the climate, characterised by 'the loveliness of the hurrying clouds, of the sun-stained green, of the rapid watery atmosphere, in which clouds have been crumbled with colour until the ocean of air is at once confused and profound' (*Essays* iii, 153). Yet, as Woolf well knew, the country house and its garden and well-stocked library belong primarily to a masculine world of provision and privilege. '[I]n all the libraries of the world', she was to write in the following year, 'the man is to be heard talking to himself and for the most part about himself' (*Essays* iii, 193, and see J's R, 90–4). Libraries were built by gentlemen for gentlemen, and this unidentified country house, like Bourton or Pointz Hall, would have looked very different from 'below stairs' – to Candish the butler, the gardener leading his pony, the scullery maid or the cook. Servants only enter the library to dust the books, not to enjoy their contents. There is no real danger of finding 'the kitchen maid curled up . . . reading Plato', or of the cook coming in to borrow the *Daily Herald*.[14] Yet if it is class-blind, 'Reading' is not entirely gender-blind, for the library bookshelves house, rather surprisingly, the writings of Lady Fanshawe, Lucy Hutchinson and Margaret Cavendish. And the history of old houses and old families is one of linguistic change, as local and particular manners gradually give way to the metropolitan, merging 'the dialect of the district into the common speech of the land . . . But what dignity, what beauty broods over it all!' (*Essays* iii, 145).

'Reading' is a highly polished essay, substantially longer than Woolf's reviews, a piece on which she evidently lavished time and trouble. Which leaves us with the interesting question of why she never published it. It appeared for the first time in 1950 in *The Captain's Death Bed*, one of a few essays that had never been published before. Leonard Woolf assumed that it was intended for 'Reading' – the provisional title Woolf gave to the book that evolved into *The Common Reader*, perhaps as an introduction, though the first mention of it does not occur until May 1921, well over a year later.[15] His supposition was probably based on their identical titles, though the library contents outlined in this essay do roughly correspond to the canon as set out in *The Common Reader*. 'Reading' underpins *The Common Reader*, rather as her essay 'Professions for Women' would later provide the seed for both *The Years* and *Three Guineas*.

The conjunction of country house, landscape and library reappears again in *Orlando* and finally in *Between the Acts*, played out against a looming threat to that particular way of life. 'Reading', by contrast, was written not in the expectation but in the wake of a major European war, some time during 1919, if internal evidence can be trusted, and probably after September when her diary records her rereading Sir Thomas Browne who figures largely in its final pages. It survives in a heavily corrected typescript among the Monk's House Papers.[16]

Was it abandoned unpublished because Woolf was 'almost ashamed' of creating a picture of an England that was 'so English'? In another essay written in the same year, 1919, and published in Middleton Murry's *Athenaeum*, she caricatures the mood of national self-congratulation on display at the Royal Academy's Summer Exhibition. Here again, we encounter the English country house in a rural setting, but this time viewed from a dramatically different angle:

> The sun is exquisitely adapted to the needs of the sundials. The yew hedges are irreproachable; the manor house a miracle of timeworn dignity . . . It is indeed a very powerful atmosphere; so charged with manliness and womanliness, pathos and purity, sunsets and Union Jacks, that the shabbiest and most suburban catch a reflection of the rosy glow. 'This is England! these are the English!' one might explain if a foreigner were at hand. (*Essays* iii, 92)[17]

Here England and Englishness have become an embarrassment, appealing as they do to spurious emotions, reflected in her choice of clichés. As a cultural critic, Woolf felt offended by the attitudes on display, the heroics, smugness and complacency that seemed to pour down from the walls. As an aesthetic critic, she was offended by the provincialism both of the subject matter and technique of the paintings. Roger Fry and Clive Bell had sought to liberate painting from precisely this kind of extraneous sentiment, the narrative appeals made by the Academy's genre paintings. Instead, they had encouraged a focus upon form intended to lead provincial English painting towards Post-Impressionism and European modernism.[18]

The versions of Englishness on display at the Academy were factitious and politically conservative. Their aesthetic poverty endorsed Fry's assumptions as to the relative strengths of literature and painting in England: whereas literature might be a legitimate source of national pride, it was usually conceded in Woolf's circle that Victorian painting had been a dead end, particularly in comparison with the French painting of the same period. As Pevsner would later observe, 'None of the other nations of Europe has so abject an inferiority complex about its own aesthetic capabilities as England'.[19]

By 1919, wider European ties had come to seem desirable, and not merely in the field of aesthetics. The Great War had left England as a major voice at the Peace Conference Table, deciding upon national boundaries in Europe, war indemnities for Germany, and generally setting the agenda (one that would lead to another European war twenty years later).

The Woolfs, like the rest of Bloomsbury, had been pacifist in their sympathies during the War, and were passionately committed to internationalism and the creation of a League of Nations as the only way to build a better and safer Europe. Leonard had contributed substantially to the establishment and maintenance of the League through his book on *International Government* (1916). In 'Reading', then, it seems that Woolf had allowed herself a private canter through her own particular English/Elysian fields, while recognising that such pleasures could only be indulged in private.

> In times of peace and tranquillity the vocabulary of patriotism is not much used. . . . Trouble changes this . . . If England seems threatened you feel that in losing her you would lose yourself; she becomes plainly and decidedly 'this dear realm of England'

wrote the poet Edward Thomas, with yet another allusion to John of Gaunt's speech, so often invoked in the context of a national threat.[20] Both before and during the Great War, Woolf had felt repelled by displays of chauvinism. They induced in her a sense of alienation that was enhanced by (or perhaps contributed to) her breakdown during the early years of the War. Her disgust with these 'violent and filthy passions' (*Letters* ii, 71) seems to have distracted her from the fears for England that would later characterise *Between the Acts*. One exception, however, may be her use of Scarborough in *Jacob's Room*. In December 1914, German gunboats had shelled Scarborough from the sea, creating the first civilian casualties of the War on English soil. Hundreds of people were killed or injured. Woolf's earliest readers would have read her account of the town's sea front, bandstand and aquarium and the houses and streets beyond, with the added knowledge of their fate to come. Her use of Scarborough (as if echoing the notorious recruiting poster, 'Remember Scarborough') is one of the novel's several deliberate reminders of the devastation wrought by the War – like the fates of Helen and Jimmy, the young men in the submarine, or of Jacob himself (J's R, 12–13, 83, 136).[21]

Woolf particularly disliked the kinds of sentiment about England and Englishness licensed by army recruitment campaigns, sentiment that appears at its most rhetorical in Rupert Brooke's sonnet, 'The Soldier': 'If I should die, think only this of me:/ That there's some corner of a foreign field/ That is forever England.' Woolf had known and liked Brooke though she mistrusted the cult of hero-worship that he attracted after his death.[22] But national pride in the institutions of democracy and empire had begun well before the War and were already being satirised in her first novel, *The Voyage Out* (completed before the War, though not published until 1915). Here she explores the meanings of England and Englishness for a right-wing, conservative, imperialist politics. At Lisbon, the little party on board the *Euphrosyne* are joined by a former Tory Member of Parliament Richard Dalloway and his pretty, silly wife Clarissa who announces that her favourite play is Shakespeare's *Henry V*, another key source of patriotic sentiment (VO, 46).[23] She parrots her husband's views with absurd inconsequence:

> I can't help thinking of England . . . Being on this ship seems to make it so much more vivid – what it really means to be English. One thinks of all we've done, and our navies, and the people in India and Africa, and of how we've gone on century after century sending out boys from little country villages – and of men like you, Dick, and it makes one feel as if one couldn't bear *not* to be English! Think of the light burning over the House, Dick! (VO, 42)

'Dick' himself is only marginally more self-aware than she is, while being, if anything, more racist. In conversation with Rachel, he admits with apparent reluctance 'that the English seem, on the whole, whiter than most men, their records cleaner', identifying skin colour with moral superiority in a revealing linguistic strategy (VO, 56). The full significance of the Dalloways' politics emerges at the end of chapter 4, when 'two sinister grey vessels [appear], low in the water, bald as bone . . . with the look of eyeless beasts seeking their prey'. This is 'the Mediterranean fleet', Dick announces, as the *Euphrosyne* dips its flag, and Clarissa, squeezing Rachel's hand, exclaims 'Aren't you glad to be English!' (VO, 60).

The vessels are Dreadnoughts, the first built in 1905, and a significant step in the arms race with Germany. Virginia Stephen had examined one at close quarters in 1910 when she took part in the 'Dreadnought Hoax'. She, her brother Adrian, Horace Cole and others, had dressed up and blacked up. Proclaiming themselves to be Abyssinian princes, they had been taken on an inspection tour of the battleship, which the navy regularly showed off to foreign powers. 'The hoax combined all possible forms of subversion', Hermione Lee points out: 'ridicule of empire, infiltration of the nation's defences, mockery of bureaucratic procedures, cross-dressing and sexual ambiguity.'[24] In *The Voyage Out*, at lunch that day, while Willoughby and the Dalloways praise British admirals, Rachel's aunt Helen remarks that 'it seemed to her as wrong to keep sailors as to keep a Zoo, and that as for dying on the battlefield, surely it was time we ceased to praise courage' (VO, 60). Woolf understood how ideas of Englishness could be exploited, even before the War had begun.

When Woolf dusted off the Dalloways and set them at the centre of her fourth novel, *Mrs Dalloway* (1925), she made them substantially more sympathetic. Richard is no longer referred to as 'Dick'.[25] At once less arrogant and more likeable, he sits on committees investigating the plight of the downtrodden – at home, victims of the police; abroad, the Armenians

(MD, 126–7, 131).[26] Now Clarissa becomes one of the novel's centres of consciousness, though it is difficult for the reader to judge just how far to identify with her. Some of the couples' former foibles are here displaced onto other characters. Clarissa's patriotism is transferred to Lady Bruton whose love for 'this isle of men, this dear, dear land, was in her blood (without reading Shakespeare)'. The earlier Clarissa's sense that she couldn't bear *not* to be English becomes entangled with sentiments echoing the words of Rupert Brooke's 'The Soldier':

> one could not figure [Lady Bruton] even in death parted from the earth or roaming territories over which, in some spiritual shape, the Union Jack had ceased to fly. To be not English even among the dead – no, no! Impossible! (MD, 198)[27]

In very different ways, both *The Voyage Out* and *Mrs Dalloway* play out insular Anglo-Saxon attitudes in contexts that expose their limitations. In the earlier novel, the Dalloways in their cabin on board the *Euphrosyne* pit themselves against the 'set of cranks' (i.e. Ridley, Helen and Mr Pepper – VO, 42). The little community of English in their hotel at Santa Marina also seem isolated, encamped on the edge of a vast wilderness into which they make a disastrous foray. In the end, the jungle apparently retaliates, seizing upon Rachel as its prey. And although *Mrs Dalloway* is set in London, at the centre rather than on the periphery, it too can be read as a conflict between the insularity of Westminster and a wider, more threatening world beyond. Clarissa herself withdraws to her narrow bed in the attic, with the sheets turned down – a kind of death. She deliberately refuses to think of the suffering Armenians, just as she does not want to invite poor, shabby Ellie Henderson to her party. Her reaction to Septimus Smith's suicide can be read either as a momentary reversal of this process, an impulse of sympathy for the outcast, or else as a confirmation of it, in which she accepts his death as the sacrifice that enables the party to go on – as if the millions of war deaths have served only to guarantee the continuance of her way of life: 'she felt glad that he had done it; thrown it away while they went on living' (MD, 33–4; 129–32; 202–4).[28]

In *The Voyage Out*, Woolf had represented the Dalloways' chauvinism as politically provocative, the kind of attitude that had brought war closer, whereas in *Mrs Dalloway*, her critique is directed against a society that has accepted the bloodshed without seeking further change or reform, a society that has picked up life where it left off before the War: Clarissa and her friends are absorbed in the London season with its sequence of 'Lords, Ascot, Hurlingham' (MD, 18)[29] as if the War had never taken place. What goes on elsewhere – whether in Albania or

Armenia, or even in the parks and mean streets beyond the little enclave of Westminster – has little impact upon her way of life.

The politics of *Mrs Dalloway* reflect insular British policy between the wars when the country looked towards the empire, rather than to Europe, for alliance and trade. Woolf's distaste for imperialism is reflected in an essay on the great Empire Exhibition of 1924 entitled 'Thunder at Wembley' which envisages a fantastic storm blowing away all the old machinery of colonialism and empire (*Essays* iii, 410–13).[30] Her next novel, *To the Lighthouse* (1927), celebrated a lost English past with a nostalgia that risked becoming sentimental (as she herself acknowledged – *Diary* iii, 107), although its central section, 'Time Passes', explores the impact of the War and was written during the General Strike of May 1926.[31] *Orlando* (1928) reworks the nexus of ideas present in her 1919 essay, 'Reading', but its narrative is so shot through with sexual and historical subversion that there is never any danger of taking it seriously. Englishness, like several of the book's other risky topics, seems to slip through customs undeclared, as Woolf makes affectionate fun of Vita/Orlando's aristocratic love of 'The Land' (O, 183, 54, 192, 215). In reality, British agriculture was as depressed as its industries, and the 1930s were marked not only by a reluctance to be drawn into European conflict but also by massive unemployment, marches and hunger strikes at home.

In 1938, the year that Chamberlain returned from Munich with Hitler's paper promises, thus staving off war for a further year, Woolf published her most explicit critique of patriotism, with its often militarist implications – *Three Guineas*. To define it, she turned to the words of the Lord Chief Justice, Gordon Hewart: 'Englishmen are proud of England . . . there are few loves stronger than the love we have for our country . . . Liberty has made her abode in England. England is the home of democratic institutions . . . Yes, we are greatly blessed, we Englishmen' (TG, 123). But she goes on to ask whether such sentiments can ever mean the same for a woman: do women have the same reasons for being proud of England, for loving England, for defending England and for feeling greatly blessed? Because of their different stakes in the community, they are made to feel like outsiders, and what can 'our country' mean to an outsider? '[A]s a woman, I have no country. As a woman, I want no country. As a woman my country is the whole world'. Yet this often-quoted assertion is followed by a less familiar qualification: for Woolf, 'some obstinate emotion remains, some love of England dropped into a child's ears by the cawing of rooks in an elm tree, by the splash of waves on a beach, or by English voices murmuring nursery rhymes' (TG, 233, 234).[32] Even while making her most unequivocal statement about the irrelevance of patriotism, Woolf could not fully disengage from the deep pull of the English landscape, the English language of her childhood.

By 1938, as threats to England's island fastness were growing, ideas of England and Englishness underwent a further transformation. Though in *Mrs Dalloway* the world of upper-class privilege apparently continued much as it had done before, fundamental social and economic changes were taking place. The days of the country house, with its 'upstairs, downstairs' split, were numbered, and 'middle England' was beginning to find a voice for itself, its values often expressed by sensible, humorous, provincial or suburban ladies. The nation of explorers and conquerors had become a nation of gardeners, decent ordinary people who muddled through with a combination of cheerfulness and good sense, more appropriate to uncertain times.[33]

During the 1930s, many towns and villages acted out their own (imaginary) pasts in secular pageants, often performed on Empire Day (24 May), though such entertainments could reflect a range of political attitudes – in London in 1936, for example, the Communist Party performed its own 'March of History' pageants, evoking a past of radicalism and resistance.[34] Woolf's friend E. M. Forster wrote two pageants: the 'Abinger Pageant' of July 1934, with music by Ralph Vaughan Williams in the form of folk-song settings, was set in the garden of the old Rectory at Abinger, enquiring in its epilogue, 'Are [houses] man's final triumph? Or is there another England, green and eternal, which will outlast them?' His second pageant, 'England's Pleasant Land' was performed at Milton Court, near Dorking in July 1938.[35] Its title refers to Blake's poem 'Jerusalem', another key text for Englishness. It had been broadcast by John Reith at the end of the General Strike of 1926 to signify that England had been saved; today it is always sung on the last night of the promenade concerts at the Royal Albert Hall, as well as by the Women's Institute, traditionally supporters of English country life.[36] By the spring of 1940, Woolf had herself become 'an active member of the Women's Institute, who've just asked me to write a play for the villagers to act. And to produce it myself. I should like to if I could' (*Letters* vi, 391). In the event, she didn't, but it was an instance of life imitating art, for she had already written Miss La Trobe and her village pageant into this final novel.

Woolf began *Between the Acts* in the atmosphere of increasing international tension of 1938, reverting to the fantasy of her essay on 'Reading' and of the country house and village fête sketched out in the '1911' section of *The Years* – yet developing these, too. It was to be 'composed of many different things', among them 'English country; & a scenic old house – & a terrace where nursemaids walk', as well, of course, as a library, for she wanted to discuss 'all lit.', and even 'all life, all art, all waifs & strays – a rambling capacious but somehow unified whole – the present state of my mind?' (*Diary* v, 135).[37]

The sense of an imminent ending to a way of life that has gone on uninterrupted for centuries is very strong in the novel. While for William Dodge the present is enough, Isa, and Giles too, in different ways and for different reasons, look forward to an uncertain future (BA, 51), and it is such anxieties that make *Between the Acts* Woolf's most English novel, the novel that records most fully her complex feelings about the English past, the English way of life, the nature of English genius and of English society, sharply ranked and distrustful of outsiders as it is. The first draft focused particularly upon English literature, and it opened with Isa and the gentleman farmer, Rupert Haines, recognising each other through a shared allusion to the poet Edward Thomas, and his poem about memory and the past entitled 'Old Man' (misremembered by Isa as 'Old Man's Beard'). Thomas speaks to Isa's generation as Byron had spoken to that of her father-in-law.[38] Woolf's initial choice of Edward Thomas to open, and perhaps preside over the novel reflects the centrality of English landscape and literature to her initial conception of the book, for these had been the main subject matter of Thomas's prose and poetry.[39] In a second draft, she cut away most of this opening scene, and in the process entirely removed the discussion of Thomas, yet his poem 'Old Man' left its shadow across the moments where Isa 'threw away the shred of Old Man's Beard she had picked in passing' or 'stripped the bitter leaf that grew, as it happened, outside the nursery window. Old Man's Beard' (BA, 69; 123).

*Between the Acts* catches up the theme of insularity, treating it socially, rather than politically. 'Our island history' unfolds within a smaller island, a microcosm of English society quietly absorbed in its activities, 'as if warm days would never cease'. At the same time, Giles (and therefore the novel) cannot forget Europe, 'bristling with guns, poised with planes', at once so far away, yet also dangerously close, 'just over there, across the gulf in the flat land which divided them from the continent' (BA, 34, 30).[40] Giles is a lone Cassandra in a society preoccupied with the threat of the cesspool or the building of new bungalows (BA, 5–6, 47), yet Woolf herself recognised during the crises of 1938 that the thought of war was so overwhelming that one could only deal with it by averting one's eyes, by concentrating on the local and trivial: 'One ceases to think about it – that's all. Goes on discussing the new room, new chair, new books. What else can a gnat on a blade of grass do?' (*Diary* v, 162).

The village society of *Between the Acts* is rooted in the past. Many of the local families have lived there time out of mind and they are well aware of who has insider or outsider status, gossiping and speculating about Mrs Manresa's Tasmanian background, about her Jewish husband Ralph and the money he has made, as well as about Miss La Trobe (BA, 46, 27, 37). Characteristically, it is the two outsiders who revitalise the flagging community. Between them, if in rather different senses, they are always 'getting things up'. Miss La Trobe's name reveals that she is 'not pure English'; indeed she is not pure anything, being both a social and a sexual outsider (BA, 37). In this role, she offers the insiders an image of themselves, an image of an England affectionately observed yet at the same time parodied, simultaneously mocking and reproducing England's favourite narratives of itself as a seafaring nation under Queen Elizabeth I, as a cheerful eighteenth-century squirearchy and as a harmonious Victorian family, with father at home, reading to the children by lamplight (a myth approached but narrowly avoided in *To the Lighthouse*). Once again Woolf turns Englishness into a joke, dissolving the embarrassment of sentiment in permissive laughter.

Ultimately, the novel reaches beyond its vision of England in 1939 to something altogether darker, older and more enduring. Miss La Trobe turns, as Woolf herself used to, from the work she has just completed to envisaging her next project, to be enacted in a time and place before England – 'It was land, merely, no land in particular' – where a couple stand among rocks, though she does not yet know what they will say (BA, 124). Her vision reaches beyond the novel's preoccupation with the current condition of England to something timeless. The final paragraphs of *Between the Acts* re-enact Miss La Trobe's vision, so that love and hate, which have engendered all the plots, are finally seen in their full nakedness as the explanation of what we are and what we do – not just the English, but all people for ever, reproducing themselves and making war. The final words of the novel are couched in the theatrical terms that Miss La Trobe had used ('the curtain would rise') and, as in her vision, English history is annihilated in a moment that simultaneously evokes an impossibly distant past and anticipates the anarchy of war to come: 'Our English past' is reduced to 'one inch of light' (BA, 124, 130; W, 174).

It was difficult for Woolf to reconcile the counter-currents of her socialism and, even more, of feminism and modernism with her love of that patriarchal myth of 'England' – itself, distinctive and elaborated, with its own recordable history.[41] As a sharp observer and analyst of prevailing ideologies, she recognised that ideals of Englishness were intended to arouse the envy of foreigners, the pride and protectiveness of its natives, and to disguise the increasingly divided and disheartened nature of a nation slipping from world leadership into economic decline. Patriotism for Woolf was normally a matter for censure or satire, or at the very least ironic distance, yet she was also in love with the language – poems and verses remembered from childhood, as well as downland walks and tumultuous clouds, and at moments her dream of a fair country merged with the reality around her – her England of the mind assumed a body.

Near the end of her life, when air raids had exiled her from it, she identified London as her only patriotism (except for a vision of spring in Warwickshire) (*Letters* vi, 460), but in her essay on 'Reading' of twenty years earlier she had created her own England, a private vision which seems to have gathered power from being suppressed. Its country house is recreated in *Between the Acts*, where the hills and woods of the parish epitomise England. If Pointz Hall owes its name to Shakespeare (Pointz is one of Hal's companions in *Henry IV*), the name of the village, Bolney Minster, combines 'Bolney' (the name of a South Downs village not far from Rodmell) with the suffix 'Minster', perhaps glancing backwards to her visit to Iwerne Minster of 1926. Though *Between the Acts* is as humorously critical of English insularity as ever – of English snobbery, conservatism, xenophobia – it is also imbued with love for a country anticipating a foreign invasion. Woolf could not resist the upsurge of patriotic feeling that the War brought, producing what Raphael Samuel has described as 'a country in love with itself'.[42] Even Churchill, a former bugbear of hers, was now redeemed.[43] The sense of imminent danger around her – and perhaps also within her – restored that ideal vision. 'The searchlights are very lovely over the marsh', she wrote to Ethel Smyth in the summer of 1940, 'and the aeroplanes go over – one, a German, was shot over Caburn, and my windows rattled when they dropped bombs at Forest Row. But its like a Shakespeare song today – so merry, innocent, and very English' (*Letters* vi, 402).

## Notes

1. Raphael Samuel, *Island Stories: Unravelling Britain* (*Theatres of Memory*, vol. II), (London: Verso, 1998), pp. 24, 49.
2. Samuel, *Island Stories*, p. 4; Philip Dodd, 'Englishness and the National Culture', *Englishness: Politics and Culture, 1880–1920*, ed. Robert Colls and Philip Dodd (London: Croom Helm, 1986), p. 1.
3. Alun Howkins, 'The Discovery of Rural England', *Englishness*, pp. 62–84; Peter Brooker and Peter Widdowson, 'A Literature for England', *Englishness*, p. 141; see also Richard Jefferies, *Wild Life in a Southern County* (London: Smith, Elder, 1879), a work often considered his best.
4. Dodd, *Englishness*, pp. 16–19; Raphael Samuel, *Theatres of Memory*, vol. I (London: Verso, 1994), pp. 218–19; Howkins, *Englishness*, p. 79.
5. E. M. Forster, *Howard's End* (London: Penguin, 1941), p. 133 (end of ch. XIX); Shakespeare, *Richard II*, Act II, sc. 1, 46. Stuart Clarke reminds

me that Virginia Woolf, like Forster, deplored the destruction of the countryside by motor-cars in 1924 (*Essays* iii, 440), though in 1927 the Woolfs bought one themselves.

6. 27 April 1926, *Congenial Spirits: The Selected Letters of Virginia Woolf*, ed. Joanne Trautmann Banks (London: Hogarth Press, 1989), p. 207.
7. Brian Doyle, *English and Englishness* (London: Routledge, 1989), pp. 1–4.
8. Nikolaus Pevsner, *The Englishness of English Art* (1956; London: Penguin, 1997), pp. 16–20.
9. P, 128, 135, 154–8.
10. 'The most rich inheritor', W. B. Yeats's 'Meditations in Time of Civil War'–3 (*The Tower*, 1928 – Woolf reviewed this volume – see *Essays* iv, 544–5); Winifred Holtby, *Virginia Woolf: A Critical Memoir* (London: Wishart, 1932) entitled her first chapter 'The Advantages of Being Virginia Stephen'.
11. Though T. S. Eliot's outlook ('royalist in politics, and anglo-catholic in religion') was utterly different from that of Woolf, his *Four Quartets* and her *Between the Acts* sometimes seem to echo one another, as Gillian Beer points out (BA, xii, xxvii, 134, 142).
12. One possible model for the house in 'Reading' could have been the moated Elizabethan manor house at Blo' Norton, where the young Stephens stayed in August 1906. This had dark Jacobean panelling but did it also have a library? Blo' Norton is described by Sonya Rudikoff in *Ancestral Houses: Virginia Woolf and the Aristocracy* (Palo Alto, CA: Society for the Promotion of Science and Scholarship, 2000), p. 183, and by Vanessa Curtis in *The Hidden Houses of Virginia Woolf and Vanessa Bell* (London: Robert Hale, 2005), pp. 180–2.
13. 'It was the Elizabethan prose writers I loved first & most wildly, stirred by Hakluyt' (*Diary* iii, 271). Woolf first wrote on *Traffics and Discoveries*, either just before or during her stay at Blo' Norton (*Essays* i, 120–3), and again in 1917 and 1918 (*Essays* ii, 91–3; 329–33), briefly in 1924 (*Essays* iii, 450) and in 'The Elizabethan Lumber Room' (*Essays* iv, 53–5). Its influence on *The Voyage Out* and *Orlando* is apparent – see Alice Fox, *Virginia Woolf and the Literature of the English Renaissance* (Oxford: Clarendon Press 1990), pp. 20–50.
14. Woolf avoided servants disturbing her ideal library, by having 'a sallow priest . . . dusting the books and the carved birds at the same time' (*Essays* iii, 141). The maid reading Plato appears in the full text of 'Professions for Women' (P, xlii), and the Georgian cook borrows the *Daily Herald* (from the drawing room, rather than the library) in 'Character in Fiction' (*Essays* iii, 422).
15. The typescript of 'Reading' is among the Monk's House Papers held by the University of Sussex Library, at B.11.d. A note by Leonard describes it as 'Typescript of Chapter for "Reading" Unfinished book'. There is also a manuscript of the last two pages (numbered 33, 34) in the Berg Collection of the New York Public Library. Woolf wondered 'how to shape my Reading book' on 23 May 1921 (*Diary* ii, 120).
16. '[E]ven in the year nineteen hundred and nineteen a great number of minds are only partially lit up by the cold light of knowledge', Woolf wrote in 'Reading' (*Essays* iii, 154), apropos of Sir Thomas Browne's *Vulgar Errors*. Narrower dating is difficult, but the discussion of Browne suggests that it

was written after a diary entry for 12 September 1919: 'I was making way with my new experiment, when I came up against Sir Thomas Browne, & found I hadn't read him since I used to dip & duck . . . hundreds of years ago' (*Diary* i, 297). It's possible that the 'new experiment' was 'Reading' (unless it was a short story), and it may be relevant that by September the Woolfs had surrendered the house at Asheham moved into Monk's House which Virginia initially compared unfavourably with it. A fantasy of an ideal house might have been the outcome of that moment of doubt, though by the end of the month, 'Monk's House improves, after the fashion of a mongrel who wins your heart' (*Diary* i, 297, 302). Another, rather different, context was the railway strike from 27 September to 6 October 1919, a spectacle of national division – see entries for 28, 30 September, 1, 7 October (*Diary* i, 301–4).

17. 'The Royal Academy' appeared in the *Athenaeum*, 22 August 1919, and was written in July and early August, whereas 'Reading' is unlikely to have been completed before September (see previous note). Chapter XIX of *Howard's End* begins 'If one wanted to show a foreigner England . . .' (p. 126). Woolf's brief notice of the Royal Academy's Summer Exhibition in the *Nation and Athenaeum*, May 1924, made several of the same points as her 1919 review: 'As a compliment to ourselves it is magnificent. As a contribution to art . . .' (*Essays* iii, 406).
18. Clive Bell, *Art* (1914; London: Chatto and Windus, 1923), pp. 28–30; Roger Fry, *Vision and Design* (1920; London: Chatto and Windus, 1928), pp. 12, 15; Woolf, 'The Royal Academy', *Essays* iii, p. 93.
19. Pevsner, p. 25, responding to Roger Fry's *Reflections on British Painting* (1934) (see also Pevsner, p. 205).
20. *The Last Sheaf* (London: Jonathan Cape, 1928), p. 91, quoted by Edna Longley in *A Language Not to Be Betrayed: Selected Prose of Edward Thomas* (Manchester: Carcanet, 1981), p. 222. Thomas's point is frequently made; see, for example, C. F. G. Masterman in *The Condition of England* (1909): 'Never . . . has the land beyond the city offered so fair an inheritance to the children of its people, as today, under the visible shadow of the end' (quoted in Brooker and Widdowson, *Englishness*, p. 136), or Slavoj Zizek in *For They Know Not What They Do* (London: Verso, 1991), p. 802: 'national identity constitutes itself through resistance to its oppression – the fight for national revival is therefore a defence of something which comes to be only through being experienced as lost or endangered'.
21. The Scarborough raid was witnessed by the sixteen-year-old Winifred Holtby – see Martin Gilbert, *First World War* (1994; London: HarperCollins, 1995), p. 110; David Bradshaw, *Winking, Buzzing, Carpet-Beating: Reading 'Jacob's Room'* (Southport: Virginia Woolf Society of Great Britain, 2003) pp. 12–15.
22. 'I never think his poetry good enough for him, but I did admire him very much indeed', Woolf told Ka Cox (*Letters* ii, 75). She was particularly critical of Edward Marsh's hagiographic account of Brooke's life (*Letters* ii, 267–8; *Diary* i, 171, 172).
23. For patriotic readings of *Henry V*, see Howkins, *Englishness*, p. 119 (the first dissenting voice was that of Gerald Gould, significantly in 1919 – see essay 1, p. 13).

24. Hermione Lee, *Virginia Woolf* (London: Chatto and Windus, 1996), p. 283; Stephen Barkway, 'The "Dreadnought" Hoax: the Aftermath for "Prince Sanganya" and "his" cousins', *Virginia Woolf Bulletin*, no. 21 (January 2006), pp. 20–27.
25. Woolf may have been familiar with the slang sense of 'Dick' as the penis – in military use from circa 1860, according to Eric Partridge, *The Penguin Dictionary of Historical Slang* (London: Penguin, 1972) p. 254.
26. In *Virginia Woolf* (Basingstoke: Macmillan, 2000), pp. 104–5, Lyndon Peach suggests that Dalloway was involved in negotiations for the Lausanne Treaty, 'the final act of betrayal' of the Armenians. Vita's husband, Harold Nicolson, actually was involved, and described the conference in *Some People* (1928) – see essay 10, pp. 158–60.
27. The allusion is, once again, to John of Gaunt's speech, although we have been told that Lady Bruton 'never read a word of poetry herself' (MD, 115). A very different juxtaposition of John of Gaunt's speech and Rupert Brooke's 'The Soldier' occurs in A. S. M. Hutchinson's best-selling novel, *If Winter Comes* (1921) – see John Lucas, *The Radical Twenties* (Nottingham: Five Leaves Publications, 1997), p. 58.
28. 'Mrs Dalloway in Bond Street', the short story from which the novel derives, is even more explicit: 'Thousands of young men had died that things might go on' (CSF, 158–9).
29. Compare 'everywhere . . . there was a beating, a stirring of galloping ponies, tapping of cricket bats; Lords, Ascot, Ranelagh and all the rest of it' (MD, 5). Gertrude Bell, writing during the General Strike of 1926, made the same point: 'It is so amazing that the world seems to go on just the same – Ascot and parties are what I read of in *The Times*', quoted by Martin Gilbert, *A History of the Twentieth Century*, vol. 1: 1900–33 (London: HarperCollins, 1997), p. 708.
30. See Samuel, *Island Stories*, pp. 88–90.
31. Kate Flint, 'Virginia Woolf and the General Strike', *Essays in Criticism* 36 (1986), pp. 319–34. For an account of the General Strike as 'a battle for England', culminating in the broadcasting of 'Jerusalem', see John Lucas, pp. 217–21. Lyndon Peach makes the point that when Lily Briscoe first appears in the MS of *To the Lighthouse*, she is an 'English' painter of thatched cottages and hedgerows, p. 116.
32. Woolf's 'As a woman, I have no country' alludes to the *Communist Manifesto*: 'The working people have no country', Karl Marx and Frederick Engels, *Selected Works* (London: Lawrence and Wishart, 1950), vol. 1, p. 44.
33. Samuel, *Theatres of Memory*, p. 218–19; *Island Stories*, p. 68, 82–3. John Lucas cites Orwell on the 'cult of cheeriness and manliness, beer and cricket, briar pipes and monogamy', p. 35. Alison Light explores 'Femininity, literature and conservatism between the wars', as well as self-division in Woolf, in *Forever England* (London: Routledge, 1991), especially pp. 2–19.
34. Samuel, *Theatres of Memory*, p. 207.
35. 'The Abinger Pageant' is reprinted in Forster's *Abinger Harvest* (1936; London: Penguin, 1967) pp. 369–84. On 'England's Pleasant Land', see *Diary* v, 156; *Letters* vi, 255, 258.
36. '[T]he absurdity . . . is matched by its nastiness', commented John Lucas, on Reith's broadcasting of 'Jerusalem', p. 220.

37. I read 'capacious', rather than 'capricious'.
38. *Pointz Hall: The Earlier and Later Typescripts of Between the Acts*, ed. Mitchell A. Leaska (New York: University Publications, 1983), pp. 38–40. Although she refers to it as 'Old Man's Beard' (usually wild clematis, rather than southernwood), Isa is thinking of Thomas's poem 'Old Man', in which the speaker shreds and sniffs a handful of southernwood (also known as 'Old Man or Lad's Love'), and meditates upon childhood, love and loss. We do not know when Woolf first read this poem, though a reference to the crushed leaves of verbena and southernwood in her 1919 essay 'Reading' may also allude to it: 'If we could see also what we can smell – if, at this moment crushing the southernwood, I could go back . . .' (*Essays* iii, 145).
39. Reviewing Thomas's *A Literary Pilgrim in England* for the *TLS* in October 1917 (six months after his death in France), Woolf declared 'He had a passion for English country and a passion for English literature'; she had seldom read a book 'which gives a better feeling of England than this one' (*Essays* ii, 161, 163).
40. See Gillian Beer, 'The Island and the Aeroplane: The Case of Virginia Woolf', *Nation and Narration*, ed. Homi K. Bhabha (London: Routledge, 1990), pp. 265–90.
41. Brooker and Widdowson note that these counter-currents failed to produce a literature of 'socialist-feminist modernism' before 1920, *Englishness*, p. 158.
42. *Theatres of Memory*, p. 218.
43. Churchill had been a notoriously right-wing Home Secretary in November 1910 at the time of 'Black Friday' and the Tonypandy strike (see essay 8), and had later been militantly opposed to the General Strike, which the Woolfs had supported (see *Diary* iii, 78; *Letters* iii, 261). Woolf had mocked his style in the first draft of *A Room of One's Own:* 'huge leather arm-chairs & vast mahogany tables & turkey carpets so thick that the foot sinks in them somehow write like this when they are alone after dark in an office', *Women & Fiction: The Manuscript Versions of A Room of One's Own*, ed. S. P. Rosenbaum (Oxford: Blackwell, 1992), p. 156. Yet by 13 April 1940, he had become 'Winston' (*Diary* v, 279), and a letter to Ethel Smyth noted 'the admiration this war creates – for every sort of person: chars, shop-keepers, even much more remarkably, for politicians – Winston, at least' (*Letters* vi, 434).

Essay 14

# Between the Texts: Virginia Woolf's Acts of Revision

I want to read largely & freely once: then to niggle over details. (*Diary* iii, 127)

Near the end of *A Room of One's Own*, in a coda as cunning and surprising as any of Beethoven's, Virginia Woolf declares, 'The truth is, I often like women. I like their unconventionality. I like their subtlety. I like their anonymity. I like – but I must not run on in this way.' Or so the passage appears in the special limited edition published in the United States on 21 October 1929 and in Britain on 24 October, in the British and American first editions (also published 24 October), and in all subsequent American editions.[1] Yet in the second British impression, published less than a month later, on 9 November 1929, Woolf liked 'their unconventionality. I like their completeness. I like their anonymity'. This revised version continued to appear in all British editions of the text until January 1992, fifty years after her death, when Virginia Woolf's work came out of copyright in Britain. In new editions published by Penguin and Oxford World's Classics, editions that reset the text from the British first edition, Woolf reverted to liking women's 'subtlety'.

As the general editor of the Penguin reprints, I was one of those responsible for the decision to return to the text of the first British edition on the grounds that this would be a practical way of shedding the accumulated errors of later editions. This decision seemed further justified by the widespread assumption that, though Woolf revised her work extensively in the stages before and sometimes during publication, she lost interest in it thereafter, so that any post-publication changes that occurred were probably non-authorial. Since 1992, however, I have become steadily less confident of this assumption: an example such as I began with must call it in question, while the assumption has itself functioned to deter further investigation into Woolf's post-publication revisions.

In what follows, I shall discuss and illustrate the grounds for my growing distrust of some of the editorial assumptions that underpin the way Woolf's texts are currently edited. Given the high levels of critical interest in Woolf, surprisingly little attention has been paid to her practice as a reviser of her own work, and what research there has been has focused largely on individual texts, rather than addressing her practice as a whole, as I shall do here. We need to know more about Woolf as reviser, a role in which she reveals herself both as a modernist and a feminist, the author of a developing series of texts characterised by change, variation, difference, and the refusal to provide a definitive or final version. We need to acknowledge the proliferation of variants that are the result of that process, and to begin, as critics, to recognise that there is more than one text, and to learn to distinguish between them, to consider what difference it makes when Woolf changes 'subtlety' to 'completeness', when she deletes a passage or expands a footnote to suppress or express her impatience with her blinkered society. In Britain, Woolf's work has been extensively re-edited since it came out of copyright in 1992 (temporarily, as it turned out), but her editors have consistently failed to identify the range and difficulty of the problems created by her processes of revision. My aim is to clarify the present state of knowledge, and to clear the ground for better-informed research and editorial policies in the future.

In describing Woolf's practice as a reviser, I shall begin be examining how and why she made the textual change described in my opening example. Unfortunately there is no surviving evidence to show precisely how it was effected, but it is possible to make an informed guess: as it required the top line of page 168 of the British first edition to be reset, Leonard Woolf would have written to instruct R. & R. Clark of Edinburgh, the firm that regularly printed large runs on behalf of the Hogarth Press, and had already produced the British texts of *Jacob's Room*, *The Common Reader*, *Mrs Dalloway*, *To the Lighthouse* and *Orlando*. Although no such letter has come to light, the Hogarth Press archive at Reading does include a carbon copy of another letter from Leonard to the Clarks concerning an alteration to the fourth impression of *A Room of One's Own*. This letter instructs them to correct a title that appeared in the first footnote to page 31 as *Life of Miss Emily Davies* to *Emily Davies and Girton College*[2] (no equivalent correction was made in American editions of the text).

While one can suggest how the change from 'subtlety' to 'completeness' was made, the question of why it was made is more complicated. As originally printed, Woolf's sentences emphasised women's eccentricity and self-effacement, reducing the effect while retaining the spirit of the passage as it had appeared in the typescript that Woolf sent to Donald Brace in New York:

> The truth is, I often like women. I often find them very interesting to talk to. I like their unconventionality. [I like to be able to say half a sentence and have the second half understood.] <I like their subtlety.> [Also] I like their anonymity. I like their courage. [I like their amateurishness.] I like – But I must not run on in this way.[3]

The alteration of 'subtlety' to 'completeness' counteracts the marginalising implications of the neighbouring terms. It may even have been intended to modify the effect of the notorious passage occurring earlier in that chapter in which Woolf had asserted the need for male and female elements within the soul to come together, so that 'the art of creation' ('the act', in American editions[4]) might be achieved. By characterising women as 'complete', Woolf reasserts women's self-sufficiency: we include both male and female elements within us. A different kind of explanation is suggested by the position and appearance of the page as it was first printed: page 168 is the third page from the end, and the top line could easily have caught Woolf's eye as an experienced printer, both because it is loose and because it includes a double word-break. In the first edition, this line reads 'tionality. I like their subtlety. I like their anony-'. Such a visible fragmentation of women's attributes works to reinforce the suggestion of marginality, whereas 'completeness' responds to and actively repudiates it. However we choose to explain Woolf's intervention, 'completeness' makes a stronger claim than 'subtlety', and so anticipates Woolf's own trajectory towards a less anxious and more openly articulated feminism in her writings of the 1930s. 'Completeness' thus stands, in more senses than one, as a figure for what can be learned from examining as many states of Woolf's texts as were published in her lifetime.

It is hard to imagine that the change from 'subtlety' to 'completeness' would have been authorised by anyone other than Woolf herself, and in this respect, it is an excellent example, if an unusual one. It makes the point, no less valid for being familiar, that for Woolf, as a modernist and feminist, no text was ever finished. She continually revised her own work, and a great deal of material recording or relating to its early development has survived, including her working and reading notes, manuscripts, typescripts and marked-up proofs, as well as passing comments on her work in progress to be found in diaries and letters. With so much information available, it has been possible to trace the progress of individual texts from conception to publication. Scholarly editions of holograph drafts of *The Voyage Out* (as *Melymbrosia*), *Jacob's Room*, *Mrs Dalloway* (as *The Hours*), *To the Lighthouse*, *Orlando*, *A Room of One's Own* (as *Women and Fiction*), *The Waves*, the '1880' section of *The Years* (as *The Pargiters*) and *Between the Acts* (as *Pointz Hall*) have occasioned full and detailed accounts of how these books came to be written.[5] In the cases of *The Common Reader*, *Mrs Dalloway*, *To the Lighthouse* and *Orlando*, the proofs that Woolf marked up for her American publisher, Harcourt, Brace, have survived.[6] Those for *Mrs Dalloway* and *Orlando* have occasioned important bibliographical essays,[7] while the Shakespeare Head editions of *Mrs. Dalloway* (1996), *To the Lighthouse* (1992) and *Orlando* (1998) have adopted these proofs as their copy text. Yet despite ample evidence of Woolf's extensive revision of her work before publication, there has been a reluctance to admit that the process of revision also extended beyond initial publication.

As co-publisher of her own work, Woolf was exceptionally well placed to put her publishing intentions into practice. Founded by the Woolfs in 1917, the Hogarth Press owned Woolf's copyright and until recently continued to publish her texts, so that it might well be assumed that these exist in peculiarly authentic and therefore unproblematic versions. Yet while their authenticity is irrefutable, it is also multiple; and while the traditional editorial concept of a 'final intention' is on occasion invoked by her editors,[8] it makes little sense when applied to a writer as sharply alive as she was to the fluidities and proliferations of selfhood. It is generally known that Woolf created numerous revisional variants between the American and British texts of a number of her novels; but it is also the case that such variants crop up in the several British impressions and editions issued by the Hogarth Press during her lifetime. These variants stand as a tribute to her sustained creative energy, repudiating the concept of the closed text or final version both at a level of 'niggling' detail, and 'largely & freely' at the level of structure. Editors have been slow to acknowledge the existence of the later variants in the British transmission of Woolf's texts and as a result their occurrence has only been intermittently recorded, and even more seldom set out in any published edition. When Woolf's work first came out of copyright in Britain in January 1992, there had been scarcely any serious attempts to edit individual texts according to contemporary scholarly practice, and her editors did not know what problems lay ahead. They were hardly equal to the task of formulating appropriate textual policies, far less of implementing them. The resulting editions thus have more to tell us about the biographical, literary and cultural evolution of any particular novel than of its textual history.

Brenda Silver's incisive article, 'Textual Criticism as Feminist Practice',[9] provides an excellent overview of the extensive research into the changes Woolf made when revising her original holographs, and the impact this research has had on critical studies of Woolf. But Silver's concern here, as she is the first to admit, is not with particular editorial and bibliographical problems arising from Woolf's complex publishing history. Instead, she demonstrates how feminist scholarship on Woolf's early drafts has contributed significantly to changing concepts of editing, and how the recovery and publication of those drafts has radically altered our sense of what kind of writer Woolf is. This excavation and reconstruction of Woolf's creative processes has been immensely exciting, and, understandably, has taken precedence over more traditional forms of textual investigation. One unfortunate result has been that the collation of British impressions and editions that would once have laid the foundations for further bibliographical study has never taken place at all. Indeed, in comparison with the flood of critical writings on Woolf, traditional textual criticism has scarcely amounted to a trickle.

The present lack of interest in the nature and states of Woolf's texts stands in contrast to that of a previous generation of critics, however, and some of the sharpest questions on textual issues are among the earliest. A letter to Leonard Woolf from the critic Joan Bennett registers a number of misprints in *Granite and Rainbow*. Another from the distinguished textual scholar J. C. Maxwell not only comments on the various obscurities and typographical problems in *A Writer's Diary*, but also directs our attention to a notable textual crux in *To the Lighthouse* – it serves as a reminder of how seldom such points have been discussed and how puzzling they remain.[10] In the course of his three-page letter, Maxwell proposed that the following long and difficult sentence required emendation: the first 'though' should read 'thought', having lost its final 't':

> But then, Mrs. Ramsay, though instantly taking his side against all the silly Giddingses in the world, then, she thought, intimating by a little pressure on his arm that he walked up hill too fast for her, and she must stop for a moment to see whether those were fresh mole-hills on the bank, then, she thought, stooping down to look, a great mind like his must be different in every way from ours. (*To the Lighthouse*, London: Hogarth Press, 1927, p. 112: 1–9)

In his reply, Leonard pointed out that '"though" is in the first edition and all subsequent editions. I am not sure that it is not what she wrote – it does just make sense – though I agree that your emendation may well be right'.[11] Maxwell's conjectural emendation is persuasive in terms of the rhythm of the sentence, so it is regrettable that there is no independent evidence for it: the fifteen words after 'Ramsay' do not appear in the holograph draft at all,[12] and were probably added while Woolf was typing up her manuscript. As the typescript has not come to light, these words first appear in the proofs, where Woolf passed over at least two opportunities to restore the missing 't', if it was indeed missing. On the other hand, it could be argued that the proofs include other significant errors that she failed to notice, and would undoubtedly have corrected, had she done so.[13] As published, the syntax of this sentence is uncharacteristically clumsy, though it can be defended on the grounds that it reflects Mrs Ramsay's rambling thoughts. As far as I know, Maxwell's proposal has never been seriously considered by any editor, though it voices a serious concern for the meaning of the text – and, as Leonard admitted, it 'may well be right'.

The early drafts of Woolf's novels generated a great deal of excitement for the reasons set out by Brenda Silver in her article – that they represent a less inhibited and more fully articulated impatience with social prejudices concerning the nature of women and of their bodies, and perhaps with class distinctions as well. It is undoubtedly true that Woolf cut from her published work passages that might offend her readers, such as the one from *Jacob's Room* describing the intimate physical acts performed in Mrs Pascoe's cottage,[14] or her discussion of the exhibitionist (under the unexpected heading of 'street love') in the third essay of *The Pargiters*.[15] Even her account of the woman writer's need to practice self-censorship, read to the National Society for Women's Service in January 1931, exists in a longer and more explicit version.[16]

In revising her work for publication, Woolf often practised self-censorship, yet her self-awareness was such that the texts themselves remain fully conscious of whatever processes of silencing they may have undergone: Rachel, the heroine of *The Voyage Out*, is preoccupied with prostitution, the dark knowledge that society hides from itself; Jacob, in chapter V of *Jacob's Room*, reads aloud his attack on literary expurgation. Woolf was often amused when not annoyed by the prudishness of contemporary biography: *Orlando* is a novel that repeatedly draws attention to its acts of concealment by presenting them as elaborate jokes. Woolf cut from the text at proof stage a passage in which the narrator

> dropped into the kitchen grate two days ago Shakespeare's own account of his sonnets which Greene happened to have on him and gave to Orlando as a keepsake . . . But when truth and modesty conflict, who can doubt which should prevail? [17]

In *The Years*, the narrative compares the trivial obscenity of mentioning sanitary towels in conversation with the unspeakable obscenity of the Great War.[18]

Woolf's revisions thus buried some but by no means all of the passages that told uncomfortable truths about the body and its loves; yet she did not invariably reduce or dilute her impatience with the attitudes of her society. During the 1930s, she kept three scrapbooks in which she collected newspaper cuttings recording notable instances of male hypocrisy or misogyny. As the source for many of the examples given in *Three Guineas*, these notebooks are crucial to an understanding of the text and they serve, as Woolf's allusions usually do, to reveal her active engagement with contemporary politics; but then so do a number of the textual revisions that she made to the endnotes.[19] Note 41 of chapter 2 in the American edition includes an extra paragraph that never appeared in any British edition:

> Presumably the need for a scapegoat is largely responsible, and the role is traditionally a woman's. (See Genesis.) It is a curious fact that although the 'practical obliteration' of her freedom is assured if certain characteristics generally if erroneously associated with aggravated masculinity remain unchecked, the educated woman not only accepts criticism, but if publishers' lists are to be taken as evidence, makes no attempt to return it. This may be attributed to poverty which, as the poet says, makes cowards of us all. (*Three Guineas*, New York: Harcourt, Brace, 1938, p. 239: 2–11)

Feminist anger is as much in evidence in this addition, made while correcting the American proofs, as at any of the earlier stages of composition. She may even have expressed her anger more openly here in response to a sense that her American readers were more likely to share her impatience with British patriarchy.

The revision in the form of expansion of several notes in the American edition of *Three Guineas* is unexpected, both because of their outspokenness and because such additions more often occur in the British, rather than the American editions. The note described above is one of many examples of the textual differences that exist between Woolf's British and American first editions. These differences are extensive and substantial, and are particularly in evidence in the novels of her middle years, from *Mrs Dalloway* (1925) to *Flush* (1933), though they can also be seen in *Three Guineas* which has a substantial number of changes in wording and additions to the notes, including the example quoted above.[20] Differences between the states of Woolf's British and American editions first attracted attention in the early 1970s, when J. A. Lavin examined the variants in *To the Lighthouse*,[21] but, without having Woolf's marked-up proofs to check against, he mistakenly concluded that the American edition represented the latest and best state of the novel, 'superior to the one published in England by Mrs Woolf's own company'.[22] He nevertheless provided the first list of variants between American and British first editions, as well as a further list of variants drawn from the 1938 Everyman edition.[23]

Examining 'The American Edition of *Mrs Dalloway*' two years later, E. F. Shields made use of Woolf's marked-up American proofs as a way of analysing the relationship between the British and American first editions. For this novel (and frequently thereafter), Woolf revised two sets of proofs supplied by R. & R. Clark independently, sending one set to Donald Brace in New York, from which the American edition was set, and returning the other, sometimes a single signature at a time,[24] to the Clarks in Edinburgh where they were printed on behalf of the Hogarth Press. By marking up her revisions either wholly or partly independently of one another, Woolf created two distinct lines of textual transmission, as both Lavin and Shields noted, so that, in effect, her British and American readers encounter different novels. This, in turn, has contributed to the surprising differences between Woolf's reception in the United States and the United Kingdom.

Shields recognised that the two texts posed the question as to which was superior, but she preferred the British first edition on the grounds that Woolf had exercised greater control over its publication, and critical opinion has usually followed her. Though Shields does not say it in so many words, there is evidence that Woolf worked through the pre-publication revisions for R. & R. Clark more thoroughly, and perhaps more slowly than those she prepared for Harcourt, Brace. Shields warned critics quoting from one edition of the novel 'that the other edition of the novel might not contain the same passage or might contain it in a greatly altered form',[25] a warning that has largely gone unheeded. British readers would have been surprised and perhaps shocked to learn from the first volume of Gilbert and Gubar's *No Man's Land* that 'Clarissa Dalloway responds to the news of Septimus Warren Smith's death by deciding that his sacrificial suicide "made her feel the beauty, made her feel the fun" of her own existence',[26] since this sentence had never appeared in any British edition; if it had, it might well have affected the novel's interpretation in the United Kingdom.

A year before Shields' article appeared, Carolyn Heilbrun's *Towards Androgyny* (1973), one of the founding texts of feminist criticism, had examined that 'sentence of significant syntax' in the American first edition of *To the Lighthouse* in which Mr. Ramsay reaches out for his dead wife:

> [Mr. Ramsay, stumbling along a passage one dark morning, stretched his arms out, but Mrs. Ramsay having died rather suddenly the night before, his arms, though stretched out, remained empty.] (Harcourt, Brace, 1927, p. 194: 1–4)

British readers, however, would not have encountered the sentence in this form, since the British edition is worded significantly differently:

> [Mr. Ramsay stumbling along a passage stretched his arms out one dark morning, but Mrs. Ramsay having died rather suddenly the night before

he stretched his arms out. They remained empty.] (Hogarth Press, 1927, p. 199: 28; p. 200: 1–4)

The Uniform Edition of 1930 added commas after 'but' and 'before', further disturbing the syntax: 'but, Mrs. Ramsay having died rather suddenly the night before, he stretched his arms out. They remained empty' (Hogarth Press, 1930, p. 200: 1–4). Stella McNichol, in her edition of the novel for Penguin, conjectured that Woolf intended 'before' as a conjunction governing the clause that follows, rather than as part of the phrase 'the night before' (meaning 'the previous night'), so her proposed emendation replaces the full stop after 'empty' with a comma, thus:

> [Mr. Ramsay . . . stretched his arms out one dark morning, but, Mrs. Ramsay having died rather suddenly the night before he stretched his arms out, they remained empty].[27]

The revised punctuation of the Uniform Edition attempts to redefine a sentence that, like Mr Ramsay's sense of himself, remains hauntingly incomplete through its various transformations.

The textual differences between the British and American editions are both numerous and sufficiently substantive to create problems in any classroom where students bring their own texts. Those in *To the Lighthouse* are particularly disconcerting because this is the most familiar of all Woolf's novels: for example, in the first British edition, the first part, 'The Window', ends with the words 'And she looked at him smiling. For she had triumphed again' (p. 191: 6–7). The American edition adds a further sentence: 'She had not said it: yet he knew' (p. 186: 6). Critics need to be able to identify such differences readily, yet they have never been easy to locate. The *Concordances* to Woolf's novels produced on microfiche by James Haule and Philip Smith Jr during the 1980s included comparative lists of variants between the British and American first editions, which were assumed to be reliable since they had been produced electronically, but in reality they were often incomplete and seldom corresponded precisely with independent listings.[28]

*To the Lighthouse* and *Orlando* present especially large numbers of variants, and in working on them Woolf had clearly decided to revise her British and American proofs separately and 'sent out different versions, different texts'.[29] Why she did so has never been satisfactorily explained, but one possible reason emerges if we examine the history of her American editions, beginning with the publishing anomalies that resulted from her revisions to her first novel, *The Voyage Out*. The possibility of an American edition of it prompted her to wonder whether it ought to be distinguished in some way from the British edition. In November 1919, she wrote to her friend Lytton Strachey

> An American publisher wants to bring out Night and Day and the Voyage Out . . . would you be so angelic as to tell me if any special misprints, obscurities or vulgarities in either occur to you. I have to send the books off on Monday and they say the more alterations the better – because of copyright. I've just glanced between the boards and see that the whole thing must be rewritten from the beginning – and only 2 days to do it in! (*Letters* ii, 401)[30]

The wording of this letter and her subsequent practice suggest that Woolf thought that any differences she introduced would help to establish a distinctive American copyright, and thus make piracy from the British editions more difficult – at this period, almost all English books published in the States were in any case required to be reset and printed there. Accordingly, she made a number of deliberate alterations to the text of *Night and Day*: most of these consisted of necessary corrections – one syntactic change was suggested by Strachey in response to this letter, while another substantive alteration corrected a list of works by Sir Thomas Browne. But in addition to these, there are around twenty further small and unnecessary changes of wording, mainly clustered in the first few chapters, and again near the end.[31] Although Woolf did not specify in her letter to Strachey which of her first two novels required such drastic rewriting, she revised *The Voyage Out* for American publication by cutting more than three thousand words, mainly from chapter XVI.[32]

*The Voyage Out* poses a problem for editors concerning the choice of copy text since the novel was published in Britain in 1915 by Woolf's half-brother, Gerald Duckworth, and then in a heavily revised version in the States in 1920 by George H. Doran. Sheets of the American version were then bound and reissued in Britain by Duckworth, first in 1920 and again in 1927. The remaining sheets and copies were then bought up and reissued by the Hogarth Press with a 'cancel-title' as the 'Third Impression' in the spring of 1929.[33] In September of the same year, the Hogarth Press reissued *The Voyage Out* in the Uniform Edition, but this time it reprinted the original, uncut British edition of 1915. Elizabeth Heine has suggested that this may have been because it was a more convenient size for reproduction in the Uniform series than the American edition, which had been set on fewer but larger pages.[34] Woolf's earlier anxiety to reduce the novel's autobiographical content must necessarily have diminished in the wake of the outspoken *Orlando*. However we interpret her decision, the publication of the novel in two different versions within eight months of one another further compromises any notion of a 'final intention'.

Woolf's third novel, *Jacob's Room* (1922), was not published in America until 1923, and in this instance she seems to have forgotten the point she had made in her letter to Strachey. At any rate, she made no significant changes to the American edition. The multiplication of variants begins in earnest with *Mrs Dalloway* for which Harcourt, Brace had set up an arrangement for simultaneous publication in the States. When Leonard Woolf asked in what form he wanted the copy, Donald Brace specifically asked for 'finally corrected page proofs',[35] apparently expecting to receive a 'final' copy text identical with the one to be used for the Hogarth first edition. He was not to do so, either then or later.

Woolf maintained her practice of correcting American and British proofs independently in several of the novels that followed, though the number of variants has diminished by *The Waves* (1931) and *The Years* (1937). By contrast, *Flush* (1933), first serialised in the US in the *Atlantic Monthly*, includes around fifty variants of individual words or word order.[36] While none of them are especially notable, more than a third occur in chapter IV, in which Flush's abduction exposes the risk to safe, respectable, middle-class Wimpole Street from 'outcast' London, waiting just around the corner to pounce on the careless or unwary.

How deliberate was Woolf's practice of independently proof-checking for American and British publication? And what view did she take of textual revision as a whole? From holograph to typescript, from typescript to corrected proofs, there is ample evidence to show that she was prepared to take extraordinary pains with her writing, even though she found the final stages of revision and correction stressful. Her diary for 14 January 1927 records the completion of *To the Lighthouse*: 'I have finished the final drudgery . . . Since October 25th I have been revising & retyping (some parts 3 times over) & no doubt I should work at it again but I cannot' (*Diary* iii, 123) – and compare her note two years earlier: 'I revised Mrs D[alloway]: the dullest part of the whole business of writing; the most depressing & exacting' (*Diary* iii, 4). A letter from Leonard Woolf to an unidentified enquirer records her discarding as many as six or eight drafts of a particular article.[37] She certainly continued to make substantial changes to her novels up to and during the proof stage: three vivid pages invoking Mr Ramsay's life as a widower, addressing an audience of elderly women in a fog-bound lecture hall on the absence of God, appear in the surviving proofs of *To the Lighthouse*, only to be deleted before they reach publication.[38]

The proliferation of variants between British and American versions might in itself be regarded as further evidence of Woolf's fascination with the process of revision since it would undoubtedly have been easier and quicker to have restricted herself to transferring corrections from one set of proofs to another, yet she never seems to have attempted to reduce the work involved. On one occasion, she specially prepared and sent a set of proofs of *Mrs Dalloway* to amuse her friend Jacques Raverat as he lay dying. This set includes several alterations that she never made elsewhere. Here, the news of Septimus Smith's suicide produces sensations of 'insolence' and 'levity' in Clarissa which, G. P. Wright thought, altered her character appreciably 'in ways for which the novel itself offers little justification',[39] although the American text, in which Septimus Smith's suicide made Clarissa 'feel the beauty, feel the fun', approaches this tone more closely than does the British. Alison Scott's analysis of the marked-up *Orlando* proofs reveals at least two distinct stages of proof correction: alterations were first made in pencil and then rubbed out, or else confirmed by being overwritten in violet ink: 'she had gone through them at least twice . . . She had corrected eighty typographical errors and made over *six hundred* substantive changes to the text' (Scott's italics).[40] Woolf seems to have found the process of revision more absorbing than she was prepared to admit.

Although there are several discussions of the differences between Woolf's British and American editions, there have been few general accounts of her practice of revision across the board, and even fewer attempts to assess or record the post-publication changes made within the British line of textual transmission. This is partly because they are less remarkable than the American variants, but also because even copyright libraries are not equipped to provide copies of individual impressions and such volumes are even harder to obtain in the States, where most of the serious textual research on Woolf has taken place. J. A. Lavin's article on *To the Lighthouse*, referred to earlier, is exceptional in recording variant readings from the 1938 Everyman edition, while Glenn Patton Wright's edition of *Mrs Dalloway* for the Hogarth Press (1990) is exemplary in providing a much-needed collation of later British editions of the novel,[41] though he encounters some characteristic problems in the process. With insufficient data, it is very difficult to estimate the extent of the changes made within the different impressions and Uniform Editions published during Woolf's lifetime, or to know how much time Woolf spent revising them; nor is there any obvious source of external evidence to turn to for further information. The Hogarth Press archive at Reading includes carbon copies of several of Leonard Woolf's letters to R. & R. Clark, and the Clark ledgers, now in the Scottish National Library in Edinburgh, include sums charged to the Hogarth Press for 'alterations', but most of Leonard's correspondence with the Clarks (including, presumably, the authorisation for my opening example) was destroyed during the war, so that the presence of post-publication changes can only be identified by drawing up full collations. Given the possibility of small but significant changes within individual impressions, all the states of the novels published by the Hogarth Press during Woolf's lifetime now need to be examined.

Until this task has been carried out, we must treat with a degree of scepticism the often-cited assertion, made by G. P. Wright at the outset of his article on 'The Raverat Proofs of *Mrs. Dalloway*' and repeated in his edition of *Mrs Dalloway*, that 'After a novel was published, she rarely tinkered with the text – the notable exception being *The Voyage Out*'.[42] Indeed, his own collation of *Mrs Dalloway* identifies several revisions made in the second impression of the first edition as well as in the Uniform Edition, although, as he points out, these are minor and might be classified as corrections or clarifications. Thus, they might have originated with other readers, including Leonard; none is as clearly authorial as my opening example.

Wright's collation is nevertheless of great importance, and not least because it throws down a challenge to the accepted bibliographical classification of Woolf's novels. Defining an edition as a version of a text that includes variant readings, he reclassifies the second and third editions of *Mrs Dalloway*. In doing so, though he does not make this point himself, he effectively reinstates their original descriptions by the Hogarth Press as the 'Second Edition' and the 'Uniform Edition'. Kirkpatrick's otherwise excellent *A Bibliography of Virginia Woolf* had re-described them as the 'second impression' (A9a) and 'First edition – photo-offset reprint' (A9d), respectively. In this case, Wright's evidence justifies the Hogarth Press's own descriptions which Kirkpatrick had dismissed, but the difference between Kirkpatrick's definition of a new edition as one that requires the text as a whole to be reset (a definition in accordance with modern bibliographical practice) and Leonard's definition as one that requires partial resetting reflects no more than a tightening of bibliographical terminology. Kirkpatrick's usage unintentionally misled scholars into assuming that there were no significant differences between the different impressions of an edition. As we have seen, this was not the case.

A comparable problem arises with the Uniform Edition of *To the Lighthouse* (1930), which the Hogarth Press announced as a 'New Edition' – 'incorrectly', according to Kirkpatrick, who reclassified it as the fourth impression of the first edition (A10c), on the grounds that it was offset from the first, although it included several minor alterations, as well as some new errors.[43] As a result, textual scholars such as J. A. Lavin bypassed the Uniform Edition in favour of the 1938 Everyman edition, described by Kirkpatrick as the second English edition

(A10d), but the variants Lavin found and listed in the Everyman edition seem to derive from the Uniform edition.

In the cases of *Mrs Dalloway* and *To the Lighthouse*, the claims made by the Hogarth Press and effectively by Leonard Woolf, a person of scrupulous honesty and integrity, turn out to have had a basis in observable fact, even though they beg further questions as to the distinction between a new impression and a new edition, a distinction further highlighted by my opening example from *A Room of One's Own*, since, in this instance, both the Hogarth Press and Kirkpatrick are in agreement in describing the text that this variant appears in as the 'second impression' (A12b). Although Wright's arguments suggest the need to think more carefully about the implications of Kirkpatrick's classifications, we lack the data by which to judge them. A first step might be to acknowledge that the Hogarth Press's original claims have some basis in observable fact, while recognising that these too can be misleading and that any individual impression may include any number of small changes. What Wright establishes is that, in Woolf's case, an impression (though he wants to redefine it as a new edition), while consisting largely of identical text and page numbers, may still include substantive textual variants. When Woolf made changes in her published texts, she was printer enough to ensure that they corresponded exactly to the space available.

Thus a widespread confusion or ignorance as to the actual differences between individual texts prevailed when, in January 1992, British copyright was lifted on the books Woolf had published during her lifetime (it has since been re-imposed, with the adoption of European Union copyright laws, until 1 January 2012). Her literary reputation had risen sharply during the eighties, and though it stood even higher in the States, as many as four British publishers decided to undertake major reprints of her work: the Hogarth Press and Blackwell's Shakespeare Head imprint did so in hardback, and Penguin and World's Classics (Oxford University Press) in paperback. There was a further flurry of singletons: Virago (which had not been able to publish Woolf's work before) brought out an edition of *Orlando* to coincide with Sally Potter's film; Everyman, which had first published *To the Lighthouse* in its 'Library' in 1938, reprinted their old text with a new introduction, and went on to publish *Mrs Dalloway*; Macmillan brought out the three most popular novels in a single volume edited by Stella McNichol – and this list is far from complete.[44] There have been several comparative reviews of the resulting volumes,[45] but no comparable consideration has been given to their respective merits as edited texts, nor has there been any discussion, as far as I am aware, of the way in which the task of text-editing was interpreted within the various series.

By the 1980s the Woolfs' own Hogarth Press, like so many older London publishing firms, had lost its independence and dwindled to an imprint within the American conglomerate, Random House (traditionally, the rival of Harcourt Brace Jovanovich, Woolf's American publisher). The Hogarth Press anticipated their loss of copyright with a pre-emptive strike, bringing out a 'Definitive Collected Edition' in 1990 with introductions by Woolf's nephew and niece, Quentin Bell and Angelica Garnett, the acknowledged 'guardians of the flame'. Until the 1990s, Woolf's novels had been published without annotation, despite their use as texts for study and the accumulation of Woolf scholarship. The Definitive Collected Edition provided neither notes nor 'Further Reading', and only two of its volumes had named editors: one was G. P. Wright's important edition of *Mrs Dalloway*, already discussed. Although Wright described his text as 'conservative',[46] the implications of his argument (that we must examine all the post-publication states of Woolf's novels to appear in her lifetime) are far-reaching and constitute the most serious challenge so far to the current consensus on editing Woolf. A second volume, Elizabeth Heine's edition of *The Voyage Out* (1990), also provides a full and detailed account of the textual changes the novel underwent, but after these two, the series lost momentum, and other volumes make do with what looks like in-house editing and a list of British and American first edition variants derived from Haule and Smith's *Concordances*.

Two major paperback publishers, Penguin and World's Classics, compete commercially and hold watching briefs on each other's policy decisions. Their editions are aimed at students and Woolfian common readers, but during the 1990s, their output increasingly came to reflect academic and scholarly concerns.[47] Even so, the typical volume 'editor' was more likely to be a critic than a textual editor, someone who could provide a readable introduction and annotate unfamiliar names, places, quotations and allusions. The text itself was normally reset from a first edition or some other reliable source; any further textual information was an unexpected bonus. There are evident similarities between the Penguin and World's Classics editions of Woolf: the great majority of them adopt the British first edition as their copy text.[48] Both series restored material which had dropped out of earlier reprints, such as the photographs used to illustrate *Three Guineas*, or those from *Orlando* first omitted from the Uniform Edition of 1930, though in that case, presumably, with Woolf's knowledge. Both editions of *The Years* added as an appendix the 'Two Enormous Chunks' that Woolf cut from the proofs. Kate Flint's edition of *Jacob's Room* (for World's Classics) transcribed a number of passages from the holograph, while Sue Roe's edition of the same novel for Penguin reprinted the original chapter X, later published separately by Woolf as ‘A Woman’s College from Outside’.[49] Penguin also provided a map of London in the 1920s in several of their novels, a plan of the 1924 British Empire Exhibition to accompany Woolf’s essay ‘Thunder at Wembley’, and Vanessa Bell’s original woodcuts for *Monday or Tuesday*.[50]

The lifting of copyright provided enormous opportunities while imposing a number of constraints: the Penguin series had originally been conceived as a sequence of individual volumes radiating from a core that consisted of Woolf’s several uncompleted autobiographies set out in the form of a consecutive narrative. In the event, the necessary permissions could not be obtained, though the ambition to create a coherent Woolf library is still reflected in the selections of short stories and essays published. The series was also distinctive in being designed as explicitly, if variously, feminist, and the editors represented a range of viewpoints within feminist criticism. The Penguin policy on textual editing was necessarily determined by the limited time and resources available: British first editions provided the copy text, supplemented by some account of the major variants. In 1992, there were very few experienced textual editors of Woolf in Britain. One was Stella McNichol,[51] who edited the texts of *Mrs Dalloway*, *To the Lighthouse* and *Between the Acts*, and in so doing, unavoidably complicated the meaning of ‘editor’ as used elsewhere in the series. These three novels and *Orlando*, edited by Brenda Lyons, were published with the clumsier but more precise formulation, ‘Edited by . . . with introduction and notes by . . .’). The volumes edited by Stella McNichol were exceptional in listing selected readings of later British editions where these seemed of interest. The rest of the series attempted to register differences between British and American first editions, relying mainly on the listings supplied by Haule and Smith’s *Concordances*, even though independent checks cast doubt on their reliability. Any close attention to Woolf’s texts tended to expose numerous small discrepancies, suggesting that they existed in more variant states than Kirkpatrick’s classifications had allowed for.

The more recent of the new editions, Blackwell’s Shakespeare Head imprint, promised more and better attention to Woolf’s texts than the paperback series had been able to provide: it would have academic resources to draw upon, work to a slower timetable, and would cost ten times as much as the paperbacks. A committee of five experienced Woolf editors would set its agenda and among its prime movers were Andrew McNeillie, co-editor of Woolf’s *Diary* and sole editor of a genuinely ‘definitive’ edition of Woolf’s *Essays*,[52] and Pat Rosenbaum of Toronto University. Thirteen American and Canadian Woolf scholars agreed to edit individual volumes for this essentially British publishing project. The series could not call itself 'definitive' since the Hogarth Press had appropriated that term, but it aimed to succeed where the Hogarth Press had failed in publishing 'reliable texts, complete with alternative readings and explanatory notes'. Disappointingly, its initial statement of textual policy failed to take into account the post-publication British variants, concentrating instead on the British and American variants and, where these were available, on Woolf's marked-up proofs.

Of the eleven texts published in this series, most have adopted British first editions as their copy text – thus, their editors have generally made the same choice of copy text as did Hogarth, Penguin and most of the World's Classics volumes. The exceptions are Susan Dick's edition of *To the Lighthouse* (1992), Morris Beja's edition of *Mrs Dalloway* (1996) and J. H. Stape's edition of *Orlando* (1998), which adopt Woolf's marked-up American proofs as copy text on the grounds that these provide an exact record of her intentions, uncontaminated by further editorial intervention, and thus serve as a reliable guide to her writing practice. On the debit side, however, is the fact that 'the first English edition contains more revisions than the first American edition', as Dick acknowledges in the case of *To the Lighthouse*,[53] so these texts reproduce a transitional stage in a larger process of revision, whose later development this series has chosen to overlook. Stapes's *Orlando* responds to this objection by incorporating later revisions made for the first British edition, but a text based on proofs lacks historical standing, a relevant consideration in editions of modern texts.

The volumes published by the Shakespeare Head edition to date – *To the Lighthouse* (1992); *The Waves* (1993); *Night and Day* (1994); *The Voyage Out* (1995); *Roger Fry* (1995); Mrs. Dalloway (1996), *Orlando* (1998), *Flush* (1999), *Three Guineas* (2001), *Between the Acts* (2002) and *Jacob's Room* (2004) – provide the fullest and most reliable accounts yet available of the differences between the British and American first editions, and they are welcome on that account as on others, but their editorial policy, both generally and individually, has not considered the possibility of later changes within the British line of transmission. Beja asserts that 'there is no evidence that Virginia Woolf had any role whatsoever in any corrections or revisions after the initial publication of *Mrs. Dalloway*';[54] yet a number of minor changes were made, and it is hard to imagine that either Leonard, or anyone else at the Hogarth Press, would have made them without at least consulting the author. J. H. Stape's edition of *Night and Day* collates the second impression of the first British edition, but ignores the Uniform Edition which may or may not include further variants. In the course of her introduction to *To the Lighthouse*, Susan Dick refers on three separate occasions to the difficult 'question of the author's final intentions', noting that 'it remains unanswered'.[55] A more traditional approach to 'final intentions' would have included the substantive changes made in the Uniform Edition of the novel and perpetuated in the 1938 Everyman edition.

It would have enhanced our knowledge of Woolf's texts had the Shakespeare Head editorial committee revisited its policy of ignoring most post-publication variants, but there are alternative approaches. In her excellent article on the *Orlando* proofs, Alison Scott suggested a variorum edition,[56] and Woolf's multiple versions would be well suited to parallel electronic texts. Most of her published writings, and much that is unpublished is already available on CD-ROM edited by Mark Hussey, in Primary Source Media's 'Major Authors' series, though the material is set out as a library for the literary rather than the textual scholar. Thus, no special preference is given to early editions or those published in Woolf's lifetime, and there is no easy way of comparing texts with one another: while it is possible to move from Rosenbaum's edition of the holograph, *Women & Fiction*, to Woolf's typescript of *A Room of One's Own*, to the American text of 1981 (as I did, in the process of writing this account), the disc was not designed to facilitate this particular task. A collection more closely focused on textual states would have included the first British edition of *A Room . . .* but, even had it done so, 'completeness' would still have been absent from the text provided; nor, in a more general sense, would it have been achieved so long as the post-publication revisions remain uncharted.

It is, of course, possible that my opening example of 'completeness' is unique – possible, but unlikely. Recent textual scholarship has focused too exclusively on the proofs Woolf corrected for Donald Brace and the revisions Woolf made for American publication – fuelled, perhaps, by an unconscious desire to appropriate one particular version of a very English writer for her American readers, though paradoxically this textual policy is enshrined in an edition whose very name – Shakespeare Head – gestures towards English canonicity. Woolf herself showed no further interest in her American variants, and she certainly made no systematic attempt to incorporate them into the editions published by the Hogarth Press that developed independently, accumulating further small changes and corrections at later stages[57]. And though it cannot be proved beyond a doubt that Woolf was personally responsible for making those changes, she did, on occasion, elicit them from her friends: 'The Trouble I took with that Lighthouse! Its going to be reprinted so send me any corrections', she wrote to Vita Sackville-West in June 1927 (*Letters* iii, 388). And though there is no unequivocal evidence of her hand in the Uniform Edition, a parenthetical diary entry for 25 November 1929 enquires 'ought I not to be correcting To the Lighthouse', in preparation for its reissue in the following February, while a further entry five days later adds 'Reading The Lighthouse does not make it easier to write' (*Diary* iii, 267, 268).

Woolf put enormous effort into revising her work at every stage, and reacted with annoyance when she missed the opportunity to make changes in the third impression of *Roger Fry*, as letters in the Reading archive reveal.[58] If our knowledge of Woolf's texts and the revisions she made to them are to keep pace with the critical study of her work and support it appropriately, we now need full collations of the various impressions and editions published by the Hogarth Press in Woolf's lifetime, and we need to recognise that 'completeness' is just as important as 'subtlety' for a proper understanding of her texts.

## Notes

1. *A Room of One's Own* (New York: Fountain Press, 1929), p. 155: 12–14; (London: Hogarth Press, 1929), p. 167: 25–6, p. 168: 1–2; (New York: Harcourt, Brace, 1929), p. 194: 6–10.
2. Leonard Woolf to R. & R. Clark, 13 December 1929, Hogarth Press Archive, folder 570, University of Reading Library.
3. In my transcription, angle brackets indicate insertions, square brackets deletions. Typescript of *A Room of One's Own* (2nd) p. 145, MH/B15.1, Monk's House Papers, University of Sussex Library.
4. *A Room of One's Own* (London: Hogarth Press, 1929) p. 157: 13; (New York: Harcourt, Brace, 1929), p. 181: 20.
5. *Melymbrosia: An early version of The Voyage Out*, ed. Louise DeSalvo (New York: New York Public Library, 1982); *Jacob's Room: The Holograph Draft*, ed. Edward L. Bishop (New York: Pace University Press, 1998); *'The Hours': The British Museum Manuscript of Mrs Dalloway*, ed. Helen M. Wussow (New York: Pace University Press, 1996); *To the Lighthouse: The Original Holograph Draft*, ed. Susan Dick (Toronto: University of Toronto Press, 1982); *Orlando: The Holograph Draft*, ed. Stuart Nelson Clarke (London: S. N. Clarke, 1993); *Women & Fiction: The Manuscript Version of A Room of One's Own*, ed. S. P. Rosenbaum (Oxford: Blackwell, Shakespeare Head Press, 1992); *The Waves: The Two Holograph Drafts*, ed. J. W. Graham (Toronto: University of Toronto Press, 1976); *The Pargiters: The Novel-Essay Portion of The Years*, ed. Mitchell A. Leaska (London: Hogarth Press, 1978); *Pointz Hall: The Earlier and Later Typescripts of Between the Acts*, ed. Mitchell A. Leaska (New York: University Publications, 1983).
6. The marked-up proofs of *Mrs Dalloway* are in the Lilly Library of Indiana University at Bloomington; those of *The Common Reader, To the Lighthouse* and *Orlando* are in the Frances Hooper Collection of the William Allan Neilsen Library at Smith College.
7. E. F. Shields, 'The American Edition of *Mrs. Dalloway*', *Studies in*

*Bibliography*, vol. 27 (1974), pp. 157–75; Alison M. Scott, '"Tantalising Fragments": The Proofs of Virginia Woolf's *Orlando*', *Publications of the Bibliographical Society of America*, vol. 88: 3 (September 1994), pp. 279–351.

8. See below, note 53.
9. Brenda R. Silver, 'Textual Criticism as Feminist Practice: Or, Who's Afraid of Virginia Woolf Part II', in *Representing Modernist Texts; Editing as Interpretation*, ed. George Bornstein (Ann Arbor: University of Michigan Press, 1991), pp. 193–222.
10. Joan Bennett's letter is undated; J. C. Maxwell's is dated 4 December 1953; both are among the Leonard Woolf Papers, Part II, D. 1. c, at Sussex University Library.
11. Leonard Woolf to J. C. Maxwell, 10 December 1953, location as above. Leonard's reference to 'subsequent editions' refers to the fact that Maxwell had been using the Everyman edition (1938).
12. Holograph notebook of *To the Lighthouse*, p. 239 (M31, part 1), Berg Collection, New York Public Library; see also Susan Dick, ed., *To the Lighthouse: The Holograph Draft*, p. 118.
13. Notably the misnumbering of the sections in part III, 'The Lighthouse'. See Susan Dick (ed.), *To the Lighthouse* (1927; Oxford: Blackwell, Shakespeare Head Press, 1992), p. xxxii.
14. 'An earth closet out in the rain – sickness – a woman's period – copulation upstairs in the double bed – childbirth – as the room filled with bodies. It would be impossible not to think solely of these functions and desires.' See Kate Flint, 'Revising *Jacob's Room*: Virginia Woolf, Women and Language', *Review of English Studies*, N. S. vol. 42, no. 167 (1991), pp. 368–9.
15. P, 50–1.
16. Ibid., xxxviii–xxxix.
17. Alison M. Scott, op. cit., p. 299.
18. *The Years* (London: Hogarth Press, 1937), p. 362; see my introduction, 'The Story So Far . . .' to *Virginia Woolf: Introductions to the Major Works*, ed. Julia Briggs (London: Virago, 1994), p. xxv.
19. A conscientious editor will want to make both the material from the newspaper scrapbooks and the state of the textual variants available to the interested reader, as does Michèle Barrett in her edition, ROO, TG, 335–55, 362–5.
20. For a full and detailed account of these, see Naomi Black, ed., *Three Guineas* (1938; Oxford: Blackwell, Shakespeare Head Press, 2001).
21. J. A. Lavin, 'The First Editions of Virginia Woolf's *To The Lighthouse*', Joseph Katz, ed., *Proof: The Yearbook of American Bibliographical and Textual Studies*, vol. 2 (Columbia: University of South Carolina Press, 1972), pp. 185–211.
22. Ibid., p. 187.
23. In fact, these derived ultimately from the Uniform Edition, which he wrongly supposed to be identical with the first edition on the basis of Kirkpatrick's *A Bibliography of Virginia Woolf* – a point discussed later.
24. Alison M. Scott, op. cit., p. 282.
25. E. F. Shields, op. cit., p. 174.

26. Sandra M. Gilbert and Susan Gubar, *No Man's Land: The War of the Words* (New Haven, CT, and London: Yale University Press, 1988), p. 95.
27. TTL, 261. For a recent discussion of the textual problems involved in editing this novel, see Hans Walter Gabler, 'A Tale of Two Texts: Or, How One Might Edit Virginia Woolf's *To the Lighthouse*', *Woolf Studies Annual*, vol. 10, ed. Mark Hussey (New York: Pace University Press, 2004), pp. 1–29.
28. In the case of *Night and Day*, Haule and Smith's *Concordance* (Ann Arbor, MI: University Microfilms International, 1988) only attempted 'A Selected List of Variants' (pp. 6–10), but these do not correspond to the list provided in J. H. Stape's edition of *Night and Day* (1919; Oxford: Blackwell, Shakespeare Head, 1994), derived from a computerised collation of the first British and American editions (p. 434). As Stape records, one of these alterations was the subject of the exchange of letters between Woolf and Lytton Strachey discussed above, p. 217.
29. Brenda R. Silver, op. cit., p. 196.
30. For Lytton's reply, see *Virginia Woolf and Lytton Strachey: Letters*, ed. Leonard Woolf and James Strachey (New York: Harcourt, Brace, 1956), pp. 118–19.
31. G. P. Wright comments on the clustering of Woolf's revisions on p. 247 of his article 'The Raverat Proofs of *Mrs. Dalloway*', *Studies in Bibliography*, vol. 39 (1986), pp. 241–61. Woolf elicited further corrections for her first two novels from Saxon Sydney-Turner and 'Bob' (R. C.) Trevelyan on 25 January 1920 (*Letters* ii, 418–19).
32. Louise DeSalvo, 'Virginia Woolf's Revisions for the 1920 American and English Editions of *The Voyage Out*', *Bulletin of Research in the Humanities*, vol. 82:3 (Autumn 1979), pp. 338–66, especially p. 340.
33. B. J. Kirkpatrick and Stuart N. Clarke, *A Bibliography of Virginia Woolf* (1957; fourth edition, Oxford: Clarendon Press, 1997), pp. 3–7.
34. Elizabeth Heine, ed., *The Voyage Out* (1915; London: Hogarth Press, 1990), p. 400. Alternatively, as Stuart Clarke has pointed out, the size of the edition may have originated in a mistake of Richard Kennedy's – see Kennedy's *A Boy at the Hogarth Press* (London: Heinemann, 1972), pp. 79, 84.
35. Donald Brace to Leonard Woolf, 16 December 1924, Berg Collection, New York Public Library.
36. Haule and Smith did not include *Flush* among the nine novels they concorded. This figure is based on my own rough collation and endorsed by Elizabeth Steele's edition of *Flush* in the Shakespeare Head Press series (1999).
37. The letter, dated 14 June 1942, begins 'I feel that you have some doubt whether I was not exaggerating in saying that my wife made 8 or 9 revisions of an article', Leonard Woolf Papers, part II, D.1. f, University of Sussex Library.
38. Susan Dick, ed., *To the Lighthouse* (1927; Oxford: Blackwell, Shakespeare Head Press, 1992), pp. xxiii, 207–8.
39. Wright, 'The Raverat Proofs of *Mrs. Dalloway*', p. 256.
40. Op. cit., p. 283.
41. Lavin, op. cit., p. 211; *Mrs Dalloway*, ed. Wright, pp. 177–8.

42. Wright, 'The Raverat Proofs . . .', p. 241; see also *Mrs Dalloway*, ed. Wright, p. 175. Stuart Clarke also makes the point that a conscientious editor would collate not only extant proofs and the first U.S. edition, but also 'all the U.K. editions, impressions, and reprints that appeared in Woolf's lifetime' in 'The Application of Thought to Editing Woolf's Texts', *Virginia Woolf Bulletin* no. 8 (September, 2001), p. 19.
43. Kirkpatrick, op. cit., *Mrs Dalloway* editions, pp. 38–40; *To the Lighthouse* editions, 49–50. Stella McNichol's edition of *To the Lighthouse* (1927; London: Penguin, 1992) is exceptional in including variants from the Uniform Edition, pp. 260–2.
44. The current (fourth) edition of Kirkpatrick's *Bibliography* gives details of the many editions of Woolf's work published in Britain since the 1992 lapse of copyright.
45. See Jeri Johnson, 'Woolf Woman, Icon and Idol: The Canonization of a Sceptical Modernist', *Times Literary Supplement* (21 February 1992); Jane Marcus, 'An Embarrassment of Riches', *The Women's Review of Books*, vol. xi: 6 (March 1994), pp. 17–19. My article 'Editing Woolf for the Nineties', *South Carolina Review*, vol. 29:1 (Fall 1996), pp. 67–77, takes up general, rather than textual, editing issues.
46. *Mrs Dalloway*, ed. Wright, p. 181.
47. See Marilyn Butler, 'Editing Women', *Studies in the Novel* (Special number: *Editing Novels and Novelists, Now*), vol. 27, no. 3 (Fall 1995), pp. 273–83; but policy has changed again since then.
48. One exception was Gillian Beer's edition of *The Waves* for World's Classics which preferred the text of the Uniform Edition on the grounds that it corrected earlier misprints. A textual note to Beer's edition of *The Waves* (1931; Oxford: Oxford University Press, 1992), p. xxxvii, observes that the Uniform Edition corrects misprints from the first (British) impression, but the misprints cited ('rocks' for 'rooks', 'an alien' for 'am alien') appear in the first American, not the first British edition. This example is typical of the kinds of confusion that can arise.
49. *Jacob's Room*, ed. Kate Flint (1922; Oxford: Oxford University Press, 1992), pp. 254–270; ed. Sue Roe (1922; London: Penguin, 1992), pp. 189–192.
50. Virginia Woolf, *The Crowded Dance of Modern Life, Selected Essays: Volume Two*, ed. Rachel Bowlby (London: Penguin, 1993), p. 38; *Selected Short Stories*, ed. Sandra Kemp (London: Penguin, 1993).
51. Editor of *Mrs. Dalloway's Party* (London: Hogarth Press, 1973).
52. *The Essays of Virginia Woolf*, in six volumes: vol. 1: 1904–12 (London: Hogarth Press, 1986); vol. 2: 1912–18 (1987); vol. 3: 1919–24 (1988); vol. 4: 1925–8 (1994).
53. *To the Lighthouse*, ed. Susan Dick (1927; Oxford: Blackwell, Shakespeare Head Press, 1992), p. xxxi. The only volume so far dedicated to these problems is *Editing Woolf: Interpreting the Modernist Text*, ed. James M. Haule and J. H. Stape (Basingstoke and New York: Palgrave, 2002), largely a volume of apologetics by individual Shakespeare Head editors – see my review for *Woolf Studies Annual*, vol. 10, ed. Mark Hussey (New York: Pace University Press, 2004), pp. 325–9.
54. *Mrs. Dalloway*, ed. Morris Beja, (1924; Oxford: Blackwell, Shakespeare Head Press, 1996), p. xxvii.

55. *To the Lighthouse*, ed. Dick, pp. xxxi; xxxii; xxxiii.
56. Alison M. Scott, op.cit., p. 289.
57. J. H. Stape's edition of *Night and Day* (1919; Oxford: Blackwell, Shakespeare Head Press, 1994), on the other hand, does carry out precisely this exercise – that is, he adopts the revisions Woolf made to her American text as emendations in an edition based on the first British edition (see p. xxv).
58. Letters from Virginia Woolf to Miss Perkins (a clerk at the Hogarth Press) on 25 November and 1 December 1940 ask for a number of changes to be made in the forthcoming third impression of *Roger Fry*, only to discover that she was too late for anything but an erratum slip: 'I dont think it is any use having a slip printed', Folder 569, Hogarth Press Archive, University of Reading Library. The context of these corrections is provided by Diane Gillespie in her exemplary edition of *Roger Fry* (1940; Oxford: Blackwell, Shakespeare Head Press, 1995), p. 386.

# Index